GITTA

Hidden Child of the Holocaust

Of all the crimes

conceived in fanaticism and hatred,

the war against the Jewish children,

I believe will remain as the worst,

the most vicious and the most implacable

in recorded history.

—ELIE WIESEL

GITTA

Hidden Child of the Holocaust

A Memoir

Gitta Rosenzweig

For more information contact:
www.gittarosenzweig.com
info@gittarosenzweig.com

ISBN 978-0-9964621-0-5 Paperback
ISBN 978-0-9964621-1-2 ebook

Library of Congress Number available upon request.

Book design by Dotti Albertine

To the Past and the Future

For my children and grandchildren

In loving memory of my family
My Mother, Hudesa Zajgman
My Father, Uszer Rozencwajg
My Brother, Izrael Itzchak Rozencwajg

All my relatives

Ida Rozenszajn Koper

and

One and a half million Jewish children

CONTENTS

ACKNOWLEDGMENTS

MY SINCERE appreciation and thanks to Martha Fuller for her guidance and her expertise. With patience and tenacity, she taught me the skills to write and helped me to find my voice. I could never have untangled and reconstructed the events of my life in a coherent chronology without her wisdom and editorial artistry. Most importantly, she gave me the courage and confidence to tell my story.

I would also like to thank my tireless guide in Poland, Tomasz Cebulski Ph.D., whose investigative research, intellectual passion, and knowledge of the Holocaust helped me obtain important family records and uncover evidence of my history. He found the missing pieces of my past that validated my location and experiences during the war years. He also introduced my sons to their ancestors and Jewish heritage with reliable information and clarity.

And I extend my gratitude to the many people who after hearing the story of my childhood encouraged me to write this book.

AUTHOR'S NOTE

In this true story, I have reconstructed the memories of my early years as a Hidden Child of the Holocaust to the best of my ability. Subsequent events as a consequence of this traumatic period of my life are portrayed as they occurred in my perception. In order to protect their privacy, I have changed the names of some of the people who appear in my story. The material in this book is based on interviews with family members and other survivors of the Holocaust, letters, tapes, legal documents, and historical research material primarily from the archives of Yad Vashem in Israel and the Yizkor Books.

INTRODUCTION

THE HOLOCAUST

"THE HOLOCAUST was the murder by Nazi Germany of six million Jews. While the Nazi persecution of the Jews began in 1933, the mass murder was committed during World War II. It took the Germans and their accomplices four and a half years to murder six million Jews. They were at their most efficient from April to November 1942—250 days in which they murdered some two and a half million Jews. They never showed any restraint, they slowed down only when they began to run out of Jews to kill, and they only stopped when the Allies defeated them.

There was no escape. The murderers were not content with destroying the communities; they also traced each hidden Jew and hunted down each fugitive. The crime of being a Jew was so great, that every single one had to be put to death—the men, the women, the children; the committed, the disinterested, the apostates; the healthy and creative, the sickly and the lazy—all were meant to suffer and die, with no reprieve, no hope, no possible amnesty, nor chance for alleviation.

Most of the Jews of Europe were dead by 1945. A civilization that had flourished for almost 2,000 years was no more. The survivors—one from a town, two from a host—dazed, emaciated, bereaved beyond measure, gathered the remnants of their vitality and the remaining sparks of their humanity, and rebuilt. They never meted out justice to their tormentors—for what justice could ever be achieved after such a crime? Rather, they turned to rebuilding: new families forever under the shadow of those absent; new life stories, forever warped by the wounds; new communities, forever haunted by the loss."

—YAD VASHEM ARCHIVES [1]

MURDER OF THE JEWS IN POLAND

"JEWS LIVED in Poland for 800 years before the Nazi occupation. On the eve of the occupation 3.3 million Jews lived in Poland—more than any other country in Europe. Their percentage among the general population—about 10%—was also the highest in Europe.

After the conquest of Poland by Germany and the Soviet Union in September 1939, most of the Jews remaining within the area occupied by Germany—approximately 1.8 million—were imprisoned in ghettos. In June 1941, after the German invasion of the Soviet Union, the Germans began to imprison the rest of Polish Jewry in ghettos and to deport them to concentration and slave labor camps.

In December 1941 the murder of the Jews from the Lodz ghetto began in Chelmno with gas vans. Murder of Polish Jews in Auschwitz began in March 1942. After the basic guidelines for action were formulated at the Wannsee Conference, between March and July 1942 the Germans established three death camps in Poland (Operation Reinhard) close to main rail lines: Belzec, Sobibor and Treblinka. With the arrival of the deportation trains, the victims—men, women, and children—were sent straight to their deaths in the gas chambers.

On July 22, 1942, on the eve of the Ninth of Av in the Jewish calendar, the Germans began the mass deportations from the Warsaw ghetto. By the time they ended on September

21, Yom Kippur, some 260,000 inhabitants of the ghetto had been deported to the Treblinka extermination camp.

Approximately 1,700,000 Jews, primarily from Poland, were murdered in Belzec, Sobibor, and Treblinka by the end of 1943. Between September 1942 and the summer of 1944 tens of thousands of Jews, most from Poland, were murdered in Majdanek, outside of Lublin.

In the summer of 1944 the remaining 80,000 Jews from the Lodz ghetto were deported to be murdered. Most were sent to Auschwitz-Birkenau, while some were sent to the Chelmno murder site, which was reopened for this purpose. Approximately 300,000 Jews were murdered in Chelmno, mostly from Poland. The murders in Auschwitz and Chelmno continued until the Red Army liberated the camps in January 1945.

At the end of the war, approximately 380,000 Polish Jews were still alive in Poland, the Soviet Union, or in the concentration camps in Germany, Austria and the Czech territories."

—YAD VASHEM ARCHIVES [2]

PROLOGUE

MY MOTHER was in her thirties when last seen in the Miedzyrzec ghetto in Poland in 1942 when I was four years old. The Nazis may have shot or murdered my father in Treblinka. My brother was also murdered. The final destination for my mother was the Treblinka death camp.

Those who remembered my father before the war said I look very much like him. Many said I have my mother's eyes. It is only through black and white photographs sent to relatives in the United States before the war, that I know my parents and my brother, my grandparents, my father's brother and sister, and those who remained and were killed in Poland.

During those war years I lived in constant fear. As a young orphaned child, I didn't understand that my Polish tainted by the Yiddish I had spoken at home might be a death sentence. I have only a few childhood memories, fragments at best. Other evidence of my past consists of letters, tapes, diary entries, historical documents, survivor testaments, family stories, and photographs given to me years later. In one photograph I am less than one year old, then no others exist of me until I am seven, when the war ended. During that time I had three different identities.

For years, I avoided researching and internalizing the fate of my mother murdered in this horrific way. I avoided thinking of the fate of my father killed in his mid-thirties and my brother killed at the age of eight. But in 2010, with my three sons, Jonathan, James and Judson, I undertook a trip to Poland in search of the missing pieces of my past.

This is my journey of discovery.

My Mother, Hudesa Zajgman Rozencwajg

My Father, Uszer Rozencwaig

My Brother, Izrael Itzchak Rozencwajg

Father and Brother
Biala Podlaska

Below:
Mother and Brother
Letnisko
Domaczewo, Poland

Father and Brother, Biala Podlaska

Brother, Biala Podlaska

Gitta, less than one-year-old, Letnisko Domaczewo, Poland

So long as we are

being remembered

we remain alive.

—CARLOS RUIZ ZAFON

PART I
1938 – 1979

The German attack on the Jews of Poland was not a gradual or incremental program stretched over a long period of time, but a veritable blitzkrieg, a massive offensive requiring the mobilization of large numbers of shock troops.

—CHRISTOPHER BROWNING

POLAND

The Early Years / 1938 - 1946

IN 1939, I was one year old when the Germans invaded Poland and marched into Biala Podlaska. Jews were forced into the ghetto shortly after. We lived on a street assigned to the ghetto at #8 Grabanowska.

In 1942, the transport from Biala Podlaska to Miedzyrzec passed on country roads leading through forests and small villages. During the chaos it is possible that my mother risked dropping me off at the roadside rather than face certain death. She would have told me to run into the woods and hide there until the transport passed. A farmer found me wandering alone. It is likely he knew I was a Jew as those were the only children roaming in the forests. My blond hair and blue eyes did not betray that I was Jewish, so the farmer probably sheltered me until he could place me in the orphanage. It is also possible that my father gave me to a farmer he knew, who decided to take me to a teacher by the name of Chekanski who ran a school halfway between Biala and Miedzyrzec in order to save me. In Poland, teachers were considered highly intelligent and the farmer would assume Chekanski would know how to handle such a dangerous situation. The teacher may have determined it was safer for me in the nearby orphanage.

THE ORPHANAGE YEARS / 1942 – 1945

I ENTERED the orphanage at age four, was baptized a Catholic and given the name Maria Chekanska. I went to confession and prayed a lot. I have only snapshots of strange memories from this three-year period, but I can still feel the hunger.

In one memory with no context, I sat in a highchair, eating my food. A farmer and his two shirtless sons, their backs red and sunburned, had just come in from the green fields all around us. The man whipped his sons on their backs. I heard loud shouting, so I sat very still, afraid that I would also be beaten.

My other fragmented memories take place in or near the orphanage. We were each fed an unappetizing portion of soup, porridge or bread. At times I thought there were moving insects in the soup. We were forced to drink a daily dose of castor oil. We lined up and had a large spoonful of vile thick fishy tasting liquid poured into our mouths that made me gag.

We had to use an outhouse some distance from the main orphanage building. One night I had the urge to go so badly, I made my way to it by myself. When I finished, I saw a pile of long worms that appeared to be tied together at the bottom of the receptacle. I wondered if I had expelled them from my body. I ran back in the darkness to the shelter of my bed, too mortified and ashamed to talk to anyone about the worms.

I can still see the priest in black in another fragment. Wandering around on a large farm, I came upon a priest sitting in a tower eating a plate of ripe, red tomatoes. I stopped and stared, envious of the food. I wished I could eat the delicious tomatoes. Dressed in black garments and black hat, the priest appeared lost in thought. He didn't look at me.

One night, ill with a high fever, I woke to see the priest in black with a nun wearing a headscarf at my bedside. They applied hot suction cups to my back. They looked extremely worried and this frightened me. A third person, probably the doctor floated in and out of my consciousness.

A Sister told me to go to the priest for confession in another memory. She said I had to tell him something bad I had done. Anxious, I approached the wooden booth where he waited and took my place. I sat there, confused and nervous, trying to think of what I should say. A few moments passed. "I stole some bread Father," I stammered. He absolved me, told me to say some prayers and "sin no more." I got up and left as quickly as I could.

In one snapshot we surrounded the Head Sister as she stood in her full-length nightgown, her hair in a long braid, a shawl hanging from her shoulder. I crouched, holding on to her with the other children while a dark haired, unshaven man in a short leather jacket and cap stood in the doorway and aimed a rifle at the Sister. We all cried, screamed, and prayed. The armed intruder hesitated and then lowered his rifle. In one swift movement he returned to the night. The Sisters calmed us down and we finally fell asleep.

We found an unexploded device one morning after a bombing, split in half like a giant melon, exposing wires of different colors inside. I saw myself looking at this strange object with curiosity.

In yet another frightening memory we found ourselves in a tunnel somewhere on the property of the orphanage. One of the Sisters took my hand. We carried pillows and blankets. The light from a lamp they carried illuminated the interior. Our white pillows and bedding comforted me next to the earthen walls. We lay down close to one another and yielded to an uneasy sleep.

IDA RETURNS 1945

AFTER THE war, in mid 1945, Ida Rozenszajn returned to Biala
Podlaska to lay claim to her family house, as well as to property buried by her father. One day she went into a local shop
where she met Polanka, a friend and neighbor before the war.
Polka, as Ida called her, spoke fluent Yiddish common among
Polish shopkeepers who traded with the Jewish population
daily. She greeted Ida with enthusiasm. Ida responded to her
friendly manner coupled with her sympathy and compassion
for the Jews.

Polka, who knew my parents well, told Ida that shortly
after the war she had seen the daughter of Usher Rozencwajg
in town with a large group of children accompanied by nuns.
It was on a National Polish Holiday or the day of a religious
celebration and the children were on an excursion from the
nearby orphanage. Polka was certain she had seen me because
I looked so strikingly like my father. Stunned by this information, Ida knew that she had to take action in spite of the perils
she would face. To take me from the orphanage she would have
to travel to the rural area, which would be extremely dangerous.
The killing of Jews who had survived the barbaric concentration camps was still common by some Poles. She would risk
her life if she tried to rescue me. "There were so few Jews left
and the ones that did survive the concentration camps were
homeless and in deteriorating health and I felt I had to do
something," she told me, years later. "I knew your family, and I

knew you, and I couldn't allow that beautiful blond haired little girl who I had seen playing so happily in the streets of Biala years ago, to be forever lost to us. Not after so many millions, and especially the children, had been killed. I didn't want you lost to the Jewish people. I was young, strong and enthusiastic. I spoke a perfect Polish without the trace of an accent. I had a Polish face and had no problem passing as a Polish Christian. I knew I was the perfect person for this."

Ida went to the committee in Lodz formed to help surviving Jews and to locate the missing. She told them that I had survived the war and volunteered to obtain my release from the orphanage located about 25 kilometers outside the city of Biala Podlaska.

In a photo from the day Ida retrieved me from the orphanage taken on the concrete steps in front of a wooden building, I am sitting on the lap of one of the nuns who wears a street dress. I appear very thin, my face hollow. I am wearing a plaid cotton dress with a white hat. I look forlorn and cold. I am being taken from the only home I had known for three and one half years where I was baptized and protected. I spent the war years living there as Marysia Chekanska, an orphaned little Catholic girl.

After Ida rescued me, I went to live with her in Lodz in the fall of 1945 until sometime in 1946. I was petrified to leave the confines and safety of the orphanage to go with her. I was told that she was a Jew and that Jews make Matzot of

Christian children's blood. I thought Ida would kill me, so I wouldn't let go of the Head Sister. Eventually, I realized that I had to leave.

Ida lived with her sister, her sister's husband, and their daughter Carmella who was a little older than me. We sat together at the table at mealtime. At the orphanage I received only a small portion of food, so when I went to live with Ida I asked her for my portion. She told me they did not separate their food into portions.

In the evening Carmella and I were bathed in a large portable basin in the center of the room. She always went first and then I had to bathe in her water. I couldn't understand why she would get clean water and I would not. To me the dirty bath water symbolized my inferiority.

Ida and her family spoke Yiddish. In the orphanage I spoke only Polish, but Ida chose to send me to a Jewish school in Lodz, where they spoke Yiddish. On my way there one day, I panicked at the thought of being out on the street alone, not knowing which way to turn. I stood on the corner confused and afraid. I did not know if I was Jewish or if other people thought I was Jewish. Uncertain if I had been hidden away in the orphanage because I was a Jew, I thought it must be shameful and didn't know whether to admit to it.

I didn't feel like I belonged. I was fearful of everything. When Ida saw me so unhappy, she asked why and I told her that I didn't like the new school. I felt out of place with the

Jewish environment and didn't understand what they were saying. So she decided that I could attend a different school.

I began to feel comfortable and secure with Ida. Many times she talked to me about my uncle in Paris, but I didn't understand what that meant. I loved being with her. One day she told me I had to leave to be with him. She packed all my things and we rushed out of the apartment.

"Where are we going? Where are we going?" I kept asking.

"We're going on the train. You have to go to Paris," she said in haste.

"Will you come with me?"

"Yes," she replied.

I calmed down when I knew she would be with me. But as soon as we arrived at the train station she turned, "I can't go with you. They won't let me on. Your uncle will find you." A woman pulled me away from her and onto the train. As it departed, I began to scream. Torn away from Ida, all alone and on my way to an unknown destination, I continued to yell hysterically. I don't know how long the train ride lasted. Unable to feel or see anything but darkness, I felt like a ghost.

Gitta on the last day at the Orphanage, 1945

Gitta leaving the Orphanage with Ida, 1945

Gitta leaving the Orphanage with Ida, 1945

At the Retrieval of the Rozencwajg child from the Orphanage (translated from Yiddish written on back of photograph). *Left to right:* The priest of Sitnik, a government representative of the Biala magistrate, i.e.; municipal government, Ida Rozenshayn, our representative, the administrator of the Orphanage with the child.

Gitta, Ida and the Biala Podlaska Committee, Lodz, Poland

Ida and Gitta in Lodz, Poland

PARIS

1946—1948

I ARRIVED the following day in Paris on the train. After I disembarked I found myself waiting in the midst of a crowded building that looked like an army barracks. A man, woman, and a girl close to my age approached me. My Uncle David, his wife Aunt Jenna, and their daughter Regine introduced themselves. Regine started to play with me, then after a short time she told me to pick up my little suitcase. She took my hand and walked me to the long concrete stairway. Her parents followed and whisked us into a waiting car. Just seven years old, I would begin a new life with them.

We drove to their small apartment on Rue D'Aboukir that served as their home and place of business. During the day the main room turned into their work and sales area. Uncle David did the pattern cutting and Aunt Jenna did the sewing. At night, they rolled up all the materials and made up a sleeper sofa for us. We had a bathroom closet (toilet) in the kitchen, but no bathtub. We had to bathe in a public bathhouse.

I liked my Uncle David and felt his warmth toward me. He was a handsome, quiet man. His wife Jenna showed me love and affection. I could tell she was genuine from her toothy smile and crinkled up eyes. Regine, who looked like her mother was only a little older than me, so we spent a lot of time together. My aunt's mother, Miriam Friedman, an elderly religious woman also lived with us. I did not feel at all close to her.

The transition to my new life in Paris was difficult. In the beginning, I experienced frequent nightmares. Anxious and frightened, I soiled myself at night and had to bear the shame. After a while, I settled in and became more comfortable. When Uncle David's business improved we moved to a larger apartment on Rue St. Denis with a third floor balcony overlooking the street. My aunt and uncle had their own room. Regine and I shared a bedroom and Regine's grandmother had a room of her own off the kitchen. We also had the luxury of a separate bathroom with a bathtub.

I attended the girl's public school in walking distance from our new apartment. I always looked forward to lunch at school. It usually consisted of a sandwich brought from home made of butter and small pieces of chocolate. I didn't speak the language so they put me in Regine's class. That way she could translate the French lessons to me in Yiddish. One day in math class, I knew the answer to a math problem written on the board and raised my hand to give the answer. Not realizing that I would answer in Polish, I spoke up. Everyone in class laughed at me. I was so humiliated that I did not speak up again.

Over time I began to learn French and my Yiddish improved as my aunt's mother only spoke Yiddish. I started to make a few friends. On one occasion, they asked me to get money from the house, so I took some from my aunt's purse and gave it to them. When my aunt discovered the money missing, I was afraid I would be found out. Somehow, no one ever blamed me.

Food was scarce during the war. We kept it in a traditional icebox in the kitchen. We had to buy a slab of ice from the ice peddler who hauled it up every day to keep the food cold. Because of the shortages, families were given ration cards to buy staples such as milk, butter, and eggs. Regine and I were sent to buy food with the cards. We stood in line on the sidewalk and waited while they poured milk into our metal container. One day, a man followed us on our way home. When we picked up our pace and began running, he ran after us. We made a dash into the apartment building and he followed us up the stairs. Outside our apartment we screamed to be let in. When the door opened, the man ran back down the stairs. I did not know why he chased us. The experience terrified me.

My warmest memories are of lying next to my Aunt Jenna, cradled in her arms on her sofa. When she spoke, her words comforted me. At the time she was pregnant, expecting her second child. When she went into labor, she was taken to the hospital. She never came back. The next time I saw her she was covered in a white sheet. She died in childbirth of an embolism on January 14, 1948.

Her death stunned the family and community. Throngs of mourners arrived at her funeral to grieve her sudden, senseless death. In anguish, they lamented. After all the unfathomable tragedies they had suffered: hiding from the French anti-Semites ignited by Hitler, and the death of thousands in their former community of Biala Podlaska, out of which they were lucky to have escaped, why this? They had just begun to live with newfound stability, security and the beginnings of joy. Then Aunt Jenna, a woman full of life and warmth and hope died. Her family, mother, sisters (Jenna was one of five sisters, one was killed in Poland) had to resume their lives without her.

After her death, the atmosphere at home changed. A shroud of emptiness and loneliness laid over all of us: my uncle David, Regine, my aunt's mother Miriam, and me. Aunt Jenna's distraught mother seemed to focus all her sorrow on me. Her role as a Yiddish speaking grandmother, "Bubba" to Regine, held no familiarity. Dressed in traditional loosely fitted clothes, a cooking apron, thick stockings with slippers or walking shoes, and a wig pinned in a bun denoting her Jewish orthodoxy, she looked at me so seriously, with her grief stricken eyes. I thought she blamed me. I was the orphan taken in by her daughter and my uncle, and now her daughter was dead. My mind grappled with guilt-ridden thoughts. Didn't everyone I was close to die? I had been in Paris less than two years. This tragic event would change the course of my life once again.

Regine's confidence overshadowed my feelings of inferiority but we had good times together that I remember mostly through photographs. Regine and I hand in hand in the playgrounds in Sables d'Olonne, a summer resort on the Atlantic Ocean, or on either side of Uncle David at the beach in bathing suits and rubber caps, both of us suntanned. In one, I wear a bow in my hair while Regine's hair is braided. We both look lighthearted, I look radiantly happy!

One day Uncle David called me to come into the kitchen alone with him. He held my arms and told me that he had to take Regine with him for a while and needed to leave me behind. I could see the sorrow and regret in his eyes, but he left me nevertheless. I went out to the balcony and watched them walk together down the sidewalk. Sad and lonely, I wondered if they would come back. Terrified that I would never see them again, I started to breathe heavily, and then began to cry and scream. Out of control, I became lightheaded and passed out on the balcony. When my uncle finally returned and I revived, relief flooded over me.

After Aunt Jenna died, discussions began as to whether I would stay with Uncle David in Paris or be sent to live with my father's brother, Uncle Martin and his wife, Aunt Hilda, in New York. Unprepared for another separation, I thought this distant day was sometime in the unthinkable future. When that day came, I felt an alarming and unsettling sensation. When Aunt Hilda first entered Uncle David's apartment and I was introduced to her, I sensed hostility between them.

Aunt Hilda wore a grey suit, a fashionable grey felt hat with an upturned wide brim, and laced black shoes revealing thick ankles. She had dark curly hair, small brown eyes, a large aquiline nose that broadened at the base, and narrow pursed lips. She looked nervous, harried and burdened, her voice loud and unfriendly as she talked to my uncle. She did not show any sense of warmth or gentleness and I had no desire to be with her. Her appearance and the brashness of her voice put me off.

She approached me with a smile and asked to take me out for a walk. We communicated in Yiddish and Polish. When we stopped at a *brasserie*, she offered me hot chocolate and hard-boiled eggs on display in egg holders. Eating made me happy and more relaxed. After eating two eggs, I was still hungry, but Aunt Hilda in her brusque manner refused to let me have another one. "You'll get sick if you eat any more," she said. Her harsh tone frightened me and I was relieved when she took me back to the apartment.

Aunt Hilda and I didn't get along from the start. She spent many months in Paris and worked hard to obtain a visa for me to enter the United States. As a Polish national, I was caught up in the quagmire of the U.S. Immigration laws. The allocated quota of visas for displaced persons per year was four times as numerous for persons of German and Austrian countries (25,957 visas) than those of Poland (6,524 visas). However, based on my compelling story and Poland's shifting borders, she eventually convinced the American Counsel to issue me a visa under the German quota.

During the six months that it took Aunt Hilda to obtain my visa, we spent time together in Paris. She stayed in a small walk up apartment that belonged to a friend's sister and husband, Albert and Sluva. Albert, a professional photographer, took beautiful photographs of our time in Paris together. In the photographs I am smiling and you can see the gap from a missing tooth. It is fall and I am dressed in a skirt and argyle sweater, a fur coat draped over my shoulders. My aunt wears a suit and hat. The Eiffel Tower is in the background of many photos. Some photographs are taken at the Tuileries where Albert's wife, their two children, Aunt Hilda and I pose in front of a fountain.

Aunt Hilda liked to visit landsmen, people who came from the same district and immigrated to Paris from Biala Podlaska before the war. They survived by hiding in the south of France during France's occupation. In 1940, France was partitioned into the occupied and unoccupied zones. The Nazis occupied the Northern and Western part of France. 350,000 Jews lived in the metropolitan area, 250,000 lived in and around Paris. Jews in the occupied zone had to declare themselves at a police station by Nazi Ordinance dated September 21, 1940. This registration aided the roundup of Jews in July 1942 by the French police who also rounded up children.

When I wasn't in school, Aunt Hilda took me with her to see the landsmen. She walked quickly, with the bearing and stride of a person on a mission. I wondered if she was too pre-occupied to remember that I was with her. I could barely keep up and was frightened I would lose her.

Finally, the day of our departure from France arrived in June 1948. Aunt Hilda and I boarded the SS Washington, one of the largest ocean liners, at Le Havre, France, bound for New York. Restored to its pre World War II luxurious standards, it accommodated 1,106 passengers in a single class. Once again I found myself with a woman, a stranger to me just six months before, bound for another country. I felt sad to leave Uncle David, Regine and my home in Paris, but I had no power to control my destiny. The enormous ship with its maze of rooms, decks, compartments, staircases and people overwhelmed me. I was afraid of getting lost but Aunt Hilda watched over me. We shared a cabin with other passengers. She slept in the lower bunk and I slept above her. The pitching of the ship in the vast Atlantic Ocean frequently made me seasick.

On a tour of the ship one day, Aunt Hilda and I passed a beauty salon. She suggested I have my hair washed. Going to a beauty salon was a new experience for me, especially on an ocean liner. I agreed and she left. After they washed my hair, they put my head inside the concave metal hood of a free standing dryer. The temperature became too hot and I didn't know what to do. My scalp burned and I started crying. Finally

I got their attention and was rescued from the hair dryer. Aunt Hilda raised her voice at me for not removing my head from the dryer and then yelled at the beauticians for not taking better care of me.

Food was abundant on board and all the tables in the dining room were covered with white tablecloths. At my table, I met a boy a few years older than me, traveling with his uncle to New York and eventually to South America. He too had spent the last years in Europe during the war and lost his parents. Happy to be united with his uncle, I could see the strong affection they had for each other.

After a week on the ship, we finally reached our destination. I would begin another new chapter of my life in America.

Above: Aunt Jenna
Below: Uncle David in Polish Cavalry Uniform, August 6, 1932

Gitta (at bottom) and Regine (on swing), Sables d'Olonne, France

Left to right: Regine and Gitta, Paris

Left to right: Gitta and Regine, Sables d'Olonne, France

Left to right: Gitta, Uncle David and Regine, Sables d'Olonne, France

Left to right: Gitta, Uncle David and Regine, Sables d'Olonne, France

Left to right: Aunt Hilda and Gitta, Paris

Left to right: Gitta and Aunt Hilda, Paris

Gitta and Aunt Hilda, Paris

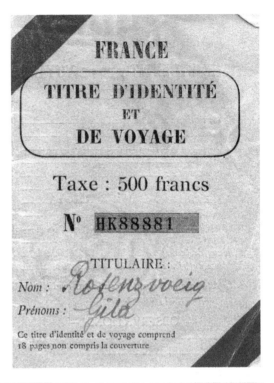

Right: Gitta's French identity and travel document

Below: Gitta's U.S. Immigrant Visa, May 25, 1948

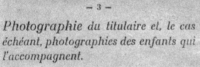

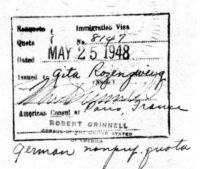

Aunt Hilda and Uncle Martin

NEW YORK

New York / 1948—1979

I WAS nine years old when we arrived in New York Harbor on June 25, 1948. A teeming crowd filled with excitement waited for the passengers to disembark. As we walked down the steep gangway, I held on to my Aunt Hilda, in anticipation of meeting my Uncle Martin for the first time.

We made our way through the maze of people until we found him. A pleasant looking man with a balding head, he had a light complexion, clear blue eyes and full lips. He was so happy to see me. He held me close, kissed and hugged me warmly.

Aunt Hilda's sister Esther, and her husband Aaron, along with Aunt Hilda's brother Nathan, and his wife Sarah, came to greet us. We exchanged many kisses and embraces making me feel very special and cared for. Aunt Esther, a short woman with dark hair and eyes made the biggest impression on me. She presented me with a doll wearing a beautiful pink silk dress. The doll had blond hair and eyes that opened and closed. I immediately sensed Aunt Esther's tenderness. She made me feel comfortable.

We drove from the Harbor to Townsend Ave in the Bronx where my uncle and aunt lived. We climbed two stories up in a new six-story red brick building and entered their apartment to welcoming shouts and cheers. After so many months, Aunt Hilda's friends were excited to see her. These people had lost many close family members in Poland. They were in a state of joy and wonder on seeing me. After a few hours of welcoming and congratulatory conversation of which I was the center of attention, I settled into the apartment that contained a living room with dining area, kitchen, bedroom and bath. Outside, a short distance away, an elevated subway passed by, making a thunderous clanging racket every fifteen minutes on its way to the nearby station.

They put a bed in the corner of the living room for me next to the window. I wasn't accustomed to sleeping by myself in a modern open space. I was used to old high ceiling apartments in Europe with large windows overlooking courtyards. In the orphanage I had slept with many children in the same room. When I lived with Ida in Lodz I shared her bed, and in Paris I shared a room with Regine. Afraid of the dark, and startled by the frequent clanging from the subway, I lay awake for a long time each night, not wanting to be there. Lonely and sad, I kept thinking about Uncle David and my former home in Paris. I missed the beautiful city, the tree lined streets and colorful shops. I longed for the family I had known there.

I was introduced to a variety of new foods. At first, I could not tolerate the richness of sour cream and cream cheese. Even the texture of bananas tasted strange to me.

Right away when my Uncle Martin was playful, I became more adventurous. He looked affectionately at me with his blue eyes. His nearly bald head was surrounded by what remained of his wiry blond hair. He often put on a T-shirt when he came home and relaxed in his favorite chair. He would pull me onto his lap and wrap his arms around me. He teased me by pinching my backside and exclaiming that he needed to fatten me up, or saying that I had very long arms. He smiled through his full lips and in Yiddish said that I had "lange lapes". Unlike Aunt Hilda, he made me feel safe and secure.

When I couldn't sleep, I risked going into their bedroom. I went to Uncle Martin's side of the bed and lay down beside him. I was never tempted to lie next to my aunt on her side. Uncle Martin would make room for me and I would fall asleep snuggly in his arms. I did this many nights. One night as I neared their bed, my uncle moved all the way over to the edge of the bed leaving no room for me. The only space left was on Aunt Hilda's side. I suspected this was planned, as my aunt resented my choosing to lie next to my uncle, which I had overheard them discuss. Reluctantly, I dutifully went over to my aunt's side and lay down. I didn't like being that close to her or pressing against her body. I didn't question this incident, but it was the end of my nightly visits to their room. I missed sleeping next to my uncle and the physical closeness that soothed me, but I did not speak up. I didn't want to chance making my aunt angry.

Early on in our relationship, Aunt Hilda exhibited her unpredictable behavior. I had only been in the United States a few weeks, when she and I were standing on a crowded subway platform during rush hour in New York after visiting the family doctor. I held on to her hand. The train made its way noisily through the tunnel. As the train approached and eased toward the platform, people held on to their hats against the gust of wind it created, as skirts and trousers were plastered against the bodies of those in the front. The train came to a squeaking stop. The people crowded inside maneuvered and made their way to the doors of the subway cars.

Hardly waiting for the passengers to exit, the crush to enter overwhelmed me. I felt like I was drowning in a sea of people and held on to Aunt Hilda's hand in desperation as she pulled me toward the door. Propelled by the crowd, she pushed forward onto the train. Unaccustomed to traveling with a child, she did not take sufficient care against the tugging and pushing of people to ensure that I was not separated and our handgrip was broken. People continued to rush in and the doors closed. The train pulled away and I was left standing on the platform. Through the glass door of the slowly departing train, I saw my aunt's frantic face. She mouthed words and gestured with her hands. I understood that she wanted me to remain on the platform. Panic washed over me. I stood there, alone and abandoned. Was I to stay there? Would she come back? Afraid to turn my head or move my body, it seemed an eternity that I waited for her. Other trains came into the station. People approached me, but I could not speak. I did not understand what they were saying and I could not make myself understood. Finally I saw my Aunt Hilda running towards me, her face distressed and flustered, her lips pursed. She was out of breath. The relief at the sight of her enveloped me. "Don't tell Uncle Martin what happened to you," she said, after we boarded and settled into the train. She knew he'd be furious. When I saw him, I ran to him. When he held me, I couldn't help but tell him what had happened. His eyes flashed with anger. " Why didn't you listen to me," he shouted at Aunt Hilda, "I told you not to take the subway."

Aunt Hilda had left her hometown of Biala Podlaska in Poland at the age of twelve after her mother died of mushroom poisoning. This was not an uncommon occurrence in Poland where hunting for mushrooms was a family tradition and the wooded landscape offered many varieties. It was easy to mistake a deadly one that looked similar to a regular one before it opened.

Aunt Hilda's older sister Esther immigrated to the United States, so my aunt went to live with her. Uncle Martin owned a bicycle shop in Biala Podlaska and married Hilda when she returned in her early twenties as an American citizen. Although my grandparents were Orthodox Jews, my father, Uncle Martin, and the other siblings appeared from their photos and their occupations to be assimilated and modern. Uncle Martin had a girlfriend he was enamored with in Biala Podlaska, but the opportunity to leave Poland in the 1930s by marrying Aunt Hilda was irresistible. The political and economic instability during the 1920s and creeping anti-Semitism caused him to make this decision. As history unfolded, this choice proved to be a lifesaver. He never saw his family in Poland again.

Until I came to live with them, Aunt Hilda earned a living as a hat maker in a millinery factory. She had a passion for socialist political movements, which characterized the Jewish community in their quest for a utopian society. This fervency continued after I joined them. She was active in the Jewish Federation Workers called the Bund. Through her charitable actions and donations, she gained a reputation amongst outsiders, the Jewish community, and strangers. At times, however, she could be naïve. At one point she met a homeless, alcoholic man who she hired to perform odd jobs around the house. Her sympathy for his plight prompted her to invite him to live in our basement. She made him promise to give up drinking. Overjoyed by her generosity, he readily agreed, but his temperance lasted only a few weeks. It shocked me that as time went on, she even cleaned up his vomit. When this continued, she finally asked him to leave.

Uncle Martin arrived in the United States in 1933 during the height of the depression. He had great difficulty finding work. The country with the reputation of having sidewalks paved with gold morphed into hardship, struggle and deprivation. His health became a problem. For several years he suffered with ulcers. His diet was severely restricted and he had one surgery after another, crisscrossing his torso with scars. For years after his arrival, he endured abdominal pain, and the effect on his temperament took its toll.

On one of his jobs, he met Frank Piotrowski, a Polish American. They decided to open a business together, one of the first ballpoint pen factories, Ballerina Pen Co. under the manufacturing name of Framar (Frank and Martin). Uncle Martin ran the machine shop where his accent and poor English didn't matter, while Frank managed the office and sales. The business grew quite profitable and with success as a businessman, Martin became conflicted about his politics. He still leaned toward communism believing like many others that Stalin saved Jews during World War II. He did however vote for Rockefeller for Governor.

⌒

During the 1950s, Frank invited us to their annual family Christmas dinner. I met his wife Marie, a well-mannered, reserved woman older than Frank, and their young children. I was delighted as I entered their small, comfortable house illuminated by the lights of a Christmas tree. Following brief introductions and conversation, we sat down at a table decorated with holiday ornaments and were served turkey dinner with trimmings. After we ate, I opened my unexpected present near a cozy fireplace. This novel holiday celebration, which I experienced for the first time filled me with warm, affectionate feelings.

Aunt Hilda and Uncle Martin spoke Yiddish to each other at home and to their friends and relatives. While living in the Bronx, I attended P.S. 64. My main task was to learn English. I had a wonderful teacher, Miss Dora Adams, a middle aged woman with short thinning hair. She paid special attention to me and wanted me to succeed. Every afternoon after school I sat at the pull down desk in the living room where I did homework, and learned vocabulary by writing words ten times each. I caught on to English quickly. I even entered a Spelling Bee in class, but I stumbled on a very common word *ice*. I just could not visualize the sound of the word. Miss Adams was sympathetic and consoled me. I knew she was rooting for me. I took my schoolwork seriously and excelled as a student. I loved cut-out fashion books and also coloring books. I always made sure I colored within the lines. I worked well with rules and boundaries established by assignments. I maintained good grades, received awards, and had a reputation as a bright student. I never missed school except for illness, and received a Certificate of Attendance in 1950. At Wade Jr. High School I was presented with a Scholarship Award for the period ending 1951, and two others undated.

In 1950, Uncle Martin and Aunt Hilda decided to adopt me. Soon after we went to the lawyer's office and they signed the official documents. I thought this very special and confirmed their love for me, but it was Aunt Esther, who I came to really love. She had a totally different temperament than her sister Hilda.

Aunt Esther slept over on many of her visits from nearby Yonkers, which gave her an opportunity to spend more time with me. Once after sleeping over, I asked her to stay another night. "I can't, I have to go home," she said. I found comfort in her company and tried to think of a way to make her stay. She had large breasts like Aunt Hilda so I decided to hide her brassiere in the back of a bookshelf close to the floor. Women of large breast size wore corsets or long brassieres that attached to the stiff foundation garment. They would not go out on the street without wearing one so I knew Aunt Esther would not leave without her brassiere. I was delighted with my mischievous act, but sure they would find it. To my surprise, when I came home from school, she had not found the brassiere after hours of searching. I didn't think the hiding place was all that elusive. She sat in the living room looking trapped and forlorn. Aunt Hilda started screaming hysterically at me. "Do you realize what you did? Esther had to go home. She had a doctor's appointment, she had to go shopping and prepare dinner for her husband. How could you be so inconsiderate? Why would you do such a thing?" I located the brassiere, but she continued to yell. She could not see the humor in the situation, nor control her rage. Aunt Esther conveyed her sadness at Aunt Hilda's harsh treatment of me.

In photographs of Hilda as a young woman, she appears attractive, full bosomed with a trim figure, about five feet tall, with rather heavy legs. Her dark hair is curly and unruly. She has small brown eyes, a long nose and thin lips. With age she became heavier and lost her shape. Her hair turned grey and became more unmanageable. She relied on her corset to mold her body into shape. She wore it only when she left the house, wearing either a smart tailored suit or dress and a hat. When she took the foundation garment off, her large breasts sagged revealing marks from the pressure of the stays and lacing. Her heavy thighs and legs were marbled with veins for which she eventually had painful surgery. Unaccustomed to seeing a mature, naked woman, the sight of her undressed disturbed me. I hoped I would never look like that. At home she wore a housedress to cook and clean, as was the custom at that time, and did not make any attempt to improve her appearance. When she did go out to weddings, or on other occasions and wanted to dress up, she asked me to put her makeup on for her. I happily applied pancake foundation, eyeliner, eye shadow, and mascara. I then applied her lipstick. She seemed satisfied with my effort, and I liked the way she looked too.

In 1951, we moved from the small apartment in the Bronx with one bedroom and one bathroom adjacent to the elevated subway, to a spacious house in the suburbs of Queens. This newly built community consisted of a large parcel of land equivalent to six streets in Hollis Hills near Bayside where the choice was a two story or a ranch house. We bought a two-story house, a happy occasion for everyone. Uncle Martin's business was doing well. He paid twenty-one thousand dollars in cash. Paying cash in full was not unusual. Uncle Martin looked down on newly originated credit card payment. It characterized a person without money. Whenever buying a new car or any household furnishings, food or clothing, everything was paid for in cash. "Vell, if you don't have the money, you don't buy it," he would say.

The closest major thoroughfare, Union Turnpike, provided access to buses. The walk from the house to the bus was approximately one half mile each way and then a forty-five minute ride by bus to the subway. We entered the house through a small vestibule with a coat closet on the right. The living room opened to the dining room on the left. The entrance hallway led to the staircase on the right and two doors; the first door opened to a flight of stairs to the basement and the other door opened to the guest bathroom close to the kitchen which had its own dining area overlooking our back yard. The odd proximity of the bathroom and basement doors never entered anyone's mind.

On occasion when both Aunt Esther and her husband Aaron came to visit they slept over to avoid traveling back home in the evening. She slept upstairs and Uncle Aaron, a short, thickset, quiet man with grey hair slept on the living room sofa. One morning, I came down from my bedroom late, to a room full of weeping, despondent people. "What happened?" I asked. Uncle Aaron had mistaken the basement door for the bathroom door and they found him dead of a broken neck at the bottom of the basement staircase. In spite of this tragedy, they never put a lock on the door to the stairs.

Popular for entertaining, homeowners often added a wood paneled room in the basement with a built in bar. Ours had cedar walls, a bar, and a separate walled in space for the laundry and boiler area. When I was older, the room provided privacy for partying with my friends if Aunt Hilda and Uncle Martin were away for the evening. I took dates down there to listen to music on the Victrola. We danced and kissed and explored!

Newly planted hedges separated our backyard from our neighbors to either side and in back, but provided no privacy. The street behind us sloped down hill exposing it to floods from heavy rains that inundated the basement and street level of the houses, and left them looking like boats marooned at a marina. Possessions floated down the street. We were distressed for our neighbors, but relieved that we hadn't chosen a house there. The second floor of our house had three bedrooms and two baths. I had my own bedroom and bathroom. A lovely, aromatic lilac tree flourished under my window and bloomed profusely for a short time every spring. In the front yard, maple and birch trees thrived.

We usually all ate dinner together unless Uncle Martin came home late from the machine shop. Then he would take off his hat, coat and jacket, and sit in the swivel chair in the living room for almost an hour, while Hilda waited in the kitchen wearing her apron, until he was ready for dinner.

"Do you want to eat now?"

"A bit later," or "not yet," he'd say. "I have to get this noise out of my head. A whole day I am in the machine shop with the rattling and clanging and banging of the machines. My head is spinning. I have to settle down, I can't put food in my stomach yet."

Hilda prepared his favorite broiled rib steak, or sometimes lamb chops or roast chicken.

When she entertained in the dining room illuminated by a crystal chandelier, she seated the guests at the mahogany table covered with a white tablecloth. She would start the meal with a chopped liver appetizer served on a leaf of iceberg lettuce with a few slices of tomato. She made a variety of dishes of Jewish Polish origin such as brisket, flanken, roast chicken with stuffed derma, potato pudding, *latkes, luckshon* (homemade noodles), a variety of organ meats such as brains, sweet breads, calves liver with fried onions, and pecha (gelled cows feet). She made her own pasta dough and stuffed it with meat.

She also cooked breast of veal stuffed with potato and onions, roast beef, side dishes, and soup with kreplach, similar to ravioli or wontons. She generally served three different meats as entrees. She also did her own baking, particularly Mandelbrot, a form of biscotti, and coffee cakes.

Martin couldn't conceal his irritation and disapproval at the variety of dishes Hilda prepared and served, while everyone else complimented her. "Why are you serving so much food? Isn't one main dish enough? Why all this cooking?" He didn't hide his annoyance or even try to be cordial for the sake of the company. He just made surly comments. People ignored him and ate with gusto. I waited for the ticking bomb to explode, which it did many times and turned into shouting.

I don't know why Martin was so unappreciative of Hilda's talents and all the energy and enormous amount of work that went into her preparation and cooking. Eager to please, Hilda very much wanted his affection, but Martin always gave off an air of dissatisfaction and hostility. I never saw Uncle Martin and Aunt Hilda holding hands or kissing, not even a loving glance. They did have long conversations though as they walked around the block together.

The one thing I did love about Aunt Hilda was her cooking. She prepared everything meticulously. She often rendered chicken fat and placed the fat in a large glass jar to solidify and use for cooking. When she accumulated more jars of fat than needed, she gave them to visiting family members. She gave me the bits of crispy chicken skin that did not melt down, on a piece of bread, called *gribenes* in Yiddish. Although delicious, it gave me an introduction to heartburn. As a special treat for me, she made potato gnocchi (soft dumplings Polish style) with fried onions called *kluskie*.

On holidays Hilda prepared the traditional dish of Gefilte fish that consists of carp, pike and white fish, chopped in a wooden bowl with a hand chopper, mixed with other ingredients and boiled with the fish heads and bones for flavor. A regional dish served sweet or unsweetened, hot or cold, depending on the country of Eastern Europe or Russia you originated from. It was slightly sweetened and served warm in its own sauce with a piece of sliced carrot on top. We also ate it cold after the fish was refrigerated and the sauce turned into a jellied texture.

The smell of Hilda's cooking also irritated Martin, so she cooked at night while he slept and she couldn't. She closed all the doors to the kitchen, to the hallway, and to the bedroom. She put the vent on in the kitchen and opened the outside door to air out the odors. Sometimes I stayed in the kitchen with her as the frying and baking scents orbited the room. I knew she wanted my company. She rambled on for hours, but I didn't pay much attention. She expressed her gripes, grievances, and sadness as she chopped, stuffed, kneaded, and sliced. I was happy to be liberated when she said, "It's time for you to go to sleep."

At some point we bought a barbecue for the back yard and Martin discovered that he loved to grill. He had found his calling. No matter the heat, he stood shirtless with sweat dripping from his face flipping burgers, steaks and hot dogs for us and sometimes for guests.

Sundays were days when people dropped by for a visit, whether friends or family. There were no invitations or formalities. Hilda and Martin had many married friends who originated from Biala Podlaska. In the case of four or five of the couples, the men had married women (sometimes older) who could provide them with American citizenship. They didn't have children but they remained together. Visitors arrived unannounced dressed in suits, overcoats, and hats during the cold weather, and slacks and shirts during the summer. Aunt Hilda put out her spread of tea, percolated coffee, fruit, dried fruits, coffee cake and cookies. Chopped liver and crackers, prepared in advance, were also served. Her brother Nathan or "Net" the Jewish pronunciation for Nat, and his wife Sarah visited often. They took the subway and bus until he bought a car. Arriving by car was an event. We stood at the open door and watched through the screen while Nat attempted to parallel park. The car somehow ended up at an odd angle to the sidewalk. Aunt Sarah would then get out of the car to direct him, motioning him to turn the wheel. Many times when he was unsuccessful, out of frustration he just left his car in the middle of the street and Uncle Martin ran out of the house to park it for him.

Both Nat and Sarah worked in millinery shops. Uncle Nat,

a staunch communist and anti-Zionist, a reader of the *Freiheit*, had a fiery temper when it came to discussing politics. Aunt Sarah, soft spoken and gentle, was supportive and calming. Uncle Nat was convinced that communism would produce a just society and argued passionately with Uncle Martin, a leftist, and Aunt Hilda, who belonged to the Lincoln Brigade for women. Their tone became increasingly elevated and turned into raucous yelling as arms waved. I didn't understand what the fuss was about.

I frequently heard words and names shouted out such as: Vladimir Zabotinsky, Knut Hamsun, Bundism, Stalinism, Leninism, Socialism, Communism, Trotskyites, nihilism, anarchism, Zionism, Polish leader Pilsudski, and poets such as Bialik, Perez, and Tchernikhowsky. The political exchange based on the numerous political theories and philosophies at the end of World War II and the devastation to everyone's family fueled passionate discussions. Arguments became intense, aggressive, and opinionated. They struggled to reconcile their humanitarian views of Stalin who had joined Hitler after the invasion of Poland, and changed his allegiance to the Allies after Hitler invaded Russia. One time, Uncle Nat paced back and forth in an agitated manner as he disagreed with Uncle Martin who argued harshly from his swivel chair, and then Uncle Nat stormed out of the house. Aunt Sarah not surprised at the outcome of the argument, but surprised by the timing, gathered her things and ran after him. Their visits stopped for months. Eventually Aunt Hilda coaxed Uncle Nat to visit again and the same drama and exit replayed. I grew up thinking all political arguments were mortal combat. When I matured, I stayed away from any discussion involving politics.

In the summer of my eleventh year, Hilda and Martin sent me to a Hebrew camp where my cousin Malka and her husband Benjamin Rudavsky, a Reformed rabbi, were head counselors. I enjoyed Benjamin's boyish charm, and I immediately liked Malka, a dark haired, dark eyed loving woman. The first time I met her she wore a full skirt with lace stitching at the hemline, shaped wide by a crinoline, the fashion in the late forties. She read *Grimm's Fairy Tales* to me that captivated my heart. No one had ever read to me before. I didn't want her to leave.

Martin and Hilda meant well by sending me to Camp Massad in the beautiful Poconos Mountains with shimmering lakes. I enjoyed spending the summer with people my own age in a camp structure and I liked the athletics. I did not like the religious rituals and the Hebrew cultural activities though, such as theatre and events that involved instruction in Hebrew. I found myself again in an environment where people around me spoke a foreign language. I assumed that was the norm. As speaking Hebrew was preferred, I avoided conversations when the counselors were nearby.

During my second year at Massad, I developed a crush on a boy named Sheldon who also liked me. When I returned home after the summer, I was overcome by feelings of separation and loneliness. To me this was not just a teenage summer crush; it took on the dimensions of losing my one and only love. Nothing would console me. My chest felt as though squeezed by pincers leaving me breathless. When I finally worked up the nerve to telephone him and say hello, he responded nonchalantly as if to say the summer is over. That was then, and now is now. I was devastated. This marked the beginning of the road to many entanglements, romances, and relationships that I would handle in a yearning lovesick way. Each day of uncertainty would be torture; my sense of self immersed in feelings of worthlessness and dependence on another's response to me.

When I went to live with Uncle Martin and Aunt Hilda, they were childless. It was one of the factors that tipped the scale toward my being sent from Paris to live with them, along with the untimely death of Aunt Jenna. I was nine and one half years old then. They had been married for over 20 years and they assumed that Hilda could not have children. In 1951, three years after my arrival and subsequent adoption, Aunt Hilda became pregnant. It was not totally welcome news to her as she was in her early forties. One day, she stood leaning against the piano, her hair unkempt, angry about something I had done. "I wish I wasn't pregnant, how does it look? I am too old for this," she screamed. Enraged, she yanked me off the piano stool and slapped me. Stunned and furious, before

I could think, I raised my hand and hit her back. She stood there, shocked. She never hit me again, but the news of her pregnancy shattered me.

Soon after Marcia's birth, I began to lose Martin's attention. His new baby girl captivated him. Hilda and Martin were not comfortable being new parents. They continued to rely on their general practitioner, Dr. Weinstein, who delivered Marcia and became her pediatrician. One night Marcia became sick. Dr. Weinstein either prescribed an adult dosage of medication or they gave her the wrong dose. She had difficulty breathing. They called Dr. Weinstein and he advised them to immediately give her teaspoons of coffee until her breathing became regular. Martin ran down the stairs in a panic to get the coffee. When the first teaspoon proved insufficient, he did this repeatedly. Eventually she responded and they took her to the doctor's office.

Marcia's birth dethroned me from my status of only child who received all their attention, a position I had occupied for a short time. Once again I would take second place. I began to feel insecure. Would I be safe with them? Would they keep me? After all, I thought Uncle David had sent me away because I wasn't wanted. Regine had remained with him because she was his natural child.

After my adoption Aunt Hilda and Uncle Martin had asked me to call them *mother* and *father*. At the orphanage, I had called the nuns *sister* and the priest *father*, so to assign a family title to newfound relatives, first in Paris and now in New York, confused me. To call them by the parental terms of mother and father seemed foreign and uncomfortable when not long before they had been strangers to me. But following Marcia's birth, after much mental anguish, I forced myself to refer to them as *mother* and *father*. At thirteen I reasoned that if I used those endearing titles I would be in a safer position. I didn't want to become an outsider again. Although I called them Mom and Dad from then on, it didn't feel natural to me. In my mind they were still Aunt Hilda and Uncle Martin.

Marcia, a sweet, cute little girl, and fun to play with, went on trips with Hilda (Mom) and Martin (Dad). I was left behind, distressed at not being included. I focused on my being adopted, whereas Marcia was their natural child. On my birthday, I sensed they thought it more of a duty to give me a birthday present than a cause to celebrate. "We'll get you a present, but we're not sure what, and possibly in a few days." On one of my birthdays I received a watch, but the other birthdays were not memorable. I began to feel undeserving of recognition, not worthy of receiving presents.

During the time of Hilda's pregnancy and Marcia's birth May 23, 1951, I attended Public School 109 in Queens. In June 1952 I received an Honor Roll Certificate and a Service Award for lunch guard duties both date stamped by the principal Charles Veit. In September, I moved up to ninth grade.

The trip to Jamaica High took approximately one hour: a long walk to the bus stop, a change of buses followed by another walk to finally get to school. I was lost in the multitude of students, but I excelled in my studies particularly the languages of French and Hebrew. I graduated in fifth place in the January 1956 class. I was awarded Certificates of Scholarship for my earned averages for all the years I attended, 1952 through 1955. I also received Certificates of Excellence in Hebrew and a Certificate of Merit in French.

During my high school days, Marcia was a toddler. She frequently came to my room and wanted to play while I tried to concentrate on my homework. She wanted my attention, but we were thirteen years apart and I had little patience for all the interruptions. I would rush her out of my room so I could continue with my studies. She balked and fussed. I took care of her when Hilda and Martin were out, but we circled on different paths.

In all types of weather, Aunt Hilda took me for piano lessons on the Grand Concourse Blvd. in the Bronx. We walked in pelting down rain against gusts of wind that turned our umbrella inside out, our hair flying out like branches of a tree. Hilda sat in the dim waiting room during my lesson.

When we moved to Queens, Hilda arranged for me to have a new piano teacher who made house calls, Mr. Rubini. He always dressed in a suit and tie and wore a hat. On cold days he put on an overcoat. He walked from the bus to the house and back, regardless of the weather. We bought an upright piano and positioned it against the wall in the living room. I sat on the piano bench, and he sat on a chair next to me as I practiced the scales and played the assigned compositions from music sheets. Many times I peeked over at him during lessons and caught him dozing. I didn't wake him or say anything. I felt sorry for the short, bespectacled, even-tempered man. I was not a very talented piano player, and did not possess the gift of playing by ear. I had difficulty reading the notes until we realized that I needed glasses. The glasses made a big difference at school and they allowed me to actually see the written notes, but my confidence did not improve measurably.

I dreaded playing in front of people. According to Hilda, playing the piano promised a social entree and acceptability. "At a party if you are asked to play for people, look how popular you will be? You'll be such a hit," she said. I imagined playing the piano flawlessly at a gathering, surrounded by people, my hands nimble and proficient, playing tune after tune to the delight of the onlookers. What a fantasy! When guests came to the house, I would repeatedly be asked to play. I couldn't say I didn't feel like it, so I played quickly and nervously to the expected praise after I finished.

Mr. Rubini had a recital every year, where his students gathered to perform in front of all the parents. Each one of us selected a favorite piece and rehearsed it for months. I had progressed to playing difficult compositions and I chose "The Malaguena," by Ernesto Lecuona, music of a Spanish dance similar to the Flamingo. It is very dramatic and I loved playing it. I practiced it for many months and had become quite proficient, but performing it in front of people was another matter.

After playing the first section, which repeats and intensifies in volume, I could not continue. My anxiety and fear took over. I replayed the first part three or four times, hoping I would relax into it, but I finally gave up. I received applause and Mr. Rubini smiled with understanding, but I felt like a failure.

On a daily basis, Aunt Hilda asked, "Did you practice today?" I practiced everyday for an hour as I watched the clock. Having failed so miserably at the recital, I told Mr. Rubini the next time we met, after getting Aunt Hilda's permission, that I had decided to stop taking lessons. I found it difficult to voice my decision. I felt empathy for him, as he appeared so weary when he arrived and I thought I had let him down. I knew nothing about his personal life although he had taught me for several years. We never spoke about private matters, but I did think it might be a hardship for him to lose a student.

As for my dance lessons, girls were expected to take ballet classes, but ballet did not have the same social advantages as playing the piano. Hilda took me by subway to Carnegie Hall every Saturday. We rode the bus to the subway and then changed subway trains until we arrived to the West side at Seventh Avenue and 57th Street. We travelled over an hour each way. We sat together while she talked obsessively. Many times in the subway car she would remove a bundle of cash and methodically count her money. I did not understand why she did that in public and her behavior made me apprehensive. People seated across the aisle watched her with curiosity, but we were never accosted or robbed. Perhaps some of the money was part of her *knipple*, set aside secretly for a rainy day, as was the custom in the Jewish culture for women. When Aunt Hilda died, her *knipple* was discovered under the kitchen sink hidden among the potatoes and onions revealed to us by a neighbor in whom Hilda confided.

I loved ballet and excelled at it. I practiced in the basement of our house using a bar installed on the wall. I donned my ballet slippers and practiced the steps voluntarily. Being tall, slim and graceful, I looked like a young ballerina. I was asked to demonstrate steps by the instructor in front of the class, as I was more proficient than many of the other students. As I started to receive recognition, I began to take on my own identity and I became confident. I felt like a real ballerina, elegant, light and airy.

In the dressing area I watched other girls take on the appearance of ballet dancers. They applied mascara, tied their hair back, wore headbands, a scarf around the neck, tights and snug fitting tops. I had the same bodysuit and top, black tights and pink ballet slippers made by Capezio, the renowned manufacturer of ballet shoes. Aunt Hilda always watched me like a hawk. I couldn't do anything without her permission, but I took the chance of secretly applying mascara and makeup in the dressing room, hoping that she would not notice. The day I applied mascara, I came home from ballet class and went upstairs to my room to change. Aunt Hilda yelled up to me with her usual question, "Gitta, are you doing anything important?" To this, I always replied, "No," because I didn't know what she considered important or not. Was washing up important? Was reading important? Was looking at myself in the mirror important? "Come down to the kitchen," she shouted. Uncle Martin sat at the linoleum dinette table surrounded by windows overlooking the backyard. Hilda scrutinized my eyes, "Are you wearing mascara?" she asked in front of him. Nervous, I said, "No." She looked at my eyes again and said she didn't believe me. Right after that exchange she told me that she wouldn't be taking me to ballet classes any more, but that I could go there by myself. Mortified and unnerved, I knew I couldn't. Traveling alone was too frightening an experience for me to contemplate. It never occurred to me to map out the route to Carnegie Hall so that I could get there on my own.

I assumed that our Saturday journeys together would continue anyway. When Saturday came along and she made no indication of taking me, I announced I didn't want to take ballet anymore. The ballet school called and asked why I didn't come to class. I hesitated and said that I would come the next Saturday, hoping that Aunt Hilda would change her mind and take me. They called again the following week and I told the woman I wouldn't be taking any more classes. "You should continue, you are a good dancer," she said. I couldn't tell her the truth. I felt so shaken and forlorn. I never asked Hilda to take me again, or give me a chance to learn the route to see how comfortable

I might feel going alone. The thought didn't enter my mind. I had to do what I was told. I would never negotiate. It was a predicament I couldn't work my way out of other than to suppress my emotions. I believe Aunt Hilda knew that I wouldn't go by myself. She always needed to have control over me. She could not accept my love of ballet classes, nor could she accept my independent behavior of applying mascara without her permission. She knew she could stifle and control me by instilling fear. Her temper, aggressiveness and yelling elevated my insecurity. Although I feared her, I was dependent on her.

I spent a lot of time alone in my room either studying or reading. My friend Rochelle, an English major who lived in our neighborhood introduced me to the classics by English and Russian authors. She loved to read and spent most of her time after school reading to keep away from her two older brothers who had very different interests. I loved to sit for hours in a comfortable chair by my window reading as a means to escape.

During those teenage years, I hung glossy photos of movie stars on my mirror in the bedroom. Frightened and empty, I longed for the same illusion of perfection in myself and measured others by their appearance. Wasn't my life saved during the war because of my looks? Society worshiped the image of Marilyn Monroe and I looked forward to developing breasts like her. Instead I barely filled out an A cup, which made me more insecure and depressed. To be a woman, feminine and desirable I had to have large breasts. I could not convince myself otherwise. Any remark about my small breasts from Uncle Martin or a friend on the beach who criticized my choice of bathing suit because of my small breasts, further damaged my self-esteem.

When the original 1940 film *Gone With the Wind* was rereleased, I yearned to see it and made plans to go with friends. "You can't go to see that film," Hilda said when she found out. I did not challenge her decision. Instead, I decided to make amends for making her angry by cleaning the entire house. When I finished, she said. "Didn't you want to see the film? "Why didn't you ask me?"

I never bonded with Hilda. Her sudden outbursts of anger sprang from a lifetime of frustrations, but made no sense to me. She spoke about love, telling me that she loved me more than Marcia, her natural born child. She usually said it after she yelled at me. I found her statements confusing. She set up a rivalry between us. "I love you more than Marcia," she said. Was I to be grateful? Was that to dispel my negative feelings about her sporadic harsh treatment of me? People would say, "You know, she told me that she loves you more than Marcia." Contrary to her words, she took Marcia on vacation with her and left me at home. Both Martin and Hilda travelled with Marcia without asking me to join them. This treatment opened the old wounds of feeling unwanted.

Aunt Hilda knew no bounds. She always had center stage.

She was loud, dictatorial and intrusive. I had no privacy. When my friends came over, she sat with them and took over the conversation. When she wanted to reprimand me, she wouldn't wait until I came home from school, but pursued me to the play area and proceeded to scream and rage at me in front of everyone. Of course, I had to follow her home. Even as the years went by she wouldn't let go of her need to control and dominate me. When attending college I went shopping without her and bought a coat with a fur collar. "How could you buy this coat without me? It has a fur collar. Do you know what that means? You bought it without me, without my permission." I tried on the coat and she threw herself on the floor and hit her head against the wall continuously. "Stop it, stop it, I'll take it back," I screamed. Frightened, I didn't know what to do. I had seen her agitated and unhinged many times, but not to that extent. I kept apologizing to her until she calmed down.

One time, when I was in law school, she went through my chest of drawers and purses. She found a diaphragm in a drawer that I had covered with clothing and she interrogated me. If I kissed a young man I dated as we sat on the living room sofa, I felt her presence in the shadowy upper part of the staircase watching us. She never offered an instructional discussion about issues of life, particularly sex. I had the impression that Aunt Hilda considered it "dirty" and definitely something to stay away from. I had visions of her engaging in sex with teeth clenched and a dutiful attitude.

Aunt Hilda loved to sing and hum as she busied herself about the house cleaning, doing laundry in the basement, or cooking. She introduced me to many Jewish folksongs. One of the songs she sang frequently was a Partisan Song (Partizener Lid) called "Never Say."

YIDDISH
Zog nit keys mol az du geyst them letstn veg,
khotch himlen blayene farshteln bloye teg
kumen vet nokh undzer oysgebenkte sho
s'vet a poyk ton undzer trot: mit zaynen do.

TRANSLATION
Never say that this is the final road for you
Though laden skies may cover over days of blue
As the hour that we longed for is so near
Our step beats out the message we are here.

Written in 1943 by a young songwriter, Hirsh Glick, while an inmate in the Vilno Ghetto, the song was adopted by a number of Jewish Partisan groups operating in Eastern Europe. It became a symbol of resistance against Nazi Germany's persecution of the Jews. With sadness on her face, Hilda sang in Yiddish in a resonant, expressive voice that sometimes sounded like choked tears.

Jewish folksongs represent the life, culture, and religion of the Eastern European Jews. They include cradlesongs, marriage songs, and love songs usually sad and plaintive due to the separation of lovers owing to parental displeasure, interference, absence of a dowry or pedigree. The collection of songs is extensive and Hilda had a huge repertoire. I learned many songs listening to her singing the Yiddish lyrics.

In my early and mid teens, I attended meetings of the Biala Benevolent Society with Hilda and Martin. A group of people from Biala Podlaska—who either survived the concentration camps, eluded the roundups of the Nazis, or left before the war—met on the West downtown side of New York for their monthly gatherings. They were conducted in Yiddish, although some people spoke English with a thick Polish accent. The group performed charity work, made funeral arrangements, and organized social events. They served a delicious assortment of herrings, smoked salmon and bagels as well as coffee, tea, rugelach and coffee cake. They wanted to maintain the attachment to their old community.

At the meetings, I sat stiffly and ignored people such as Ida's sister and brother in law, Moshe Schneidman, who I lived with in Lodz, who might have provided information about my parents, my brother and my childhood. I never approached them at the meetings. I kept to myself and avoided contact until it was too late. Having been conditioned to behave unobtrusively so as not to be recognized, I reacted in an overly inconspicuous manner. Feeling a sense of duty and loyalty to Hilda and Martin, and also a fear of rejection and abandonment, I kept quiet and did not ask questions. I felt awkward and troubled knowing I was ignoring them, but I couldn't bring myself to acknowledge them. I did visit my Aunt Haya's husband Fiszel Lebenberg. Aunt Haya and their son Izrael were murdered during the Holocaust but somehow Fiszel survived. He suffered from dementia and provided scant information of my family and childhood. Much later when I was ready to grapple with my past, Ida's sister and many others were no longer alive.

From the age of fifteen on, I spent many summer vacations in Mexico City with relatives on my father's side who had left Poland, but could not enter the United States. I loved being with them. They were affectionate, pleasant and generous with me. Eva, my father's cousin, was a warm, attractive woman with dark hair and a sense of humor. She was married to Max, who had wavy blond hair, blue eyes and a Roman profile. They had three children: Hildita who was my age, and two younger brothers, Abraham and Moises. Max had a successful manufacturing business. They lived in a spacious, Spanish style home with wood beamed ceilings, tiled interior, and cobblestone floors. We went on family trips together to various resorts in Mexico. Max, an attentive guide made sure that he pointed out all the sights to me. "Look, look, give a *kuk*," he'd say, not wanting me to miss anything. We made fun of him as he said *kuk* in Yiddish. At the end of the month, I didn't want to return home. At my request, Cousin Eva called Aunt Hilda and asked her whether I could stay longer. I dreaded going back. Eventually I had to return and was given the cold reception from Aunt Hilda and reprimanded for wanting to extend my visit.

In 1954, when I turned 16, Uncle David and Regine planned a trip to New York. I looked forward to their visit. From the eleven-year-old girl I left in Paris when we separated, Regine was now an eighteen-year-old young woman. Short in stature, she looked very fashionable in a fitted two-piece suit, with thickly penciled eyebrows over her dark eyes, and her hair styled in a chignon.

Uncle David (my mother's brother) was not related to Uncle Martin and Aunt Hilda, so when I spent time with Uncle David and Regine, they usually did not accompany me. The relatives on my mother's side included Aunt Blanche, Uncle David's sister, and her husband Ben, sweethearts from their youth in Poland. Aunt Blanche had left Biala before the war to marry Ben who had immigrated to the United States. A soft-spoken woman with blonde hair and blue eyes, she and her dark haired husband had two children. Gloria was a few years older than me, and her younger brother Irwin. Ben cleaned fish for a living, even though Uncle David offered to finance a business for him, but he didn't have that ambition. He and Aunt Blanche, a housewife, preferred to lead a simple life in the Bronx. In Poland, Aunt Blanche had been a close friend of my father's sister Haya. Uncle Max, Uncle David's brother, was not as sophisticated and well-groomed as Uncle David. A short man with thinning hair, Uncle Max worked as a laborer. With his wife Celia, a short, heavy woman, they had two good-looking sons, Noah and Howard.

We celebrated the family reunion and had dinners together at the Pierre Hotel, where Uncle David and Regine stayed. A photographer took photos of Uncle David, Regine and the family, as well as members of the New York Biala Benevolent Society to commemorate the time together. We also celebrated Regine's upcoming engagement to Marc, her boyfriend since her early teens.

Regine married shortly after this trip. They had a grand, opulent wedding ceremony and reception. They sent me an invitation. I had looked forward to going, but an unspoken, unresolved lack of communication between Uncle Martin, Aunt Hilda, and Uncle David existed. I can only surmise that this rift concerned money paid to the orphanage for my release. I do not know whether Uncle Martin or Uncle David paid the large sum. In those days, no one would discuss it or attempt a compromise. They simply took a stand and stuck to it, or held a lifetime grudge. Martin and Hilda thought Uncle David should offer to send me an airline ticket and pay for my expenses to attend the wedding, but they never communicated that to Uncle David who wondered why they did not send me. "If they would have asked me, I would gladly have paid and even if you had come without my financial help, I would have paid them back," he told me years later. He assumed money was not an issue as he heard that Martin was doing so well in his ballpoint pen business. Apparently to them, it was a matter of principle. "He should have written and sent you a ticket along with the invitation. It's his daughter's wedding and he should pay for it if he wants you there." Sadly, I did not get to attend the wedding.

After high school, I decided I wanted to go to an out of state university, but Hilda and Martin would not agree to it. They gave me no convincing reason other than they wanted me to live at home while going to university. They even promised me a car if I stayed with them, but they never followed through. During our relationship, Hilda and Martin broke several important promises. I felt powerless to argue with them. I looked into schools in the New York City area and Long Island. In 1956, I chose Adelphi University in Garden City, Long Island knowing that it probably would not be very demanding. When my Hebrew teacher in Jamaica High, Mr. Karp, discovered that I was to attend Adelphi University he told me he was disappointed, and that I should be attending Columbia University or another prestigious, challenging school, as my academic record was certainly commensurate with their requirements. When I did go to university I had to use Hilda's car when it was my turn to carpool.

I majored in Political Science, was chosen to join a popular sorority, and made friends. I felt unsure about taking science courses and especially a class in Shakespeare. On attempting to read his works the first days of class, I experienced such anxiety trying to understand his writing, which seemed like a foreign language to me, that I requested a change of class. I was relieved when it was granted. I performed well in some subjects and mediocre in others. My results were not as stellar as in high school and gradually I began to feel the slow peeling away of whatever emotional strength I had built up. The demands of school and the social interactions required a reserve I did not possess. I suffered physical symptoms during times of stress, particularly before examinations. Of course, there were days of jovial feelings and partying with friends, but never to excess, and I could never completely free myself. Never did I have a wild sense that my spirit could fly, that words and laughter would happily spew forth without consequence. Never did I feel in control or confident just being myself.

Hilda frequently spoke about her cousin's son Morton, a medical student who she thought was the perfect match for me. We saw each other at family dinners. A tall young man with brooding eyes and a serious expression, I was reticent in his company. Hilda insisted we were to be engaged and eventually married. She instilled this to the point of indoctrination. In 1959, after medical school he was recruited into the army as a physician under the rank of captain. We saw each other before he left. He looked attractive dressed in his military uniform, but detached. He said he would keep in touch and write to me.

After he left, I thought of him every night and the fact that I didn't hear from him. Before I went to sleep, I lay in my dark room illuminated by the faint glow of the streetlight below, and sank into depression. I found this strangely comforting.

My physical and emotional symptoms had escalated during my late teens and early twenties. In 1960, I earned a BA from Adelphi and entered Brooklyn Law School. My symptoms became even more pronounced. I experienced feelings of isolation and depression that manifested in stomachaches, shortness of breath, and unrelieved crying. From intense periods of anxiety and panic, I finally had a complete nervous breakdown. Nothing could relieve the black hole I had entered: no amount of encouragement or negotiating could lighten the darkness that engulfed me. I had difficulty sleeping and when I did, it brought no rest. I woke up feeling the same exhaustion and lethargy I had before going to bed. I stopped eating and lost weight. I no longer communicated. I felt myself shrinking, with no care or thought of my future. Unable to function I took a leave of absence from Law School. No joy or light remained. I had to be fed and walked to the bathroom. I surrendered into the melancholia that consumed me.

By 1961, Hilda and Martin, concerned and frightened contacted Dr. Weinstein, their family doctor. He referred us to his nephew Dr. Michael Wainston. He was in his mid to late thirties. A short, solidly built man with thinning light hair, he wore frameless, bifocal glasses and dressed in a suit or sports jacket, or sometimes just a shirt and tie.

Dr. Wainston had recently completed psychoanalytic studies in the traditional Freudian method of psychoanalysis. He prescribed antidepressants for me. The Tricyclic antidepressants produced severe side effects including dizziness, nausea, disorientation, confusion and abnormal heart rhythm. I went through trial periods of dosage and brands until I received some relief. Dr. Wainston cautioned me to call him immediately if any of the symptoms were intolerable. I felt uncomfortable about bothering him, so I let the side effects make me sicker than the underlying illness, until things became so bad that Hilda called him. Dr. Wainston made the necessary adjustment and reprimanded me for not calling him sooner as he had instructed.

In the summer of 1962, during my second medical leave of absence from law school, I flew to France to spend the summer with Uncle David, his new wife Ady, Regine and her husband Marc. My emotional state was fragile. I had not seen Uncle David since I was sixteen when he came to New York with Regine before her marriage. He remained single until she wed in 1956. Then he moved out of the apartment they shared at 51 Ave Burgenaud so that Regine could live with her new husband there. In 1958 Uncle David moved to 8 Rue Leroux.

Flying to Nice and then on to St. Tropez should have been an adventure for me, but I was so tense on the flight that I spilled the salad dressing on my outfit. Even without the greasy spots, I already felt inappropriately dressed in a woolen skirt when I arrived in the warm climate. Uncle David had rented a beautifully furnished villa open to the Mediterranean summer breezes, with cushioned light furniture on the decks. The house was close to the village and the port. We enjoyed the fresh fruit and daily baked French breads and pastries. The beds in the larger bedrooms were draped with sheer fabric that billowed in the wind. Regine and Marc occupied one of the larger bedrooms. My bedroom was much smaller. *"C'est tres petite. Je crois que c'est pour la bonne,"* Regine remarked, when she came to see my room. Small and thin, when she smiled her prominent teeth showed, her eyes crinkled up, and she gave off an air of haughtiness. Her conceited manner brought out my feelings of discomfort and shyness.

Regine's four-year-old son was spending the summer in the mountains with his nanny. Regine claimed the mountain air benefited the health of children. In front of me, she and Marc confided to Uncle David and Ady that they were busy the night before trying to conceive their second child. Once again the different languages posed some difficulty. We spoke French to each other and some English, but my French was rusty and her English rudimentary. We did not communicate extensively and I spoke Yiddish to my Uncle. Next to Regine's confident manner, my insecurities made me feel insignificant and unimportant.

We spent lazy days together at the beach. Not used to seeing topless women, I couldn't help but stare at the almost naked bodies, shocking to me at first. I was too shy and self-conscious to disrobe. When I put on my bathing suit, Regine's husband Marc looked me up and down. *"Elle n'est pas mal,"* he said in a surprised tone.

In the evening, we took slow walks on the promenade amidst the bustle of privileged people and listened to the rhythmic sounds of the sea. We dined at outdoor restaurants on fresh grilled fish, crudité, and luscious desserts against the background of table talk, the clanking of wine glasses, and smells of cooking that delighted my senses. Other evenings we walked up the narrow hilly streets of the town to find good places to dine.

I sat at a cafe one sunny morning at the port of St. Tropez taking in the colors of the houses, the azure skies, the expanse and calmness of the sapphire blue Mediterranean with the luxurious yachts moored at the cove. I watched the young sun-tanned crowd dressed in the new chic of St. Tropez, sipping cafe au lait. I felt privileged and optimistic. I picked up a newspaper and stared at the headline. *"Marilyn Monroe se suicide!"* A blast of reality replaced my lightheartedness with shock, sadness and confusion. The news that someone like Marilyn Monroe could commit suicide was unfathomable to me.

Toward the end of the trip, Regine started screaming at me about getting ready to drive back to Paris. "You are not getting ready fast enough!" Her yelling shattered my insecure foundation. Being so vulnerable to verbal attack, I did not know how to handle my emotional weakness. The combination of my depression, the headline, the shrillness of Regine's voice and being separated from Dr. Wainston, made me so emotionally fragile during the drive to Paris. When we returned to my uncle's apartment I became bed ridden. Upset, Uncle David did not know what had happened to me. He telephoned Martin and Hilda in New York. 'What did you do to her?" I heard him ask.

I reached the peak of my depression in 1962. By 1963, at the age of twenty five, I saw Dr. Wainston three to four times per week, sometimes as often as five times per week. His office was located in New York City on 35th St. off Third Avenue. I took the elevator up to his office and sat in the waiting room painted and furnished in beige, with a freestanding air conditioner and fan intended to obscure the noises from the adjoining offices until he called me in.

My personality and his Freudian analytical training came to an impasse during our first year. To verbalize my feelings and allow my mind to enter a state of thought association became impossible. I was not in the habit of expressing my feelings and thoughts. I had not had that luxury since before the age of four. On the contrary, in order to survive, I had to remain silent. Years later my diagnosis would be labeled PTSD, a term that had not been coined then. I sat in his office and cried during many months of treatment as he sat with a pad and pencil looking at me. He waited patiently, hoping for me to speak, while fidgeting from side to side. We spent many hours from session to session just staring at each other. After more than a year of labored and forced communication and learning to identify feelings such as sadness, anger and joy, I finally reached a point, similar to a blind person whose sight is suddenly restored. "I can feel, I can feel," I said. I had never known this liberating sensation. I kept taking big breaths so my lungs could fill and exhale rhythmically. For over twenty years I had suffocated my emotions. Finally, I experienced the ability to feel.

When I first began suffering from depression years before, I became tense as a coil and would release the tension by crying uncontrollably. At times Martin took a walk with me along our street and questioned the cause of my sadness. I tried to explain between my tears that I felt insecure. "Why do you feel like that?" he said. "I have plenty of money and when I die you and Marcia will share it. That's the only reason to feel insecure. Money brings you security and respect. You have nothing to be insecure about. When I came to the United States, I had nothing. I went through the Depression and now I have made something of myself and people respect me because I made money. That's what's important in life. Money brings you security," he said. I listened and experienced some relief, but it only lasted a short time. As soon as we returned to the house, it evaporated. I looked at the same striped wallpaper and the armchair with flowered covering in the living room. I went upstairs to my bedroom where I spent many lonely evenings. I pondered and ruminated, but could not pinpoint the depth of my sadness and grief. Martin's focus on money as my salvation created more problems and ruined the tenuous relationship we had. He was actually miserly. He did not come to my aid when I needed him the most.

As I matured, I had less and less interaction with Martin. Still habitually quiet and shy, unless Martin was dissatisfied or politically aroused, we rarely communicated. We didn't share conversations involving guidance of my future, assistance in school, or just family talk around the table. He did not have a higher education. He finished an apprenticeship in carpentry and was accepted in the guild in Poland at the age of 19. In June 1946, at the age of 39, he completed a certificate in Evening Elementary School in the Bronx. I could not ask for help with my academic work. He and Hilda did however stress the importance of higher education, a common aspiration in all Jewish families. "Education is better than money in the bank; that's something no one can take away from you," he said. They supported my desire to attend law school. In those days most women became teachers, so they praised my choice. I chose law school as a way of dealing with the absence of rights and justice in my life. I believed it would empower me. With hardly a complaint, they paid the relatively low tuition for both schools. Martin dropped me off at Brooklyn Law School on his way to his manufacturing business in Williamsburg, Brooklyn. He joked frequently that he was entitled to one half of my diploma for driving to law school everyday.

Uncle Martin in Paris

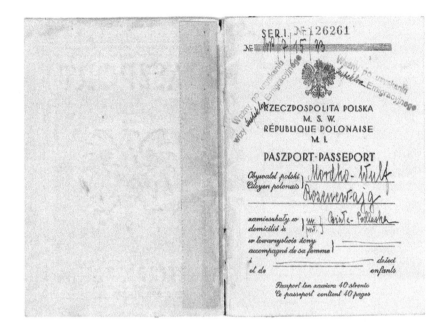

Uncle Martin's Polish Passport, 1933

Aunt Esther, Uncle Aaron and Gitta, Yonkers, NY Apartment

Huguette, friend Gitta
stayed with in Paris

Gitta and Marcia,
backyard of house,
Queens

Camp Massad, Gitta, 4th row (eighth from the right)

Regine and Marc, Engagement Day, Paris

Mother's Family / *Front row left to right:* Max (Mother's brother), Blanche (Uncle David's sister) and Uncle David. *Back row left to right:* Noah (Max's son), Irwin and Gloria (Aunt Blanche's children), Regine, Gitta, Howard (Max's son) September 1954

Uncle David and Mother's side of family and members of Biala Benevolent Society, New York

U.S. Department of Justice, Customs Bureau, New York, 1965

REPARATIONS AND PSYCHIATRY / 1963

ON SEPTEMBER 10, 1952, West Germany and Israel entered into an agreement known as the Reparation Agreement declaring that West Germany was to pay Israel for the slave labor and persecution of Jews during the Holocaust and to compensate for Jewish property stolen by the Nazis. On March 27, 1953, the agreement came into force. Holocaust survivors outside of Israel made individual claims against Germany. I was 24 years old, and at the apex of my depressive illness when Hilda and Martin contacted an attorney, Frederic Alberti, who specialized in filing such claims. He succeeded in obtaining for me small sums for "loss of parents" and "loss of liberty." Some years after the initial agreement, West Germany decided to pay monthly disability to survivors of the Holocaust whose lives were damaged because of mental and emotional illness perpetrated by German atrocities. Mr. Alberti advised Hilda and Martin that I should also file a claim for disability and emotional illness perpetrated by German persecution. This procedure required that I meet with a psychiatrist chosen by the German government. I was 25 years old. I had two sessions on April 20 and May 7, 1963 with Professor, Dr. Ernst Herz, the appointed psychiatrist to my case. Based on the limited background information that Hilda provided, he compiled the following case history and subsequent report based on his findings. The document translated and distilled below was written in German, as was all correspondence with the German Government.

Case History: Dr. Herz stated that I was born in Biala Podlaska, Poland in 1938. My father worked for the Polish Government. I could not remember my parents or brother who lost their lives due to "the national socialist persecutions." I was taken to a Catholic children's home, somewhere in Poland, and I cannot remember the events of my early childhood. After the war, when I was about 7 years old, a brother of my father who had lived in the United States since 1928 looked for and found me. He arranged for me to live with a Polish family at first. In 1946, I travelled by myself to Paris and lived there for one and a half years with my mother's brother. (This of course is not the whole story, but Hilda may have wanted to take credit for my rescue so she never mentioned Ida.) In 1948, my uncle brought me to the United States and adopted me in 1950. Dr. Herz noted that I currently lived in my uncle's house and therefore did "not have any financial problems" because my uncle supported me totally. I went to public school at the age of 10 and graduated in 1956, at the average age of 18. I attended college and earned a BA degree in 1960 within the normal four-year period. I then began to study law at Brooklyn Law School, but my studies were interrupted for six months in 1961 and again in 1962 for one year. I was therefore one year behind. I was also not married.

The direct verbiage of his report continued: She can no longer remember the separation from her parents. Nevertheless she knows that she was hidden several times when the Germans came into the children's home because the leaders were afraid that she might be discovered. She was baptized and went to church with the other children. She felt like a stranger. Unlike the Polish children, she felt that she did not belong there. She did not feel well physically and there was insufficient food. She could not remember any details from her early childhood. In Paris, she was treated by the family physician because she complained constantly of stomach spasms. She was fearful all the time and did not want to stay alone at home. Life in a family seemed peculiar to her. She felt uncomfortable and even afraid of her uncle. At school she had problems because she had to learn a new language. She felt isolated from the other children who did not play with her much. During the first years in New York, she was a good student, but still had difficulties in her relationships with other people. She had trouble seeing her aunt and uncle as substitutes for her parents and was also uncertain if the relatives who had taken her into their family would view her positively in the further course of her presence. She had difficulty with attachments to other young people. She was introverted and could not speak about her timidity and uncertainties. She was also suspicious and wondered whether other people were honest with her and whether they really liked her. In college when an exam was announced, she always complained of stomach problems. She also saw her family physician for headaches, palpitations, and trouble with breathing in upsetting situations.

In 1959 she felt particularly low. She had a relationship with a physician and the question of marriage arose. The physician went into the Air Force and had to move to Germany. She had a lot of difficulty with this and felt inferior to him. The relationship broke off and afterwards she felt very disappointed. She had a strong feeling that no one cared for her and that she wasn't wanted. At that time she could not think clearly and thought that she was very stupid. In 1960 her studies in law school were demanding. In the summer of 1961 she had a form of nervous breakdown. The final exams overtaxed her, her parents went away on vacation, and she felt very alone. Her condition did not improve even after the exams, so her family doctor who had treated her until then, sent her to a psychiatrist, Dr. Wainston. He saw her three to four times a week, and before the exams, he saw her five times a week. She still sees him regularly even though her condition has improved.

Present Complaints: She still does not come together often with other people and leads a retiring life. Although she meets young people in law school, she develops no relationships. Being shy and particularly reserved harms her. She finds it extremely difficult to speak in front of the whole class. She avoids going out with young men because she is so frightened that a more intimate relationship cannot develop. Although she dresses elegantly and values an attractive appearance, she is shy and timid when she goes out with others. She thinks of herself as inferior and cannot get rid of the thought that people think her stupid. She feels tense and nervous at school because she thinks she cannot do justice to the requirements. She knows that she has the necessary knowledge and also the aptitude to complete her assignments. However, as she is emotionally unstable, she is not able to handle the pressure of exams. With any upset or stress, she has stomach complaints, suffers from lack of appetite and sleeplessness. Sometimes she has back pains and tension in the muscles of her back, as well as headaches. Even now she is upset again and worries about the final semester exams. She has been treated only with psychoanalysis. She has no plans yet what she will do after finishing her studies. She cannot imagine that she could become an attorney in this country.

Findings: She is orderly, answers all questions promptly, and knows how to make her feelings as well as the difficulties in her life very clear. She uses analytical expressions and is careful to elaborate in detail her affective deviances and her incorrect attitude. Her description is not artificial. She gave me the impression of an immature person who cannot adapt to the conditions of her surroundings and cannot manage the affective difficulties of her situation in life. Her intellectual level is higher than average; there is no sign of any pathological reasoning. The neurological examination showed no pathological deviations from normal findings.

Diagnosis: Affective development disturbances of a persecuted child.

Opinion: Signs of any organic damage of the peripheral or central nervous system could not be found in this examination. According to the declarations such damage was unlikely. The present psychic condition is earmarked by an immature affective incorrect attitude with uncertainty and dependency in personal decisions, helplessness and lack of easy going activity as well as failure in emotional situations with panic reactions. Her lack of self-confidence might be of importance in the emergence of psychosomatic complaints, at the bottom of which may be autonomous susceptibility. In spite of good intellectual development, she is not capable of building a life of contentment and she fails in many situations...The condition is in accordance with the affective development disturbances, as they developed and continued in persecuted children after the loss of their parents and the uprooting from their life circumstances, until these children reached a maturity and could overcome the uprooting. In this case it may be that the reactions to the uprooting never stood in the foreground, especially since she was not familiar with the old lifestyle and in the new circumstances she found possibilities in her new life which offered a certain equivalent (even without her parents). However, she did not reach an affective maturity.

Summary: The affective development disturbances of a persecuted child caused 25% impairment in development as of 1945 that remains today. Curative treatment in the form of purposeful, psychotherapeutic guidance seems necessary and promises success.

⌒

The small disability compensation I was awarded represented a minor and inadequate sum relative to the damage and repercussions I experienced in my life.

My relationship with Martin became more strained. The monthly bills for psychoanalysis sent him over the edge. I dreaded the time of the month when the account arrived and I avoided him on those days as best I could. The mail sat on the kitchen counter where it was placed daily after Hilda or I retrieved it from the metal mailbox on the front door. On opening the bills from Dr. Wainston, Martin's face took on an expression of disbelief and anger. He would sit down in his swivel chair in the living room and just stare at the paper. I would hold my breath as I witnessed his angry demeanor. I hoped that he would not talk about the money. Some months he kept quiet, but other times it was too much for him. I would peek into the living room as I walked past him in the hallway, on my way from the kitchen to the staircase leading to my room. I attempted to sniff out his mood as a hunter in antici-pation of an attack. The times he kept silent, felt like a reprieve. His resentment and bitterness at having to pay these sums every month created a perceptible chill between us. "How long is this going to continue? Do you realize how much money I am spending on you?" I didn't know what to say. Frightened, I remained quiet. I knew that psychoanalysis was my lifeline to achieving some normalcy. I dreaded the return of the deep depression I had previously experienced when I could smell the scent of anxiety my body emitted. I was determined to continue with the psychoanalysis no matter how angry Martin became, or how uncomfortable the home environment. He could afford it. He earned a large sum as a partner in a manu-facturing business. The amount he had to pay did not interfere with our lifestyle.

Martin had learned to hold on tight to his money during the Depression when work was hard to come by and money was scarce. Being a foreigner, and also suffering from chronic ulcers, made it even more difficult for him to earn a living dur-ing those years. After his success in business he liked to spend money on cars, and took great pride in driving either a Cadillac or a Chrysler Imperial. He wore his Hickey Freeman suits and well made shoes. Both Hilda and Martin enjoyed being well dressed. Their quality attire symbolized having arrived into the middle class, but doctor bills, what did they represent? Not many people in those days sought psychoanalytic treatment, particularly people of their culture and upbringing who lacked formal education.

From the time I arrived in New York, they told me to forget my past. "Forget what happened to you," they said. "It's all in the past. It doesn't concern you anymore. You don't have to think about it. There's no point in remembering or talking about it. It doesn't change anything. This is a new start, a new life, a new beginning for you." This silence about my past deprived me of my former self. Not having the freedom to talk about it and explore what had happened contributed to my difficulty in communicating in social situations. While the consequences were not as severe as in the orphanage, when it meant life or death when the Nazis were looking for me, the silencing continued to inhibit my ability to interact in a healthy way. When asked to tell someone about myself, my mind went blank. I frantically searched for a topic that I could speak about. I lost all spontaneity in communicating; afraid I would divulge something I was not supposed to reveal. I did not speak about my history or myself. A creeping sense of discomfort paralyzed me. I learned to be guarded and reticent about what was central to my life. I could not let bits slip out for fear of revealing the entire story.

Hidden and fearful for my life at the age of four, I had been forced to suppress my identity, my religion and my name. I lost my parents, my brother, my family and my home during the worst massacre of Jews in history. Now I was being forced not only to suppress my past, but also my current thoughts and feelings. Experiencing such unfathomable loss, and then being told to forget such a catastrophic past, crippled me emotionally. My mind shut down, until it erupted like a volcano spewing flames and molten lava through my nervous system. Eventually, my body powered down. With such agonizing feelings and fears, I needed to slowly process my history. I needed to resurrect my experiences to consciousness in order to repair and restore my body and mind.

I had a practice of looking blankly at people who I knew or recognized from my past. I ignored them with a vacuous stare, like a child who covers her eyes and thinks if she cannot see anyone, then no one can see her. I treated a man with whom I had a sexual relationship after law school in this manner. We saw each other whenever our desires dictated. When I called him, "Yes, I am home, come over," he'd say. Or after a call from him, "Are you in the mood to come over?" he'd ask. We said very little to each other and saved our energy for the pleasures at hand. I came home exhausted and satisfied. This no holds barred relationship lasted for many months and proved incredibly satisfying. We never talked about our relationship.

A couple of years later I saw him walking with some men, who I assumed were his colleagues, on lunch break. As I approached them I observed him saying something to the man next to him. I imagined what he was saying was about me. I became distressed and ashamed. He stopped. "Hello, how are you doing?" he said with a smile. I walked by and totally ignored him. He called my name repeatedly as I passed and he shouted at me in desperation. I kept walking as though he did not exist.

We met again not long after that incident. I was searching for an apartment and coincidentally he and a friend came to see the same apartment while I was there. On seeing me, he grabbed my arm. His friend had walked off in another direction to a different room. He threw me down on the bed, called me a bitch, and angrily began to grope me. As I fought him off, his friend returned. "What are you doing? Stop it!" He shouted and pulled him away. "Let's get out of here." I have no doubt that he would have raped me. He was furious and humiliated by my blatantly ignoring him.

On Friday, November 22, 1963, I was scheduled to see Dr. Wainston at 1 pm. I sat in a coffee shop on the East side of Manhattan on Lexington and 33rd Street drinking a glass of orange juice while I waited for my appointment when Walter Cronkite announced on television that President John F. Kennedy had been assassinated. When I walked into Dr. Wainston's office I told him about the tragic event. He would always remember I was the bearer of this dreadful news. Later, I sat in Marcia's room dressed in my navy wool bathrobe over pajamas and watched the small TV screen. No longer consumed this day with my own emotional illness, I commiserated with the nation over Kennedy's assassination. On November 24, totally immersed in grief as was the rest of the country and riveted to the television, I watched as Jack Ruby shot Lee

GITTA: HIDDEN CHILD OF THE HOLOCAUST

Harvey Oswald at 11:21 am in the basement of the Dallas Police Department in full view of the public.

Kennedy's funeral and burial took place on November 25. I was on a leave of absence from law school having succumbed to severe anxiety and depression. Martin with his steely blue eyes came into the room as I watched the television coverage of the sad farewell to Kennedy.

"If you are not going to school you need to find a job. You can't stay at home and do nothing. It isn't good for you," he said without sympathy. "You have to get out of the house. You need to keep busy. I'll find work for you in my factory, in the office. Frank will find you something to do with billing. You'll drive in with me," he continued in his direct manner.

"When do I have to go?"

"You can start tomorrow," he said and left.

This upset me. To go from being a law school student to working in a factory with Dad and Frank, reinforced what a failure I was. I had to agree. He did not understand my illness. I thought I had become a burden to him and was no longer welcome in the house.

We drove together to Williamsburg, Brooklyn to the factory in an old brick building across the river, the New York skyline visible in the distance. As we climbed the iron staircase to the plant on the second floor, I heard the clatter and pounding of machinery becoming louder as we approached the open door. A substantial space, it contained a lot of equipment and numerous workers, all under Martin's supervision. He showed me around the workshop and pointed out the machinery dedicated to the production of ballpoint pens. Most of the apparatus and tools were imported from Switzerland and assembled by Martin, but some tools were designed by him and manufactured with the help of toolmakers in the United States. A gifted machinist, Martin devoted time to visualizing the tools needed and he drew his own designs and plans. In my early teens, he proudly showed me his designs and explained their function. I listened and he appreciated my attentiveness claiming that I had a gift for mechanics, although I did not always understand what he so passionately described to me. He proudly proclaimed my ability to use a screwdriver and various tools to other people.

I worked in the office part of the plant where his partner Frank Piotrowski took charge. Always dressed in a business suit, light straight hair combed to the side, and wearing rimless glasses, he sat at his desk smoking a cigar. In his early forties, he managed sales, advertising and bookkeeping. His younger brother, Anthony worked under Martin's supervision in the machine shop. As a teenager I heard stories at home of Frank's womanizing, infidelities and heavy drinking. I felt sorry and embarrassed for Marie his wife. I had the impression she knew about the women and his heavy drinking was obvious at Christmas dinners and when sailing on his boat.

In my mid teens, Hilda and Martin allowed me to travel

with Frank, Marie and their family for a short vacation to Miami. In exchange for their treating me to this trip, I babysat their children in the evening. At the hotel I slept on the living room sofa. The door to the bedrooms occupied by Frank, Marie and the two children opened onto the living room. Dressed in my bathrobe as I prepared to go to bed one evening, I turned off the lights, when the door to Frank and Marie's bedroom opened and Frank appeared in his pajamas and robe. Through the shadows of the dimly lit room, he walked slowly toward me. He stood very close and brushed his hand against my breast. This shocked me. His bravado implied that he was testing me. His bold venture depended on my response. Without a word, he returned to his bedroom. This was a man I trusted as Uncle Frank. I didn't tell anyone. The fleeting moment left me wondering whether it really happened or if I imagined it!

With Martin's success in business came an air of arrogance and conceit. After being at home for a length of time he grew restless. "I need to get away. I want to go to Paris and stay there for a while," he said, making it clear to Hilda that she was not invited. Unlike many people, he could afford to travel. He started going to Paris on a yearly basis where he visited with landsmen from his hometown of Biala Podlaska. On his first trip Hilda travelled with him, but after that his transatlantic trips were solo, celebrated with bon voyage and welcome home parties. When in Paris he stayed at a hotel and met frequently for lunches and dinners with his friends.

Hilda didn't express displeasure or disappointment. She appeared sad and melancholy, but also liberated. Not having to prepare dinners for an ungrateful husband or otherwise engage with him, released some of her tension. When Martin returned from his trips she would organize a party with the ubiquitous welcome home banner and invite all their friends. That displeased and embarrassed him. He preferred his unaccompanied travels remain a secret. He sat on his swivel chair, looking tired and bored by the events, rested his head on his hand and waited for everyone to leave. "Why do you have to make a party? What is the big deal that I take a trip? I don't want to have all these people. I want to come home to a quiet house. I am tired and don't want to entertain anyone," he complained.

My relationship with Martin continued to unravel and took on the harshness of a bitter winter. I responded to his unkind words and behavior with the same coldness and distance that he exhibited towards me. We both needed from each other what we were unable to give. My fear and discomfort with people, and especially lack of trust even in family relationships, kept me from bonding with him. He in turn sensed my dislike of him, and my lack of warmth and appreciation. As I grew older, I felt like a stranger when I visited their house. He had a warm and loving relationship with Marcia. He idolized her. She represented an extension of himself and his lost family. Initially as his niece I represented his closest blood relative, but not any more. It did not matter to him what Marcia accomplished or whether she even succeeded. They had an inseparable attachment. His bond to Marcia reached its peak when she turned fifteen.

In my early twenties at home and during my travels I dated many men, flitting from one to another, uncertain what kind of man I wanted to settle down with or whether I wanted to settle down at all. I didn't have plans for marriage, nor had I decided whether I wanted children; my future remained uncharted. I never dreamt or fantasized of being a bride dressed in white and having a home with a picket fence. But girls my age were getting married and I felt pressure from Hilda and Martin.

While in law school, I made a conscious decision to lose my virginity. Although I had dated, I hadn't slept with anyone. I chose a handsome student who sat behind me in class. We looked at each other and became somewhat friendly, but not romantically. When I sat in class I had the habit of pushing my bottom through the lower part of the seat under the slat of the backrest while I changed sitting positions. I heard my chosen friend and the male students next to him amused at my unintended, provocative behavior. I got up my nerve to approach him and suggested we should get together.

We agreed to meet in his apartment. I made up an excuse to leave the house for the evening, and packed some underwear and a short sexy nightgown for my deflowering adventure. I drove from Queens to Brooklyn to my destination, not knowing how I arrived there without crashing. A stupendous achievement for me as I always avoided traveling to unknown destinations. My anxiety level had reached its zenith. Amazingly, I found his apartment. We didn't waste much time chit chatting or engaging in kissing or petting before we were in bed. I felt like an observer going through the motions. I had kept my virginity a secret from him. When we were lying in bed after, I told him that it was my first time. He acted surprised and said that he would not have known. I was pleased as I didn't wish to appear a novice, but the whole matter of sex with him disappointed me. It had satisfied my curiosity, but shattered my illusions. After that experience I had short lived romances during my travels and at home. I made choices based on my feelings rather than curiosity, and went out with educated and eligible men.

I decided that I should find a place of my own so that I could study for the bar without family distractions. It was common for students to move out of their home to a hotel room or apartment. I told Hilda and Martin, "I need to move out of the house and live in Manhattan so I can attend the review courses and prepare." They objected strongly, but I stood up to them and rented a hotel room in Manhattan. I had enough money from my German Reparations to be able to afford it. I moved out for a few months so I could study without getting involved in the household conflicts. Hilda refused to speak to me.

For my law school graduation present, she bought me underwear and pajamas. I told her how upset I was at her lack of recognition of my achievement and how inappropriate a gift she gave me.

～

A high achiever in law school, I graduated second in my class and was a desirable candidate for government employment. In 1965 I took my first job working for the Justice Department, Customs Bureau.

Government positions provided excellent medical insurance and when I learned their policy covered 80% of psychiatric treatment I took the job without hesitation. It gave me the opportunity to continue with psychoanalysis and I hoped the treatment would bring me as close as possible to a normal life. I gave the impression that I was in control of myself. I appeared calm and composed, but my inner turbulent life pitched like a paper boat in a stormy sea.

When I told Martin the news of my new employment at the U.S. Customs Bureau and the coverage for psychotherapy, his eyes lit up. It was an enormous relief for me, and especially for Martin, to have a job that paid for my costly treatment. I began my career as an attorney at the historic building designed by Cass Gilbert, built between 1902 and 1907 located at the southern tip of Manhattan next to Battery Park at 1 Bowling Green. A masterpiece of the Beaux-Arts style, it embodied the City Beautification movement planning principles that combined architecture, engineering and fine arts.

I worked at this landmark in the legal department for one and a half years under the supervision of Attorney Samuel Blecker, a solicitous, middle-aged man always professional in his behavior. At my interview for the job, he sat across the desk from me serious in demeanor and asked me about my background. I told him about my experience as a child Holocaust survivor. We never discussed the subject again.

Throughout my employment he complimented me on my work. He showed his approval with a cordial smile and sympathetic brown eyes. My duties consisted of reviewing cases involving passengers who returned from abroad and failed to declare their purchases and pay the duty as required by law. The fines were steep. On some occasions the traveler would request a hearing, usually accompanied by an attorney, to plea for the reduction of the fine and forfeiture. As difficult as it was not to show compassion given the mitigating excuses presented, I did not have the discretion to forgive the violation or reduce the fine. The penalty for the failure to declare the goods was four times the value of the undeclared item as well as confiscation.

After eighteen months of working on identical types of cases, I agreed to take a job offer with the National Labor Relations Board, known as the NLRB that would give me a higher salary and a wider range of experience. I told Mr. Blecker that I planned to transfer. "I understand your desire to acquire other experience. I appreciate your work here. I am sorry to lose you. I admired the fact that in all this time you never spoke about your childhood Holocaust experience with the intention of taking advantage of a situation or garnering sympathy," he said. This comment surprised me and made me think of my need to remain silent about my past. Mr. Blecker, showed his high regard for me by contacting the head of the Customs Department in Washington D.C. They offered me a job based on Mr. Blecker's glowing recommendation, but I had to be willing to relocate. Although flattered, I was not ready to reorganize my life.

At the NLRB, my office consisted of a windowless cubicle, where I sat from 8:30 am to 5:00 pm. The workday seemed never-ending. On many days, I found that last half hour intolerable. I learned and became accustomed to running union elections and working on cases involving union disputes. Being out of the office on union election assignments shortened the days. Cooped up in a windowless partitioned office space triggered my restlessness and anxiety. I felt like a caged animal. One day I had a severe headache and left the office. To flag down a taxi required walking to the curb and opening my eyes slightly to the blinding sunlight. The heat and pain it caused made it feel as if the sun's proximity to earth had shifted closer. When I arrived at my apartment, I shut myself into a dark room, closed my eyes and lay on the floor for most of the day until the pain and nausea subsided. I had never experienced such an intense migraine.

On restless days, I escaped from my office as if from a jail and went for a walk. My immediate supervisor, a short man with a limp depended on a cane to get around. At the beginning of my employment, he berated me a few times for what he perceived as my rudeness. I walked in and placed my finished file on his desk, regardless of other attorneys waiting for his attention. "You have to wait your turn like everyone else," he said in a brusque manner. He assumed that I took advantage of being a woman lawyer, so rare at the time.

I didn't consider my behavior to be overbearing or ambitious. I responded to my feelings of insecurity in new situations inappropriately. If I were at ease with myself I would have simply asked, "What is the procedure here?"

One day, the topic of skiing came up in conversation. "Do you ski?" I asked. He looked at me angrily, not realizing that I was attempting to ignore his infirmity. But in my distorted way of thinking, I attempted to convey to my limping supervisor that I did not notice his disability.

"No. I do not," he said.

It came as a shock to me when I was elevated to the next level to do trial work. Reassured that I would be supervised at each stage did not diminish my apprehension. I would have to speak in front of strangers and present cogent arguments. This realization sent me into a state of anxiety that spiraled downward. In August when I received this news, Dr. Wainston was on his month long summer vacation along with all the psychiatrists in the city. Unnerved and frightened, I could not wait for Dr. Wainston. The only way to obtain relief would be to quit my job. After giving notice, I began to breathe normally again and sleep at night.

When Dr. Wainston returned I told him that I resigned from the NLRB.

"I could not imagine in my wildest dreams doing trial work," I said. "It would be impossible."

"Why didn't you wait until I returned?" he asked, revealing his disappointment at my decision with a frown.

"I couldn't wait for you to come back. I had to do it."

The compulsion to extricate myself from this terrifying situation overcame any rational thought to wait for him and discuss it. He shifted in his chair. The fear of speaking never went away after leaving the orphanage. The warning not to speak as a young child, lest the Nazis discover I was Jewish and kill me, controlled my life.

I experienced panic far beyond the common anxiety associated with public speaking. Fear engulfed me with a faceless evil. These alarming feelings magnified my sense of inferiority. I would attempt to speak and after a few moments my mind would freeze. My body became overheated and my heart raced. Caught up in the fear and anxiety of speaking, I jabbered incoherently no longer rooted in the present or aware of my surroundings.

⟿

In 1966 while still working as an attorney for the National Labor Relations Board, I met Bernard at our Christmas party. Private attorneys specializing in labor law were invited. After I entered the room, I removed my winter coat at the entry closet just as Bernard attended to his coat. He introduced himself and scarcely left my side for the entire evening. Over six feet tall, with closely cropped black hair, dark eyes, and chiseled features, I found him extremely handsome. My long, straight hair was combed back and pinned on the right side. I wore my favorite tweed suit with brown silk facing on the collar and a matching silk shirt. High leather boots completed my outfit. I looked stylish and felt comfortable with my appearance. Bernard talked openly and had a great sense of humor. My discomfort with speaking dissipated. Each time he recalled our meeting in later years, he said, "You reminded me of a Russian princess." At the end of the evening he took my phone number. We each had a small apartment in Manhattan and from then on we began to meet frequently.

Bernard worked for a law firm representing the union side of labor. He came from a low-income family. His grandparents had emigrated from Poland and Russia, and his mother and father came to the United States as children. His father, a slim grey haired man, worked in his own small business as an upholsterer. His mother raised Bernard, his younger brother and older sister.

We dated often and a few months into our relationship, I invited him to meet my family, Martin, Hilda and Marcia in Queens. Although very slim, Bernard was on a protein diet composed of eating an unspecified quantity of meat. I mentioned that to Hilda who gladly prepared broiled rib steaks and lamb chops to please him. We sat at the mahogany dining table on the matching chairs with seats upholstered in black and beige striped silk fabric. Bernard and Martin conversed with ease. In the midst of their conversation, Bernard leaned back with his weight on the rear legs of the chair. He continued to balance himself in such a fashion when suddenly the frame cracked under his weight and he fell onto the floor. The beautiful armchair lay broken in two pieces. Shocked by the sudden fall, Bernard sat on the floor with the remains of the chair. "I am sorry," he said. "I'm so sorry. This has never happened to me. I'll pay for the damage. Please forgive me. I am so embarrassed." Even though the suddenness of the breakage and Bernard's fall surprised me, I found it amusing, but kept it to myself. Martin did not. His rage erupted. "What kind of way is that to sit on a chair? This is quality furniture. Why would you balance yourself like that on a chair? We have this furniture for so many years and this has never happened. That's not the way a person sits on a chair." Hilda ran to Bernard and helped him up. "It's ok, it's ok, we'll fix it," she said. Martin eventually accepted Bernard's apology. He actually made a good impression on him other than the furniture debacle. "He's an intelligent man, a lawyer. He's easy to talk to. I like him," Martin said. Hilda enamored by Bernard's attractive appearance, also loved that he enjoyed her cooking. He ate portion after portion, complimenting her with every mouthful.

Bernard invited my family to meet his parents Sophie and Sol, his brother, sister and husband, and various other family members. His parents lived in an old, brick six- story apartment building in a modest section of Brooklyn. We entered the building through a shabby looking lobby; the floor covered with worn whitish grey tiles.

We followed Bernard into the apartment on the left side of the lobby. Obviously nervous, he knew his parents' ordinary apartment and simple possessions would bring home the reality of his financial situation to me. He worked hard to orchestrate an aura of comfort and elegance for the evening. He bought new dinnerware and created a colorful setting on an extended folding table set up in the living room just off the kitchen. Brightly colored flower arrangements dotted the room.

His mother, a heavyset woman with grey hair, brown eyes and good features was outgoing and friendly. His father, a slim man, with thinning salt and pepper hair, and a broad nose pursed his lips as though holding back a smile. He remained quiet. Bernard had warned the whole family to keep the usual lack of decorum at bay while we were there. "I read them the riot act," he said. "I told them to behave and not to shout at the dinner table. I told them how important this evening was. I really put my foot down."

As time passed Martin and Hilda asked in one form or another.

"So, when are you getting married? You're in your late twenties. It's time for you to get married. Bernard is a handsome man, intelligent; he's in a good profession, a lawyer. What are you waiting for? Time doesn't stand still." In the Jewish culture, marriage represented the next stage of adulthood. In Martin and Hilda's view, to see me married to a professional would mean they had succeeded in raising me well.

"We do love each other," I told them. "He asked me a few times to marry him, but he earns very little money. That is not the way I want to live. He is not in a position to support a family and although I am working, I want to be comfortable financially. I don't want to be stressed about money. He can't provide me with that kind of life, so this is not for me. I've told him that we can continue to see each other, but I am in no rush to get married."

Martin had drummed into my head that money was the key to security and happiness. Why would I marry someone who couldn't provide that security? Philosophically attached to representing unions rather than the company side of labor law, Bernard would not be paid as high a salary as the lawyers who represented the company in labor disputes.

I wanted to live a glamorous life, be able to dine out, dress well and travel. From my past experience, I equated being poor with inferiority and shabbiness. This prospect frightened me and I couldn't agree to marry him. Without prompting, Martin came up with a proposal. "You know," he said, "I have a million dollars, total. What if I divided it into four parts, $250,000 each for you, Marcia, Hilda and myself? Why wait until I die for you to inherit your share? Why not separate the money now. This way you can buy a house, get married, and have a little cushion in life. That way the problem will be solved." As he leaned forward and looked at me with his intense blue eyes, he appeared sincere and committed to this plan.

His unexpected idea surprised me. I knew how attached he was to his money. For him to give a large part of it showed that he really cared for me. He wanted my relationship with Bernard to succeed and for us to get married. Martins' generous offer lifted my mood. I told Bernard the good news and that I would accept his marriage proposal. I had found my anchor in this charming and assertive man.

Hilda rejoiced that she was marrying me off. It meant that her responsibility in raising me would come to a successful end and she and Martin could walk me down the aisle as a bride.

Bernard immersed himself in all the planning. From the beginning of our dating through our courtship, he played a dominant role in making decisions. Indecisive and passive, I admired his confidence and looked up to him.

We selected an elegant kosher menu serving only fish. We wanted to have a sophisticated presentation and delicious meal.

We decided on an appetizer, soup, salad, dessert and the wedding cake. As was customary, to delight the guests after the wedding ceremony and before the sit down dinner, we selected an opulent buffet of smoked salmon, white fish, and other ethnic delicacies accompanied by an open bar of liquors and wines. We settled on all the details of invitations and calligraphy, flower and color arrangements, and the band. We chose the haunting, romantic melody "Lara's Theme" from the film Dr. Zhivago that we both loved.

Although it was customary that the bride's parents pay for the wedding, the groom's parents paid for the flowers. Bernard, protective of his parents and pleased that Hilda and Martin could afford to pay for everything, said in his usually compelling voice, "My parents can't afford to pay for anything. They won't be contributing for the flowers." Pleased to have asserted himself, he repeated with an air of satisfaction to the rest of his family that he stood up for his parents. He felt fully justified in pointing out the disparity of his family's economic status with mine. Martin and Hilda never pressed the issue. They liked his parents and enjoyed being with them.

Marcia, Martin, Hilda, Gitta, New York

I married Bernard on September 30, 1967 in an elegant ceremony and reception at the Hotel Delmonico on Park Avenue in New York City. I wore a loosely fitted dress of white tulle adorned with clusters of lace and pearl applique. The bottom of the skirt was trimmed with the same motif in two circular bands. A train of white taffeta attached to the upper back of my dress spilled onto the floor. I wore a small pillbox hat with a veil that cascaded down and a shorter veil covered my face. I carried a large bouquet of white orchards.

Marcia, my maid of honor, Hilda, Sophie, and the brides-maids surrounded me wearing shades of pink highlighted with burgundy. They carried pink and white orchid bouquets. Their dresses made of various textures of velvet, lace, chiffon, and brocade blended with the color scheme creating a soft, feminine mood.

Our marriage ceremony, performed by Rabbi Benjamin Rudavsky, a compassionate and understanding man, spoke to us from the heart as we all gathered together under a canopy of white flowers. I stood next to Bernard dressed in his black tuxedo with long tails and top hat. Rabbi Benjamin wore a black robe and white tallit, the ritual shawl worn during a Jew-ish ceremony.

Hilda stood beside me, her face faintly distorted as she attempted to hold back tears. Martin looked content and happy in his formal tuxedo and dark rimmed glasses. Marcia, two of the four young bridesmaids and two groomsmen stood on my side outside the canopy. Bernard's parents, Sophie and Sol, were on Bernard's side with the remaining two bridesmaids and grooms, and his best man, his close friend Rudy.

The Rabbi spoke passionately of what I had endured as a child and that I was now a grown woman on this felicitous occasion. His words transported me to my childhood and brought out feelings of profound sensitivity and vulnerability. I could not hold back my tears. As he continued speaking I had to tune out what he said. I was thrown off balance. I wished he would stop speaking and that I would stop crying. I feared the inappropriateness of shedding all those tears. The veil that covered my face made it impossible to wipe away my tears or blow my nose. I imagined my black mascara smeared all over, but thankfully it turned out not to be.

The wedding progressed happily and with exuberance. We danced to music interspersed with traditional Jewish dancing where the more muscular guests elevate the bride and groom seated on chairs up into the air. Music also punctuated the various courses and cake cutting. Bernard, a consummate dancer executed a Russian folk dance in which the male dancers squat and kick up their legs. Not easy to perform. On a later occasion, Bernard danced this folk dance and his trousers split in half at the back!

Happy and finally at peace with myself, I looked forward to a bright future. I danced with Martin, lovingly holding him to impart my gratitude for everything that he had done for me and for this beautiful event. Now as a married couple we greeted all the guests at their tables. As the dinner was served, I observed Bernard giving orders to the waiting staff outside the kitchen in his commanding manner. It was not the first time I witnessed his officious behavior so I ignored his shouting and assertiveness as it usually passed.

At the end of the evening, after our guests trickled out, we were free to go to the honeymoon suite. We undressed and made ourselves comfortable. As we lay on the bed chatting happily about the success of our evening, Bernard looked flushed with alcohol. "Let's count the checks we received as gifts," he said. We put the envelopes in the center of the bed. He lay with his feet to the headboard and I lay with my head on the pillow. He started counting the checks. Minutes after counting, he fell sound asleep.

Like any new bride I looked forward to a special and romantic evening on our first night as husband and wife. I tried to rationalize that we were intimate many times before and Bernard had exhausted himself dancing and drinking, so it was quite understandable. He apologized the next morning and we joked about it, but it didn't make up for the sadness I felt at the lack of intimacy on our wedding night.

Wedding Day: Gitta and Bernard, Hotel Delmonico, New York, 1967

Gitta (and Marcia, maid of honor to her left) with Bridesmaids

Gitta and Aunt Esther

Hilda, Rabbi Benjamin Rudavsky and Martin

⌣

I loved Bernard dearly. I was proud to be married to such a handsome and highly intelligent man with a gift for gab. We travelled to Spain and Israel for our honeymoon. We toured the South starting from Torremolinos, Malaga, making our way up the Eastern coast to Madrid. We focused on the Jewish history of Spain, the Inquisition and the expulsions, the conversos. We drove through the Andalusia region to the provinces of Cordoba, Grenada, Malaga and Seville on a road bordered by olive groves. We absorbed the peaceful landscape and watched the bright red sun relinquish the day to a pastel colored sky.

I woke up one morning in our hotel room in Madrid to the sound of traffic noises carried upwards. The breeze through the window moved the curtains to and fro. I called out for Bernard to find that he had left the room. He stayed away for several hours and my fear of being in a hotel in a strange city without him rose to feelings of panic. I looked around for a note, sure he must have left me an explanation, but I could not find anything. Finally he returned and I confronted him.

"Where were you for so many hours? You never told me that you were going out on your own. This is our honeymoon and I assumed we would be going out together."

"You were sleeping and so I decided to take a tour of the city and get my bearings. I can't believe that you are making such a fuss about it. Even though we're married, I still have the freedom to come and go."

He looked angry and irritated, but I tried to dismiss it. We patched things up and enjoyed touring the city together for the next few days. We browsed the antique shops, purchased an oil painting and a low back carved chair that is still in the family, visited The Prado Museum, and dined at elegant restaurants.

Another night in Madrid, he made plans for us to spend the evening in the outskirts of the city. We drove to a remote place that he had chosen, as the sunset carved dark shadows over the olive groves. We arrived at an outdoor restaurant surrounded by hedges and ivy covered lattice with only one of the seven tables occupied by another couple. The dim lighting projected an unwelcome atmosphere to the already unpleasant mood created by the emptiness. We consumed a scrawny chicken dish, one of the few choices on the menu. Towards the end of the meal, a blue light accented the stage where a few male performers danced the flamenco. Bernard excused himself from the table. He stayed away for longer than I expected contributing to my annoyance.

We continued on to Israel where we stayed with my cousin Yudit (on my father's side) and her husband Munio in their open apartment in Tel Aviv. Yudit's mother and my father's mother were sisters. Born in Poland she immigrated to Mexico with her parents. With strong feelings for Zionism, she went to live in Israel where she met her future husband Munio Rikover, a renowned physician. A blond soft-spoken woman with a compassionate nature, we spent time together during my trips to Mexico to visit our family, and when she and Munio and their children visited us in Queens. She studied medicine in the United States specializing in pediatrics. We often corresponded and so naturally she invited us to stay with them on our trip.

We awakened daily to the early morning light and the traffic buzz of the city. Both fervent supporters of Zionism, we loved being immersed in this young, vibrant country.

Months before our arrival, Israel had won the Six Day War after being attacked by Egypt, Syria and Jordan. They now occupied the Sinai to the South, the Golan Heights to the North, and expanded east to the Banks of Jordan. Adventurous and young, we did not heed warnings to avoid travel. Fortunately, other than some vocal outbursts and jeers, the Arab population did not confront us. We toured the Sinai and the newly conquered cities of Nablus, Amman, and Hebron, as well as Jerusalem, rich in biblical history. Now that Jerusalem was united and Jews were free to tour the historical parts of the city, we were able to visit the last remnant of the High Temple destroyed by the Romans. Known as the Western Wall, it is the most significant site in the world for Jewish people.

After we returned from the honeymoon, we looked at our wedding photographs. Everyone appeared vibrant and overjoyed. At each table, people smiled and showed great delight as they toasted our happiness. In stark contrast, at one table the guests appeared sad and despondent. We were told that Hilda's elder cousin passed away from a heart attack as he parked the car at the hotel parking lot. This cast a shadow over such a happy occasion. These relatives were grieving for him.

⌒

When Martin came up with the idea of dividing his assets and giving me a gift of $250,000.00 against my inheritance, I decided to consult my old Professor, an expert in the field, to help us with the legal work. Professor Hermann, a rotund man with balding hair taught wills and trusts at Brooklyn Law School. His yellowish brown lizard eyes roamed the class as he made derisive remarks. His reputation as a tough, sarcastic professor preceded him, but as students we did not have a choice. He was the only professor who taught this required course. When called upon to recite an assigned case or answer a question, students did not walk away unscathed. I sat in class petrified, in a constant sweat, avoiding eye contact with him as he perused the class before making his choice of student to question in his caustic manner. Miraculously or purposefully, Professor Hermann never called on me. Before commencement, I learned that he awarded me the prize for best student in wills and trusts in my graduating class. His nomination surprised me. When my name was called out for the prize at the graduation ceremony, I walked down to the front of the auditorium to receive it.

Because he had given me the award I thought he must be sympathetic toward me. Maybe he wouldn't be so difficult to talk to as I imagined, so I spoke to Martin about him. Impressed about talking to a professor, Martin agreed to have a consultation with him. Bernard and I were asked to join them after they had finished working out the issues. We walked down the hallway leading to Professor Hermann's office on the scheduled date with the expectation that an agreement would have been worked out, according to Martin's offer.

Professor Hermann, dressed in a brown suit and tie, opened the door and gingerly ushered us into his sparsely furnished office. It appeared it might have been loaned for the meeting. One barely filled bookshelf contained black bound volumes on wills and trusts. Martin sat in the corner looking glum and serious.

"Martin has thought it over," Professor Herman said. "He doesn't want to make any changes to his assets. He's not comfortable with the idea. There may be tax ramifications and, in any event, he doesn't want to separate out his money now."

I was stunned as was Bernard.

"It was his idea. He volunteered to do that," I said, shocked at his change of mind.

"He made a promise and Gitta agreed to go ahead with the wedding based on his promise," Bernard added.

Professor Hermann then unleashed disparaging remarks at him.

"You should not be looking to anyone else to support yourself and your wife. You have a good profession. You're young. Work harder and make more money. Don't look to your father-in-law for support."

We were astonished. I followed Bernard to the door as we

quickly made our exit from the office. We walked down the hallway back to the elevator. "This is incredible," Bernard said. "Hermann humiliated me. He had no right to do that. I never asked him for anything. Martin just sat there and said nothing."

It must have been Martin's idea to back down. It took very little effort for Hermann to tip the scale. It frightened Martin to part with his money, or maybe he never intended to give it to me. I don't know why I trusted him. Being a child who had been abandoned many times during my young life I should have known better? I was caught off guard. Was my need to trust, especially an adoptive father, so ingrained?

Martin had a selfish, cruel aspect to his personality. He did not express sympathy to my privation as a child. I don't know how Martin dealt with his losses, as he never talked about it. He left Poland in 1933. His father died of natural causes in 1939. The rest of his family, his mother, two brothers, sister, nephews and distant relatives were all murdered in the Holocaust. Perhaps he never took time to mourn and come to terms with his own personal and private demons. He had no regard for my feelings. During the depth of my illness my cousin Gloria, Aunt Blanche's daughter, came to visit. As I descended the stairs, I saw Martin pacing. When I entered the room to greet her, Martin's blue eyes flashed and he began to rant. "I'm sorry I ever took you in," he shouted in Yiddish, "this is more responsibility that I ever dreamed of." Humiliated, my body felt like ice dissolving under scalding water.

About a year after I married, Hilda invited me to meet her in Manhattan. We sat at a coffee shop on the East side looking out onto the entrance of the Fifty-ninth Street Bridge. We often met on the occasions when she came into the city. Bernard and I visited her and Martin in Queens quite often. We didn't have a car and Hilda volunteered to pick us up and drive us back at the end of the evening. She was generous with food and always sent some home with us. On this occasion, we sat and talked.

"I went to my doctor, Dr. Schwartz, and he told me that I have a heart problem," she said.

"Did he say what was the matter? What are you supposed to do?" I asked.

"He's not sure. He wants me to come back for another appointment. This is important to me, so please listen. I want you to promise me that you will look after Marcia if anything happens to me," she said.

I became uneasy and concerned for her. She didn't discuss her health again though, so I assumed she was fine and taking care of herself.

A year later, I was in the kitchen busy making plans with family for our second anniversary celebration when the phone rang. When I picked it up I heard my brother-in-law's voice on the other end. He and I had become very close and as my stockbroker, he often called to give me financial advice. I expected to have a conversation with him about the evening dinner arrangements. "Hilda has been in a car accident," he said in a faltering voice. "She is dead and Marcia is in the hospital. Bernard will be home right away."

⌐⌐

That morning Martin had been running late for work. While he stood in front of his bathroom mirror shaving Hilda slept in their bed. "Hilda, wake up," he said. "Get dressed and take Marcia to school. I am late." She got up, dressed in her housedress and a jacket, and left with Marcia for the fifteen-minute drive to her private high school. On the way Hilda suffered a heart attack and crashed into a tree. She died of a broken neck. The force of the impact propelled Marcia into the front windshield and her head smashed through the glass. She remained unconscious in the hospital for five days. The glass imbedded in her forehead left permanent scars even after numerous surgical procedures.

The shock of this tragedy affected everyone's life. Martin was riddled with guilt for having woken Hilda that morning to drive Marcia to school instead of driving her himself as was his usual routine.

Marcia lay unconscious in the hospital bed. When I entered her room, rays of sunlight cast through the window accentuated the paleness of the blue patterned sheets.

Her face and head were bandaged. Ringlets of her blond hair escaped from the white dressing and her eyes remained closed. We spoke to her and touched her. Martin periodically lifted the sheets to look at her unmoving body. "If Hilda had to die why did she have to take Marcia with her," he wailed. For five days we stayed at her bedside. When I arrived each day at the hospital, Martin who sat vigil in her room looked worn, his face tormented, eyes red and sunken. Eventually she awakened from her unconscious state. She slowly recuperated back to normal, but as with many head traumas, she never remembered the tragic accident.

We visited Martin and Marcia frequently after Hilda died. Martin and Hilda had reciprocal wills so that whoever survived received the other's property. Martin was now the benefactor of Hilda's. Hilda left two diamonds, one that she wore as a pendant and one as a ring. She also had gold bracelets, necklaces, earrings and several other rings. The issue of Hilda's jewelry came up during one of our visits.

"I'm going to give all the jewelry to Marcia," Martin said.

"That's not fair, how can you do that. That's not what Hilda would want," I said.

"Hilda loved Gitta like her own daughter," Bernard explained. "This is not what she would have wanted. Why can't you give Gitta some of the jewelry? They should each get an equal share."

We wrangled with Martin until he relented and allowed

me to have the smaller diamond she wore as a pendant, but he refused to concede any other jewelry. He gave Marcia the other diamond and all the rest. I left feeling dejected that I had to battle him and assert myself as a rightful daughter and heir.

I should have known he would react that way. When I had moved out of their home a few years before, I left my collection of silver jewelry that I accumulated on my numerous trips to Mexico. When I decided to go and take my jewelry, the pieces were no longer where I had left them. I asked Marcia what happened to them.

"Dad gave them to me," she said.

"But they're mine."

"Well, you left them here. He thought you didn't want them, so he gave them to me."

I did not want to confront Martin at that time and did not fight to get my jewelry back. Marcia had no qualms about keeping my silver pieces or accepting all of Hilda's jewelry, except the pendant.

In the month following Hilda's death (September 30) I had an impulse to write to Ida who I had not seen since she put me on the train from Poland to Paris in 1946. Over the years I had thought many times about trying to get in touch with her. I contacted her sister and brother-in-law who were living in New York to obtain her address. Although I had seen her relatives at the Biala Benevolent Society meetings in my teens I had never discussed the time when we all lived together in

Lodz. They gave me Ida's address in Australia. As I began to write and reflect, I realized that with Hilda's passing I experienced a sense of freedom from the constraints she had placed on me to find out about my past and to connect with other people. I knew that Ida would be able to provide details of my childhood and I hoped I would hear back from her. On October 29 I received a reply.

Dear Gita,

Thank you very much for your letter for which I have waited for 25 years. I was so thrilled and excited I could hardly sleep that night. You can imagine my joy when after all these years I finally heard from you, because although I have a family of my own, I have always thought of you as someone very close to me. I read your letter to all my family and friends who were well acquainted with your childhood. It is very difficult to write you about your past because to tell you all that happened during your childhood is like writing a book and I don't know where to begin. I don't think I will be able to write you everything you would like to know, in this letter, but I will try and relate your story in parts, in a few consecutive letters.

You were born in Biala Podlaska of parents who were fine, intelligent and highly regarded people. Your mother was a very pretty woman who at one stage won a beauty contest amongst the Jewish community in the town. Your father had a government position working in a town hall, a position that in those times was very rare for a Jew to hold. I knew your parents quite well. I first saw you during the war when you were two and a half years old.

Because of certain circumstances, my parents and I shifted to a district where the majority of Jews lived (this was the future ghetto) and here, I lived near you and your parents during which time I saw you on three occasions. You were already a pretty child, with large eyes and lovely blonde hair. Unfortunately, soon the German occupants moved in and evacuated all the Jews from the town. We were all taken to a town about 25 km from Biala called Miedzy-Rzecz where they gathered all the Jews from the nearby towns. They made a large ghetto and gradually killed off every Jew. They led us to Miedzy-Rzecz by a large kind of road that went through fields and paddocks. Wagons were piled high, full of elderly and sick people. The rest, who were able, walked by foot. We all knew that from Miedzy-Rzecz we would go to the gas chamber.

Your parents, wanting to save your life, decided to take the risk of dropping you off by the roadside and letting you run into the fields. They knew there were a few nearby farms and you could seek shelter and not be identified as a Jew because you did not at all look Jewish. In those days, to have a non-typical Jewish look was like a blessing from God and both you and I were among the lucky ones, because in similar circumstances to yours, my life was also saved. To my knowledge both your mother and father, died in the gas chamber. You must have wandered through the fields for some time, until some farmers found you and understood that you were a Jewish child who ran away from the Jews who were being transported. You were such a beautiful child, that they did not have the heart to give you away to the Germans to be killed, so they decided to have your christened and make you a true Catholic. You were sent to a

Catholic Orphanage that was part of a convent situated halfway between Biala and Miedzy-Rzecz called Sitniki. You were given the name of Maria Czekanska and you stayed there for about three years until the end of the war.

When the war finished I came back to Biala and a Polish neighbor told me that she saw a girl who looked like Rozencwajg's daughter, being part of a group of Catholic orphans who came into Biala for a day excursion. I had heard of a few cases where Jewish mothers gave away their children to the Poles in desperation so that at least maybe their children would be saved. Thinking of this, I decided to find out if the little girl was really you. Many, many other complications arose after this which I could not begin to relate to you in this letter, but which I will tell you about in detail in the next couple of letters.

Love Ida

I read and reread all the details in her letter. I tried to visualize the paddocks (a word I had never heard) and to imagine everything that had happened during that time. Ida's description of my story provided a piece of my life I had no memory of. I had been married to Bernard for just two years when I began this correspondence. After receiving Ida's letter our life continued, the days filled with important and unimportant events. The initial impact of her letter receded, but I looked forward to hearing from her again.

The few years following Hilda's death proved difficult for Martin. Not only had he lost his wife, and suffered the anguish of Marcia's near death experience and subsequent recuperation, but he also lost his business. His dispute with Frank, his business partner, could not have come at a worst time. It deprived Martin of his status and money, and also the consolation and distraction of his work.

Frank had a younger brother Anthony who had worked in the machine shop under Martin's supervision from the beginning of their ballpoint pen venture. Frank proposed to Martin they bring Anthony in as a partner and divide the business into three parts. This proposal galled Martin. He became furious and felt betrayed. "I started the business with Frank. His brother Anthony learned everything he knew about machinery from me." Martin could not accept what he perceived as a double cross and refused to compromise. From Frank's point of view, his brother Anthony planned to be married and he wanted to give Anthony a secure future.

I didn't live at home, but I saw Martin a few times a week. He no longer had a business to go to and fill his days productively. He appeared depressed, lonely, and defeated. During the final weeks of the anticipated breakup of the business, he took machinery and parts from the machine shop and stored the items in his garage to sabotage production. The separation had the acrimony of a divorce. Martin did not tell me whether he accepted a buy out or whether he just walked away from the enterprise with the intention of leaving Frank and Anthony stewing in self-condemnation, shame and guilt.

I lived on the third floor with Bernard in a two-bedroom apartment on First Avenue and 30th Street in Manhattan, the same building where Bernard lived as a bachelor in a studio apartment. We overlooked New York University Hospital and Bellevue Psychiatric Facility to the East and Kips Bay apartments to the North. We set up the apartment with his and her furniture from our respective studio apartments. I contributed my reproduction of a Louis XVI desk with gold trim at the edges and curved legs, a French patterned area rug and grey chenille covered day bed. Bernard brought his dark red Persian rug and heavy dark Spanish furniture. We bought a new bed with a wrought iron headboard. We also had presents from Martin and Hilda, other furnishings, linens and kitchen supplies.

Sometime after his disassociation from Frank, I received a phone call from Martin.

"You are going to receive a phone call from Frank. He will offer you stocks that he wants to sign over to you. Don't accept. Don't take his money. I will make it up to you."

Frank did call.

"I want to come over and speak with you. If it's OK, I'll come over tomorrow about 3:00 pm."

I agreed to see him in my apartment. He entered carrying a large leather covered book. He appeared heavier and older, since the last time I saw him, at least five years before. His hair was thinner. He wore a grey suit and trench coat. I felt awkward in his presence. After exchanging some short pleasant remarks, he came right to the point.

"I want to sign over a quantity of AT&T stock to you, $250,000.00, to cover what is due to Martin. Martin doesn't want to accept it, but you can use the money to buy yourself a house. You should not be living in this apartment. Martin has a lot of money. There's no reason why he can't buy you a house and set you up properly. This is a good opportunity for you."

"I can't accept," I said. "I appreciate your offer, but I just can't." Frank looked disappointed. There was nothing else to be done.

"Call me if you change your mind," he said and left. I reported to Martin what had transpired.

"That's good, that's good," he said, sounding pleased. "So he left and that was that."

That was the last time I saw Frank. In spite of Martin's betrayal of me with the Professor Hermann fiasco, I felt a sense of loyalty to him. To accept Frank's offer would have severed my relationship with Martin. I falsely assumed that he would treat me as his daughter and leave his estate to Marcia and me equally. When I asked him to provide financial assistance to buy an apartment or townhouse in New York City when the real estate market was in steep decline, he refused. He didn't give a reason. I thought he didn't favor Manhattan as a good choice for raising a family. When he died, he left three quarters of his estate plus his house to Marcia. I received the remaining quarter.

Several years after Hilda's death, in October 1973, Martin remarried an Austrian woman. Lilith, well dressed, with bleached blond hair styled in a chignon with curls on the top, and manicured fingernails, spoke with an Austrian accent. Proud of being Austrian, she accentuated the old feud that the Germanic and Austrian Jews were more cultured than the Polish Jews. Her cooking was barely edible. Martin doled out a weekly salary to her for stockings, make up and other personal needs which she complained about to me and to anyone who would listen. She accused him of being cheap and she assumed he would be more generous when she married him.

Marcia continued to live with Martin when he married, much to Lilith's displeasure. Lilith liked order and immaculate cleanliness and didn't want to have Marcia living with them. "She's twenty-one years old. She should be on her own. I don't want to live with a smoker or pick up after anyone and I don't want her friends around."

The following year Martin set Marcia up in an apartment. He and Lilith bought a condominium in Florida where they spent the winters. She died years after Martin. She remained in the condominium until her death as provided for in Martin's will.

Bernard and I settled into a rhythm as a newly married couple that gave me a lightness of spirit. I loved being Bernard's wife, and having him as my husband. An aura of security enveloped me. I had someone to be linked to, someone to protect me and stand by me. We were together as one.

I enjoyed his sense of humor, his witticisms, and intelligence. I loved to laugh and I found myself laughing and giggling frequently. Our lives took on a different routine. I worked as a full time attorney for the New York City Corporation Council's Office. I came home to our apartment to cook dinner for both of us, rather than to my studio. I took pleasure in preparing French dishes using our red and orange Le Creuset pots and following Julia Child's recipes in *Mastering the Art of French Cooking (1961)*. We looked forward to having friends and relatives over for dinner. Bernard served the food and reminded our guests of his previous work as a waiter in the Catskill Mountains. Referred to as the *Borscht Belt*, it was a common summer vacation place for college students offering an opportunity to make money, to socialize, and breathe fresh mountain air. A good raconteur, Bernard told us amusing stories of various guests' ordering and eating habits.

The Catskills provided a popular retreat for Jewish residents of New York City in the 50s and 60s. Heavily wooded with birch, hemlock, oak and maple trees, the rolling countryside and mountains displayed vibrant colors of red, chestnut, and yellow. Bluish green leaves sparkled in the sunlight. Bungalows bordered crystal clear lakes. Children played with mothers and grandparents in the absence of calendars, while husbands and fathers made the drive up to join in the relaxed rhythm between sunrise and sunset.

Mouthwatering, abundant servings of Jewish food tempted guests who ordered everything on the menu "just to taste" and waiters served multiple appetizers, soups, main dishes and deserts to each person. Hotels offered physical activities including ballroom dancing. Entertainment was provided in the evening and on weekends. Many top comedians got their start in this venue. Dalliances, affairs and romances between guests and staff blossomed in this idyllic setting, but at the end of the week they parted.

Martin, Hilda, Marcia and I spent several summer weekends in the Catskills at the Concord Hotel. One summer during college I worked at the Beekman Hotel as a switchboard operator. When a phone call came in, the light on the switchboard illuminated and made a buzzing sound. I plugged the cord with a metal head into the lighted space and answered. "Beekman Hotel, may I help you?" Then I would connect the caller to the room number with the corresponding cord. Hilda and Martin came up one weekend while I worked there. Martin came to visit while I was at the switchboard. "Well, I am the guest and you are the worker," he said in a condescending manner. I didn't know what to make of his cruel remark. He then sat on an armchair and leisurely smoked his cigar.

At the end of my long workday, I spent time with a few waiters who were not worn out by the grueling work schedule, consuming drinks and eating pizza. Not being experienced in drinking, I drank more than I could handle one night and went to my room to lie down on my bunk bed. When I closed my eyes, the room began to spin out of control. I barely managed to open my eyes when I started to regurgitate the drinks onto the floor. One of the waiters, an Italian who I drank with, had fallen in love with me. I presumed he did because he cleaned up after me! After the second incident of heavy indulging, I got the message and quit drinking.

One day early in our marriage, Bernard started a conversation about his best man.

"I think Rudy is lonely. He's become despondent since we married. We used to spend so much time together, so it's natural. Do you mind if we invite him to come along for dinner?"

"I don't mind at all," I said. "Let's invite him." I liked Rudy, enjoyed his company and genteel manners.

A tall man with a muscular physique, Rudy had full lips, hazel eyes, and wore his wavy brown hair combed straight back or to the side. He held his shoulders in a military posture and strived for a taller appearance by stretching his torso upwards. He gave the impression of standing on his toes. Easy going in personality, cheerful, friendly and proficient at social conversation, Rudy avoided any discussion of his personal feelings. He began to spend time with us. He had been Bernard's closest friend before we married. Bernard told me of their travels together to Italy visiting Rudy's cousins, and on another occasion they skied together abroad. They had spent winter weekends at ski areas in Vermont and other popular Eastern ski resorts. In New York, they lived near each other and spent time dining together. They also both loved the opera and ballet.

Bernard told me about his former girlfriends in college and law school. He told me about Rudy's female friends who he socialized with, but never seriously. Bernard and Rudy were often invited to family functions and each brought along a date. While dating Bernard, I asked him about Rudy's relationship with women as we saw Rudy frequently either without a date or with a female companion with whom he had no romantic involvement.

"Did Rudy ever have a girl friend?" I inquired one day. "After all he's in his late thirties now."

"He's been broken hearted for a long time. He has not been able to get over his lost love." Bernard said. "He was engaged at a young age while in Italy. His beautiful fiancée of sixteen years broke off their engagement. He has not been able to find anyone to take her place. He has dated many women, but never experienced the same intensity as his first love. Years later when he went back to see her, she was married and had children. He still had feelings for her."

Rudy, an only child, conceived by his parents in their middle age, took over his late father's business, a successful venture in real estate. His elderly mother invited us to dinner one evening at her comfortable home in New Jersey. The scent of her cooking wafted through the door as she greeted us happily wearing her blue print kitchen apron. She prepared her specialty dish of pasta al dente with pesto sauce and string beans. We sat around the kitchen table making light conversation with her as she spoke with an Italian accent. Rudy was the light of her life. Her eyes sparkled and smiled at him.

⟆

In 1969, I surprised Bernard with a trip to Russia as a birthday present. Fascinated by politics in the era of communism and the cold war with the Soviet Union, I knew he would be thrilled to visit that country.

I signed us up for a tour sponsored by an association of attorneys. While traveling in Russia we were always under the watchful eye of a guide. Like all tourists at the time, we were closely monitored. With a strict itinerary, we could not move about freely. We felt adventurous though and did visit a synagogue on our own in Moscow during a Jewish holiday. A crowd of Jewish people assembled. The police standing by wanted to disperse the crowd, but the people were reluctant to move. A disturbance erupted and the police sprayed all of us in the crowd with a water hose. We still ventured out another day and met a young man on our walk in the city. "Please meet at Gorky Park this evening at 8 o'clock. I see that you are Americans and I would like to speak to you," he said. We debated whether we should take the risk. Even though we had been soaked and chastised from the previous experience, we decided to meet him.

On each floor of the large hotel in the center of the long hallway sat a stout Russian woman wearing a grey dress with a white apron, her hair pinned back. She sat at a desk overseeing the guests' movements. To enter and exit the hotel, only one door was usable and men in suits, grey raincoats and hats guarded the door. When we left the hotel we felt like undercover spies, but assumed we were protected and safe because we were Americans.

We met with the light haired young man in his early twenties. We anticipated a request to smuggle out a message or another clandestine matter. After making his grievances known to us about his country, he confessed that what he really wanted was to buy our American jeans. His desire for jeans to probably sell on the black market did not rise to the level of intrigue we bargained for. We went back to the hotel amused and safe.

During our trip, Bernard always dressed fastidiously, while all the other men on our bus tour dressed casually in sports attire. Bernard came dressed each morning with a sports jacket, shirt and tie. "You're not going to the office. Why are you dressed so formally?" said one of the men on the bus. Bernard responded with levity, but did not change his habit.

Eager to have a child Bernard initiated discussions. "I am in my early thirties and you are twenty-nine, I think it is time that we had a child." I hadn't given the idea a great deal of thought, just as I hadn't given marriage much thought. I accepted that these milestones came along in time and I allowed myself to drift or be persuaded into life changing events. We tried, but I did not become pregnant. After six months of serious attempts we decided to undergo fertility screening. Tests revealed that Bernard's sperm count was below normal. "I had a suspicion that something was wrong with me," he said with a worried look. His condition was corrected with outpatient surgery called varicocelectomy, a simple and common procedure that remedied the blood flow in the testicle. Six months after the surgery I became pregnant.

I worked at my last full time job for the government doing research, at the Corporation Counsel's Office. Interviewed and hired by a tall thin man with curly black hair dressed in shirt and tie and an overweight woman wearing creased cottons, they sat at desks stacked with piles of documents appearing dedicated to their work. I spent most of my time doing research in the law library. My first assignment, researching and writing a memo to a particular legal question was hailed as brilliant. Surprised by the extent of the congratulatory praise I was thankful to receive it. My supervisor, a short man in his late thirties with a tinge of grey hair was pleased, but appeared circumspect. Given a second assignment by the hiring attorneys, I followed a similar line of presentation. I attempted to frame this response in the same manner as the first one, but missed the mark. I sensed that my reasoning had some gaps. The result disappointed them.

I quickly fell in their esteem. This was a blow to my vulnerable self-confidence. I perceived their discontent with my work. Working at a library setting, and not having my own desk and cubicle, I had no place to hide. Feeling that I was closely watched and disliked particularly by my immediate supervisor, I wanted to leave.

The best part of the day was treating myself to an ice cream pop after lunch from the vendor in the park, or on a really good day to an Italian sausage with grilled onions. While eating, I sat on a bench with the sun warming my face and body, enjoying the beautiful early summer days. I felt free. Working in a place where I had to be beholden to the clock and to someone's appraisal of me brought back overwhelming childhood feelings of being at the mercy of strangers for my safety and security. I resigned from my full time job and stayed home during my pregnancy.

Hilda had nudged us to have a baby wanting to be a grandmother. She had attempted to entice us with material furnishings for the baby and money to overcome our financial concerns. Unfortunately she died ten months before our first child was born.

My labor proved long and painful. My doctor, a woman I had great confidence in, scheduled her vacation at the time of my due date. A male physician whom I never met covered for her. I lay on a bed in a small room, screaming and wailing as the pain increased and the hours passed. The doctor gave me Demerol for the pain and continued to do so as my prolonged labor continued. Alone and isolated, I lay drugged in the separate room. Bernard had notified his parents and Martin that I had gone into labor, so they came to the hospital and remained in the waiting area as was the custom.

After many hours of excruciating pain, I finally delivered my first son, Jonathan. He was born with a bluish pallor and had difficulty breathing because I had been given too much Demerol. Bernard properly gowned was admitted to the delivery room. He witnessed the urgent efforts of the hospital staff to resuscitate the baby. Later he told me of his anger as he watched the doctor's sleepy demeanor and movements as he examined me. This is my wife and unborn child, he thought, how can he act so disinterested? "I panicked," he said, "when they held the baby up and he didn't cry."

I had never experienced such joy as when my baby, wrapped in blue, was brought to me. My very own first love. A miracle created by my body. As close to family as I could ever possess, I had a son who belonged to me. I vowed I would never be angry with him. I promised him eternal love and protection. I felt as though something inside had mended and that my equilibrium had been restored. Yet I also experienced feelings of loneliness. Not having a mother to share this moment with, the grief and pain encoded in my cells emerged. I wanted to be surrounded by family, but I had no mother and father, and no grandparents for my baby. My lineage made itself present by its absence.

Nevertheless, I consented to Bernard leaving me for a few hours to have drinks with Rudy and his friends. Alone in the hospital room after Martin's visit, I missed Bernard's company when he left. Finally he returned.

"Why were you away so long? I asked. "It's been hours since I've been lying here alone."

"Look, I am celebrating with friends. After all, this is my first son and I am entitled to do that," he replied in an affronted tone.

I stayed in the hospital for the customary four nights and then went home to begin my life as a mother. The newness and excitement of staying home with our first baby soon wore off. The endless routine of feeding, changing diapers, doing laundry, and making dinner preparation made me lethargic. My only entertainment consisted of watching the English chef Graham Kerr as *The Galloping Gourmet* a cooking show on TV that aired from 1969 - 1971. He drank wine throughout the show and proclaimed its virtues in cooking. He also used copious amounts of clarified butter, cream and fat.

When Jonathan (born July 30) was almost two months old,

I received a second letter from Ida dated September 24. She apologized for not writing sooner.

Dear Gita,

I was very busy working and trying to manage the best I could. Time passed very quickly and now I realize it has been a very long time since I last wrote you. I was thrilled to receive your card on the occasion of your son's birth. I want to congratulate you and wish you all the best for the future. I was terribly sorry to hear about your adoptive mother's tragic death and I hope that Marcia has now fully recovered. I will now continue to tell you about your past from where I left off in the last letter.

After the war in Biala, I met a handful of Jews who survived all sorts of concentration camps and hiding places. Particularly at this time, life was not at all safe in Biala for the Jews as there were various groups of anti-Semites and bandits everywhere looking for any opportunity to murder Jews and there were quite a few of those incidents. Because of this fact, all the Jews decided to leave and to go to a larger city where there was a greater concentration of Jews. My family and I went to Lodz. I was not married at this time, but I knew my future husband.

In Lodz, a Biala Society formed to help the Biala people who had recently come from concentration camps. My brother-in-law, Moshe Schneidman, was a committee member. From my news about you being in an orphanage and all sorts of correspondence, word reached your uncle David Zajgman in Paris. I told the committee that I was interested and asked if I could inquire into the matter. Because I did not have the typical Jewish looks, they all thought that I would be the right person. However, I did not have any idea how to go about the inquiry. I went back to Biala with an official letter stating that I was representing a member of your family and asking for permission to take a girl, Maria Czekanska, out of the orphanage in Sitniki. At that time Polish friends heard that you were under this assumed name. I went to the Chief of Police in Biala, told him everything and offered him a reward if he would help me. He immediately set off for Sitniki and returned with the news that Maria Czekanska was a Catholic and that there was no Jewish child at the orphanage. The priest told him not to interfere with the church. The policeman then told me the matter was out of his hands and he did not want to do anything more about it. I went back to Lodz and found out that all the orphanages in Poland were under the supervision of the Education Department whose head office was in Lublin.

In the meantime, a letter arrived from your uncle in Paris saying that you were his niece and he wanted you found at all cost. He added that he would pay for everything. I then went to the Lublin with a letter asking for permission to take you out of the orphanage. I received written permission from them only if a witness and I could prove that Maria Czekanska was Gita Rozencwajg. In Biala, I found a Polish person who knew your parents, but did not know you and was willing to be a witness. With the letter from Lublin I went to the City Council in Biala. One of their representatives went with the witness and me to the orphanage. We hired a taxi and I took a large bag full of lollies with me. We traveled on a long road through the woods. As a Jew, I was very scared of an attack.

When we arrived at the orphanage, after showing my letter, the priest organized about one hundred little children to go out into the playground to play games. He asked the witness and me to see if we could recognize you. I was terrified that I would not be able to because it had been about five and one half years since I saw you last and my witness relied on me to point you out to him. The children were then asked to line up and come forward to me one by one to accept a lolly. I was observing each child nervously and impatiently. You were about the twentieth child in line. When I saw your face, I recognized you immediately and discreetly nudged the witness to let him know it was you. I took your hand and told you that you could have as many lollies as you wanted, showing them that my witness and I have recognized you. Later, the priest who was convinced that you were Gita Rozencwajg asked for about 100,000 zlotys for letting you out of the orphanage. One hundred thousand zlotys was a fantastic amount of money at that time. Back in Lodz, the committee tried to raise the money knowing they would get it back from your uncle and when we had the full amount I went to meet you in Biala. The priest and a teacher brought you in a taxi from Sitniki. You had on torn shoes and a summer dress in cold autumn. I tried to take you with me, but you began to cry hysterically and *struggled because you were frightened. After a long struggle, a friend and I managed to quiet you somehow. We bought you some warm clothes, a doll, and some lollies and we went to Lo... a while when you were calm and trusted me a little, you that back at the orphanage they warned you that I was a Jew who wanted to torture you and use your blood to make Matzot. On the way, you gradually began to like me as you could see that no harm would come to you. In Lodz you came to live with me, my mother, sister, brother in law and their daughter who was your age. They now live in New York. You and I slept on the same couch and you became very fond of me. You loved to cuddle up to me at night as I told you all about your parents and what they were like. You loved to listen as I told you that you were a Jewish child found by people and put into the orphanage. I told you about the Jewish people and what was happening to them. After a few days with me, you seemed more secure as you learned new things. You were always asking me questions about your parents, about yourself and every day life. I loved to buy you things and prepare your favorite food. You were so grateful for all these things because after being in the orphanage everything seemed a luxury to you.*

After some time, it became known that a few people on the committee did not approve of your staying with me. They thought that they could somehow benefit more for themselves if I was not looking after you. This would mean that they could say that they were responsible for you and for delivering you to your uncle. The committee, excluding my brother in law, then proposed to put you into a Jewish orphanage in Lodz until the time that you would be sent to your uncle. I was very against the idea because not only was I growing to love you, but also I thought that you had enough suffering in the other orphanage. When I refused to give you up, a few people on the Committee became suspicious and thought I had some material reason for wanting to keep you. I told them that when the time would come I would personally send you to your uncle. If you did not have any family I would certainly have adopted you as my own child as I was planning to get married. One person who knew your uncle personally was in continuous contact with him. I know that he told him a lot of bad and untruthful things about me because he wanted to be your guardian as he was the one who had material reasons on his mind. All these years he had been living on money sent to him from overseas. You can imagine how hurt I felt, when in the years that followed, I did not receive a word of thanks from your family. They did not even bother to let me know how you were and how you were growing up. I am sure that they had something against me. I am surprised that you have any photos of me. I am wondering whether you have the one that was taken when the priest and the teacher brought you in a taxi from Sitniki to meet me? I will continue in my next letter, which will be soon, and I will also tell you a little more about myself. I hope this letter finds you and your family in good health. Hope to hear from you soon.

Love Ida

In this letter I felt the love Ida had for me shone through her writing. I marveled at her cleverness to bring lollies for the children so that she could scrutinize the orphans and her ability to identify me so easily. The difficulty of retrieving me from the orphanage and the large sum of money required for my release astounded me. I did not understand the politics and distrust of her motives. Nor could I understand why she did not receive the recognition she deserved for her courageous deed. I could not talk to anyone about her feelings. Both Hilda and Uncle David were deceased and I never spoke about it to Martin. Even though we had reconnected after so many years we were still separated by continents. Many years would pass before I would hear from her again. I resumed my busy life and concentrated on my new role of motherhood.

During our son's eighth month, we travelled to Mexico City to visit my relatives. Bernard and I went water skiing at a resort. He fell and apparently swallowed some contaminated water. A few weeks after our return he appeared jaundiced. He was diagnosed with hepatitis and had to stay in the hospital for a month, with a period of recuperation after that. When I visited him in the hospital, he lay in bed weak and yellow from the illness. How could he get so sick doing such a simple thing as waterskiing?

Bernard's absence during the evenings and weekends

made me melancholy and morose. Taking care of a new baby alone in our apartment was such a radical change from the legal world I resigned from. Although I was not comfortable in my profession suffering from so much apprehension about my competence and interaction with people, still I felt accomplished. I had status. I drew a paycheck or collected fees. I adored my child, but staying at home left me bereft and plunged me into depression.

I broke down in tears during one of my visits at the hospital. "I can't stay home anymore, I am not cut out for this. I have to get a job and get out of the house." I said to Bernard. He expressed sympathy and agreed. He liked the idea of my working because money was tight. He was employed in a small law firm that represented unions. The married couple he worked for dictated his salary. Although they had a warm, respectful relationship, they would not increase his pay substantially. We had many discussions about his future at the firm and I felt strongly that he should find a position that paid better. I was not working full time anymore and we now had a child. He decided to resign and work for a corporation that paid a higher salary. This presented a philosophical conflict. "I feel like a traitor appearing for the opposition," he said on many occasions.

Soon after our discussion I took a part time position as an attorney working for a busy, renowned Chinese Immigration lawyer who was agreeable to work with. He always dressed fastidiously in a well-tailored suit, shirt and tie, his black hair combed back. The office just outside of Chinatown was an easy commute for me from downtown Manhattan. I found the ethnic environment exciting.

A few months into our working relationship, he asked me to join him for drinks. He made this request a few times. I wanted to keep our relationship on a strictly professional level so I kept my distance. He criticized me for my formality and aloofness. I was not certain whether his advances were just an extension of his friendship, but it made me uncomfortable. I had not experienced simply platonic relationships with men. I saw men as sexual beings and he was a very attractive man. My horizons at this stage did not include extramarital relationships and specifically not with men of another culture or color.

We went out to lunch whenever the opportunity presented itself. One day, after a few bites of the Chinese food, to my embarrassment, I became congested and my nose started to run. I needed to keep wiping it. I didn't know why this happened. Years later, I concluded that the MSG, so prevalent in Chinese and other Asian food at the time, brought on this allergic reaction.

His clients barely spoke English, just enough to pass an oral, written and history exam for citizenship. They answered simple questions involving their name and address, and yes and no responses to various inquiries on the form. They were also asked to write simple sentence such as, "I see the boy," and name the first president of the United States, to which they responded "Georgie Washington." They had to answer four questions to pass the exam.

The importance of becoming an American citizen varied in the community. One woman's last dying wish was to become an American citizen. This required me to arrange for a Federal judge to appear at her bedside and administer the oath in front of witnesses. In gratitude, the dying woman presented me with a white silk tapestry on which one hundred birds of various sizes were embroidered in colorful threads, which signified good luck.

I also accompanied clients to hearings for permanent residence status or "green cards" at the Federal Building downtown. Each hearing was held in a cubicle before a Federal agent. These interviews did not involve any English skills, but rather a pile of relevant paper work. Many of the clients I represented were Chinese cooks, a fluid occupation for the Chinese immigrant.

Although not challenging legal work, it suited my needs. I gained valuable experience and eventually opened my own practice in Immigration law. I liked having my own income that fluctuated from week to week depending on the number of hearings scheduled. I enjoyed the freedom of having money to spend for the house and on myself, as I saw fit.

I hired a full time housekeeper to take care of Jonathan and do the housework. When I came home midday or in the afternoon, I felt unburdened and happy to spend time with him. In spite of my work and the additional money Bernard now earned, we were still strapped for cash. "Let's create a budget," I said, "but first let's see where the money is going." He agreed I could look over his credit card receipts, but when I asked him about various charges that I didn't recognize, he became enraged.

"I will not allow you to check up on me and spy into my affairs. You are being intrusive."

"I don't have a problem if you look into my spending," I said.

"I still don't want you to investigate me and that's the end of it."

We never did resolve our budget dispute and money continued to be an issue. Bernard liked having money in his pocket and it was his custom to convert a large amount of his paycheck into cash. He spent money freely. When we discussed wanting to buy things for the kitchen or some outdoor furniture, he bought it the next day without consulting me whether it be dishes, furniture, or art work.

"Why didn't you wait before you bought all this outdoor furniture to see if I liked it?" I questioned.

"It was on sale and I didn't want to give up a good opportunity."

No matter how many times I asked him to let me make some of these decisions, he persisted. He used his charming humorous ways and endless persuasion until I gave up.

Always dressed in a suit and tie, he would come home from

work wearing his beige trench coat, and sporting an umbrella when the cloudy grey sky threatened rain. An avid pipe smoker, he was rarely seen without one clenched in his teeth. He had quite a collection of pipes and his love of them made gift giving easy. He often carried a package in his hand, usually a personal item he bought for himself or a family member, or a little gift for me.

Bernard continued to invite Rudy to join us. I was used to the sexual tension created by being with men. Men would often flirt with me. When I walked down the street men frequently whistled and gave me seductive looks. This never happened with Rudy. Whenever I tried to search for some deeper revelation of his feelings, he put up a barrier between us. Vaguely frustrated with him, I did not dwell on it. We often went out together as a threesome. I actually liked being seen with two good-looking men. I didn't feel any unusual or inappropriate tension between Bernard and Rudy. They engaged in a playful tug of war when it came to paying the bill. Rudy won most of the time and being well off I doubt if he minded it.

We settled into our family life and after eighteen months I was to give birth to our second son, James (1972). The labor pains this time came on quickly and it should have been straightforward. Bernard however, got it into his head to create drama. We took the car, although the hospital was two blocks away. As we passed the medical center I yelled, "Stop, you've passed the hospital!" The contractions were coming closer together and he continued to drive uptown at a high speed as I held on to my enormous pregnant belly.

"Why are you doing this? Turn around and go back!"

"Remember how long it took for you to deliver our first son? Well, why spend all that time in the hospital when we can drive around and spend the time outdoors," he said with an amused smile on his face.

No matter how I pleaded with him, he continued to drive all the way up to Harlem from 30th Street, at least one hundred city blocks from where we started. Finally, he turned around and drove me back. By then I was fully dilated. I could barely stand up in the elevator as I was rushed to the delivery room. As there was no time for the customary shave and episiotomy, I gave birth shortly after. Bernard later told me, he wanted to experience the harried feeling depicted in the typical Hollywood movie scene where the couple live far from the hospital and the husband has to drive full speed to get there on time.

"We live so close to the hospital and I thought you'd be in labor for hours, " he said.

"But you ignored my screaming at you to turn around over and over."

"I just didn't think it would happen so fast."

I was incredulous that he would put me in such a precarious position so he could live out his selfish fantasy.

As it turned out, giving birth without all the medication allowed me to hold my baby right away. The doctor placed his little body on my chest and I saw the face of an angel, round and perfect. His touch, so sweet and pure caressed my heart. I felt truly blessed again.

After the birth of our second son we resumed life in our spacious apartment in a six story red brick building on East 23rd Street in Manhattan. Our balcony overlooked a concrete circular staircase that narrowed as it rose two stories high. Situated to visually enhance what would otherwise be a flat concrete ground or a grassy area, it served as a place to sit and for children to climb.

As the children grew older we took many weekend trips with them. We enjoyed the autumn hues of the New England landscape and the various parks and play areas for the children. We also spent many Sundays with his family in Brooklyn.

Rudy remained a part of our lives. We invited him on weekend ski trips and on one particular trip to the Caribbean. In February of 1973 we went to Jamaica with our two young sons, accompanied by Rudy. We enjoyed spending our days at the beach, being touched by the warm sun and tropical breezes. The boys looked darling in their red sun hats and boxer style colorful print bathing suits. They liked to play in the sand with buckets and shovels. We took pleasure swimming and frolicking with them in the aqua marine sea. We jumped over the white crest of the gentle waves to their giggling delight. The cerulean colored pools surrounded by red, pink and yellow hibiscus known as the "fleur de Jamaica" made it seem like paradise. After a morning of playtime with the children we ate lunch at a table set up on the white sand beach. When they became rowdy, Bernard yelled and as punishment put them against a wall separating the pool area from the beach. The boys stood there sadly, their heads dangling down. I was so embarrassed to see them humiliated like that in public.

"Please don't place them against the wall in front of other people," I said.

"I don't appreciate you interfering with my interaction with the children," he shouted. I backed away knowing from previous experience that the milieu would not deter his explosive temper. I had experienced many humiliating situations where Bernard yelled at waiters, proprietors of restaurants, others and myself. Restaurants provoked his anger the most. The taste of the food not to his satisfaction, the small quantity of the portion, or a combination of both fired up his temper and bad manners. At times he stormed out without paying. Left in the position of frightened observer, I had no choice but to follow him out feeling ashamed and taking on responsibility for something that I had no control over. Bernard saw this behavior as a sign of strength; that he wasn't allowing himself to be pushed around. His temper terrified people. He used his loud voice to get his way with his family, with me, and as a trial attorney. When he screamed at me, I shut down, reminiscent of the effect of Hilda's histrionics.

After dinner that evening, we returned to our room. As we lay on the ruffled white sheets covering the twin beds pushed together, our hostile mood toward each other continued and lingered into the following day. I sensed that Bernard wanted to be some place else other than with me. He looked pained and his eyes had a forlorn and far off longing that I could not appease or satisfy. It reminded me of his distant expression on the night I agreed to marry him.

I had entered his studio apartment on that occasion, as he was lying on his bed. I sat down next to him. As we spoke and hugged, I became captivated again with the symmetry of his beautiful face and profile. He looked so downhearted I felt moved to accept his marriage proposal that I had previously turned down. I said that I would reconsider and that I loved him. Initially jubilant, he soon became despondent. "It will be so difficult to tell Rudy," he said. "He will be lonely and depressed. We've spent so much time together." I didn't know what to make of his remark.

⌐⌐⌐

After seven years of marriage, we began to detach at a fast pace. The freshness and novelty of marriage pulled away as the petals from a flower, leaving fewer and fewer attached. His magnetic personality and sense of humor, so riveting at the beginning, did not offset the loss I felt. The reserve of love and empathy disappeared leaving our exposed personalities no longer in check, and unable to deal with unfolding stumbling blocks and complications. Our voices grew harsher and shriller. Compassion and interest in each other waned and I sensed Bernard's feeling of restlessness. Increasingly more high-strung, he exercised even less self-restraint. One night he became uncontrollably angry because of a disagreement between us and punched his fist through the bedroom door. I became frightened and tentative about our relationship, withdrawn and resentful.

Many evenings I lay in bed with my body turned away from him. He sensed my depressed mood. We lay on either side of the bed like packages on a train bound for different destinations, or as stars having gone through their evolutionary history of energy and luminosity transforming into stellar remnants.

"I can't deal with your yelling, and controlling behavior."

"I'll be different, I won't do this anymore. I'll curb my temper," he pleaded.

I listened to his apologies and promises to change. He sounded sincere. I trusted him and looked for signs of his commitment in the ensuing days. But nothing changed. His promises to modify his behavior dwindled. We didn't look forward to intimacy and the act became less frequent. After undressing and putting on his pajamas, Bernard developed a nightly habit of removing his cameras from his closet and arranging them on the bed. He then tested the interchangeable lenses by looking through them at the bedroom light clicking away as he did so. After that test satisfied him, he brought three fruits to bed and read a book as he chomped on each fruit. Disturbed at this routine, I pestered him to stop.

⌐

Bernard came home from work one day and stood in the kitchen archway wearing his signature trench coat. "My sister in law announced that she was pregnant again," he said. I had not decided how many children I wanted, but the thought of her pregnancy danced in my head. If she's having a third child and his sister had four, maybe I should have three. I was sure I would have a girl. I thought this would bring us together again.

"Bernard, what do you think of having another child?"

"You think we should have another child?" He looked pleased. Neither of us brought up the subject of our marriage difficulties. We became occupied with the idea of having another child and the logistics of timing and space. "Let's look for a house," I told Bernard when I became pregnant. Happy at the prospect of having another baby, he loved the idea of finding a new house. It represented shopping on a grand scale.

As I had reached the age of thirty-five I required an amnio-centesis. On the day of the appointment Bernard accompanied me uptown. A few streets from the building amidst the hustle and bustle of a crowded street, he turned to me.

"You don't mind going by yourself do you? If you do I'll go with you. I am sorry that I have to take care of a matter in the office, but I can reschedule if you think I should."

"No, it's O.K."

Disappointed, I couldn't ask him to join me. I wanted him to volunteer to accompany me, to want to be with me. Once again I didn't feel valued and didn't want to chance another rejection. If I had said, "Yes, I want you with me," that would have provoked another conversation. He would say, "Are you sure? After all, I'll just be sitting there and not really contrib-uting to anything. I don't know if I can stay in the room with you anyway. Something important came up at the office. If you wanted me to be with you why didn't you ask me ahead of time?" Rather than engage in that dialogue, I found it easier to say, "I'll be fine."

I felt that the pregnancy was mine. My body had to go through the test so I rationalized that it didn't matter if my husband accompanied me. My amniocentesis revealed we were having a third son. Surprised at the result, I felt momentarily disappointed, but I had always favored little boys. Bernard seemed genuinely pleased. Before expressing his feelings, as was his custom, his eyes would move to the side as though calculating his thoughts and the expression of feeling would follow. In time we did look forward to another boy and happily announced the news to our families.

"Oh, another boy," they rejoiced, "well, that's wonderful."

My obstetrician Dr. Dantuano decided to induce me, as she was concerned I would deliver the baby very rapidly on the weekend when she was out of Manhattan. She would not give me an epidural as I had a disc problem. I underwent hours of excruciating pain. She had to shake me to remind me I was giving birth and bring me back to reality. I often wondered if she made the decision to induce me for her convenience as she lived a distance from the city. She didn't offer me a choice and I didn't question her motives.

After the painful ordeal, I finally saw my third beautiful son, Judson. This meant another circumcision and baby naming. Bernard loved the process of looking through name books and finding English names equivalent to the Hebrew names of departed close relatives. Jewish Ashkenazi tradition requires the naming of babies after deceased family members. Unfortunately, I had many to choose from. Although consulted, I relented to Bernard's persuasiveness and agreed to names he selected.

We found a charming colonial style two-story house in Great Neck, New York, although it needed some updating. The lightly wooded property had a large grassy area ideal for the boys to play and everyone had a bedroom of their own. The kitchen had rich brown cabinets in the spacious cooking area. Dark blue wallpaper with little white flowers covered the walls accented with white molding in the cheerful eating area. A wooden table with a built in bench that fit under the window overlooked the expansive yard. Shaded by all the trees, the living and dining room with the dark wood floors appeared gloomy. In contrast, a sun parlor with walls of windows sparkled with light. A double-sided fireplace and wicker furniture with blue and white chintz provided lightness and warmth.

We met with the owners, a couple our age, a few times. They cordially offered us refreshments each time we came and gave us the opportunity to look around and inspect while relaying a bit of the property's history. We successfully negotiated the selling price.

Just before the final inspection and signing of the documents, Bernard perused the contract and title and discovered that the actual size of the property had been overstated by a minuscule amount. He called the sellers to inform them of the mistake and met with a stunned reaction.

When we arrived for the final inspection, we received a cold reception. Bernard reiterated that the agreement exaggerated the size of the piece of land and requested a reduction in the purchase price. We went out to the yard with measuring tape in hand and walked over the winter earth that showed hints of spring as new grass and budding trees sprouted in the warm morning sun. But the confusion did not diminish. The frustrated sellers were angry that we would even attempt to measure the size of the property at this point. "Take the seven hundred dollars off the purchase price. This is unheard of; renegotiating the price by such tactics at the hour of signing off on the deal."

We signed the agreement giving us title to the house and land. Right after, they verbally chased us off the property. I felt embarrassed and humiliated. Bernard believed they knowingly deceived us. "I wasn't going to let them get away with this. He was attempting to cheat us and I am fully vindicated in asking for a reduction," he declared in his imperial tone. I was so relieved to have the mess over that I never sorted out the merits of the case. We moved into the house after our third son was born (1975).

The novelty of the third pregnancy, the birth, searching for a house and all the events of selling our apartment and buying a new home had kept our lives busy and energized. We settled into the house located off the main street in the suburbs, with the city accessible only by car or train. The children went to school except for the baby. I had opened a part time practice in Manhattan and relied on a housekeeper for childcare.

The attic with a high-pitched roof and window in the pitch contained a bedroom and bathroom to accommodate a live-in housekeeper. Soon after we moved in, I interviewed a cheerful, colorfully dressed Caribbean woman. Heavy set and energetic, seemingly playful and kind to the children, I hired her to take care of the boys and the house while I went to work. She started coming late on Mondays after being off for the weekend. I felt trapped and overwrought waiting for her to arrive. The feeling manifested itself as more than annoyance at someone's tardiness or the apprehension of being late to an appointment.

Perhaps deeply buried memories from my childhood experience in the rural orphanage caused me to overreact. I felt like a prisoner who could never leave the house. I rushed from window to window anticipating her arrival along the wooded path. When she finally arrived, the feeling of panic left as quickly as it came on and I bolted out of the house.

Moving to the suburbs after living together in the city for over seven years exacerbated the tensions between us. Encumbered with a family, a home, and the commute placed a new strain on Bernard's freedom. Life in suburbia rankled his identification. He became distant and angry. He certainly did not appear happy in the relationship.

⌒→

Bernard continued to be irritable and moody. I reacted negatively to his moods and his considerable weight gain. What still existed of our bubble of marriage, romance, union, love and parenting burst, exposing hostile strangers. I decided I wanted a divorce. I consulted an attorney I knew who specialized in family law. Bernard attempted through various intermediaries such as his brother-in-law and friends to pull me back. He promised to change, to do whatever was necessary to make the relationship work. I refused. I needed to be free from him. After negotiating the terms, he agreed to sign a separation agreement. The conditions stated that he pay reasonable child support and agree to leave our home. I could finally breathe. I felt emotionally free.

I entered the house holding the written contract that required his signature, feeling happy and amazed that everything went so smoothly. I called out his name expecting to see his packed suitcases near the door. He came down the staircase in his navy velour bathrobe. I approached him with the legal document.

"I changed my mind," he said. I will not sign the agreement. It's unfair and too costly. I am not leaving the house either."

"You agreed to it! Everything is as we decided. How can you back out at the last moment? How can you stay in the house? We can't live together."

"I have been taken advantage of and I am going to fight you," he declared.

Distressed, I pleaded to no avail. I would have to go through one of the cruelty, abandonment or adultery routes to obtain my freedom.

"Bernard, you realize that now we have to fight each other for the divorce. We could just settle it through the agreement, live apart for one year and get the divorce peacefully. This is what we decided to do. Why are you making things so difficult? You're not happy either."

"I refuse to be taken advantage of. I have to fight for my rights. I am not giving up so easily," He paced the floor tightening his bathrobe.

"This will to be agonizing for both us and for the children. We have to allege cruel and inhuman treatment. We have to expose our dirty linen for the court using humiliating and degrading language. It will only make things worse between us."

"I am not the one asking for the divorce."

He walked up the stairs to the master bedroom and closed the door. The direction he decided to take led to almost two years of abject misery. My state of mind changed. Now I needed a lawyer who was a fighter, someone who could be tough and protect me in court.

Because Bernard refused to leave the house or the master bedroom, I slept in the attic. My spirits sank. I had to face him every day and feel his angry, hostile presence morning, evening and weekends. On Sundays he invited his family over. When he stayed home on weekends, I could not be with the children. I remained quiet not wanting to stir up his anger and involve them. I'd run out of the house to the pleading questions of my oldest son.

"Mama where are you going? Why can't you stay with us?"

"I can't stay at home, I can't stay with your father."

My son looked at me with imploring eyes. I felt wretched and powerless.

Unexpectedly, Bernard moved his mother into the house. "My mother is going to stay with us. She can help with the children."

I had been on good terms with his mother throughout our relationship. She had been kind and helpful. It surprised me that she left her husband and apartment to live in my house under these strained conditions.

She walked in with him, looking drained and sad. Bernard brought her suitcase upstairs to the larger of the three children's bedrooms. She followed him at a slower pace and did not look at me directly. She moved around the house with a bearing of discomfort and strain. During the time she lived with us she seldom stayed in the same room with me. On the occasions we were together, she would stand with her head bowed and arms crossed on her chest. It became obvious that she was pressured to do her son's bidding.

One morning Bernard lost his temper and screamed at me.

When his mother heard the commotion she scampered up a flight of stairs to the bedroom level. She saw him dressed in his suit ready to leave the house, threatening me.

"Bernard, calm down. Stop all the yelling. Not in front of the children. Please get control of yourself. Stop this screaming." She held her arms out as she pleaded with him. She appeared pale, her brown eyes wide.

My four-year-old middle son, still in his pajamas, clung to my bathrobe. He asked his father to stop. Bernard took a hold of his arm, dragged him into the bathroom and slammed the door. The frenzy and pitch of his anger sealed in my fear. I stood back in silence so as not to provoke him further. His mother and I remained in the same position anxiously waiting. When they finally came out of the bathroom, my son looked frightened and distant. Bernard left.

"What did your father say?" I asked him.

"Nothing," he replied in a flat tone.

I called my attorney to get a court order removing his mother from the house. Before the matter came up for hearing, Bernard moved her out knowing he would lose in court. The case was dismissed.

One evening Bernard came home drunk. When he found me in the living room he started shouting demeaning names and pushed me to the floor. He raised his fist in a threatening manner, but did not go through with the gesture. As our relationship unraveled, no words were too hurtful to fling at each other.

Another evening, I sat at the dining room table with friends eating dinner. Bernard returned from Manhattan, breezed in and made a discourteous remark. I turned to the door and saw him dressed in a three-piece suit of light tweed fabric, trousers tightly tailored looking like a fashionable dandy. Dr. Wainston's words leaped into my thoughts.

During this tumultuous time, a friend introduced me to an Italian man of medium height, with thinning hair and a seductive look in his eye. A look that suggested he was experienced and comfortable with women. The introduction was not intended to lead to a dating relationship, but I found myself physically attracted to him and responded to his allure. "Why are you seeing him?" my friend who introduced us asked. "He's married. He has nothing to offer you. He's not in your class." Antonio himself was amazed that I dated him, but nothing could dispel the irrational love that I felt for him. His being married didn't concern me, nor did his lack of education, his non-Jewish religion, or that we came from a different class of society. We spent much of our time in hotels rooms. He loved to hear my voice and asked me many questions. To hear me speak was more seductive to him than sex. "You speak so intelligently," he said, "I am not used to that." At those times all rational thought of my future disappeared.

Bernard sensed my change of attitude, habits, dress, and smell. He suspected I was having an affair. He would fly off in a rage swearing and yelling but he never presented me with any evidence. It soon became clear that he had hired a private detective, which was a common practice between divorcing spouses.

One evening when I took a taxi to the airport a car with only one headlight followed us. It tailed my taxi for fifteen minutes. I finally waived to the pursuing driver letting him know that his cover was blown. Exasperated, he maneuvered his car into traffic. Later I telephoned Bernard. "That is a bungling investigator you hired. Who would drive a car with a broken headlight? How ridiculous is that?" I sensed from the way he exhaled his breath how foolish he felt. Trapped by the invisible noose of marriage, I knew if the affair was exposed that Bernard would sue for adultery and this would jeopardize my having custody of the children. After a time, the appeal of the Italian man dissipated as quickly as it appeared. What did I see in him that made me take that risk? I asked myself.

Shortly after Bernard's mother moved out, in a new state of contrition, he gave up the master bedroom. "I'll stay upstairs," he announced, "You can use the master bedroom. I am sorry, I should have given it to you right away." I readily agreed.

Bernard's anger and subsequent rash behavior often lead to misguided results. Provoked by thinking that people were getting the better of him, he felt the need to revisit an earlier agreement or bargain. This led him to back out of deals, sometimes at the last minute, whether the purchase of the house or the settlement. He needed to squeeze out better terms no matter how dubious his explanation and rationalization. These actions infuriated the vendors, but Bernard often ended up with the acquisitions.

I bought a fur coat from the father of a mutual friend. While at the furrier, Bernard tried on a man's fur coat.

"Are you sure men wear fur coats?" he asked the furrier.

"Of course," he replied, "they're made for men. That's who I sell them to. They've become popular. You can always return it, if you're not sure."

Bernard strutted up and down in front of the mirror.

"OK, I'll take it and see how comfortable I feel in it."

On the way home, he said, "I am not sure why I bought it. I really didn't want to spend money on a fur coat." He kept the coat for a few weeks and then tried it on. After buttoning it, he hunched his shoulders forward to see if the coat felt tight across the back. As he bent his elbows, one of the seams ripped. "It's too tight, it tore. Look at this; it's not well made. It tore at the slightest movement." He kept repeating the motion and each time another seam holding the pelts together ripped. "This is ridiculous, it's a cheap piece of junk. I am taking it back."

He called in advance to tell the furrier that the coat did not hold up and that he was returning it. When we arrived the furrier looked at the coat, astonished at the many tears of the seams. " Why did you continue to rip it after you felt the first tear and realized that it was not a good fit for you? It's outrageous. I have to re-sew the whole coat." Bernard got his money back, but at the cost of a friendship with the furrier's son.

I had to endure many postponements and continuations of the divorce case. Being an attorney, he conjured up various schemes for nonappearances leading to months and months of delay. With each adjournment my optimism for a release from my hostage situation ended in depression. I felt defeated in this psychological war.

Another court date was scheduled for the following day. I opened my eyes the next morning to look out the window at a white landscape, the aftermath of a raging blizzard. The courts were closed. I watched the storm obliterate another day of my long sought after freedom. Even the weather seemed to be conspiring against me? Despondent, I stayed in bed all day. I felt as though that snowy day would last forever.

Months went by. In 1978 Bernard finally agreed to the divorce on the condition that the alleged complaint stated we were both at fault for cruel and inhuman treatment. He demanded and received a lump sum settlement for walking away from the house, even though the money for the down payment came from my individual funds. We settled on an amount for child support. He devised a plan to divide our personal property by making a list of all the items given to us as wedding presents. Those that were given to us by his family or friends went to him. This ensured that he received the most desirable item on the list, the sterling silver flatware, given to us by his parents. He also requested all the place settings of the Spode china embellished with a sailing ship in muted orange. We bought the set together after our wedding. He justified this request by saying he chose the "masculine" design. In addition, he fought hard to retain two brass lamps with black shades, refusing to split them up. I did not put up much of a struggle.

I had replaced the first attorney with one who specialized in family law and paid him pursuant to our contract as the case progressed. We went to court to sort out the final details of the property and support agreement. After signing it the judge would be able to grant the divorce decree. To my shock, my attorney demanded an additional $20,000 in addition to the $8,000 I owed him. I broke out in a sweat and stared at him, not believing what I heard. He glared at me with a fixed cold look. "Do you want your divorce now or don't you?" he said. He was not entitled to the money. He knew how desperately I wanted the divorce. Bernard had poisoned the playing field. He made anyone involved with the case aware of his grossly exaggerated claims that I came from a wealthy family.

I knew my legal rights, but I had no energy to play out my hand and call his bluff. It was extortion. All I could think of was more time slipping by without resolution and possibly having to deal with another attorney. Just steps away from the finish line, but exhausted, I couldn't go through it. I wrote out the check. Weeks after, I heard my attorney remarried and had a lavish wedding. No doubt I paid for part of it, but the divorce was finally granted. After the proceedings, Bernard and I found ourselves together in an empty elevator descending to the lobby of the courthouse. We stood there awkwardly, no longer connected. It was a hot August day in 1978. Legally we were strangers. We could now go our separate ways.

"Will you be all right?" he asked. "I feel so sad seeing you alone."

"Yes, I'll be just fine." I said and exited the elevator. I slowly walked to my car with an overpowering sense of freedom. I inwardly celebrated having fought off a tenacious opponent.

I inhaled deeply. A huge burden had been lifted.

During the time I waited for my divorce, I received a telephone call from Neil, a friend and former neighbor. He and his wife Laura lived in the same red brick building where I moved in with Bernard. They had one child and were expecting their second.

Our apartments, located across from New York University housed many medical students and residents. A number of the other wives were pregnant. We walked around with our expectant bellies generally meeting in the lobby on our way in and out to various appointments and errands looking as though we all drank from the same fertile fountain.

As neighbors, we had double dated a few times, but didn't have very much in common. Within two years of my meeting them, Neil and Laura had three boys and Laura became pregnant again as she desperately wanted a girl. She invited me for coffee one day. "I love being pregnant," she said. "I get so much attention and it's very good for my complexion. Look at my face. See how clear it is." I received a phone call from Neil months later announcing the birth of their fourth child. "We have a daughter, we finally have a daughter," he said, emphasizing the "t" in daughter, his voice filled with excitement.

I visited Laura shortly after she delivered. They lived on our floor on the other end of the hallway in a two-bedroom apartment. Two cribs, two children's beds besides their own, and all sorts of baby paraphernalia took over the rooms. Packed boxes of clothing were stacked on top of each other in the living room in anticipation of moving. One boy of fifteen months stood up smiling in his crib with arms stretched out wanting his mother's attention. A toddler, dressed in overalls played in the kitchen. He climbed over his high chair and jumped on the kitchen chairs with gymnastic precision while using a toy hammer to highlight his landing. The oldest, four or five years of age, had an outing with his grandparents.

Laura, eager to display her progeny showed off her new daughter sleeping in the crib. Having delivered a week before, her breasts were full of milk. "I love my breasts after giving birth. They are so huge and firm," she said, her eyes wide with excitement as she stressed the word "huge." "I just stare at them in the mirror. Neil likes to help himself to some of the milk too. They really turn him on," she said with a giggle. "Neil has been offered a partnership in a medical practice in New Jersey. It's only an hour's drive to Manhattan," she consoled herself. "We'll miss the city, but it's a great opportunity for him. The houses are reasonably priced and we have all the room we need for the children. We'll be visiting the city often. It's not far."

About a year after their move we received an invitation to one son's birthday party. On the day of the party we drove with our four- and five-year-old sons to their house. As we approached their spacious tree lined street, children wearing party hats ran around with balloons. They played games and lined up with anticipation for a turn on the pony ride.

We helped our children on to the ponies. They stayed outdoors with adults in charge of party games and we went into their unremarkable, but roomy one story home. The living room painted yellow contained a fireplace as its centerpiece. As they conversed with us, Laura attempted to set the party table. Her hands shook hindering her from laying down plastic utensils and plates in an orderly way. "Let me help," I said and easily finished the task. I noticed Neil looking at me intently. His stare made me uncomfortable.

I flashed back to the time he unexpectedly knocked on my apartment door when we were neighbors in Manhattan. I invited him in. Dressed in his hospital greens with a white overcoat we sat in the kitchen and I offered him coffee. As we sipped, I wondered what was on his mind and why he came to visit me. We spoke about the time I telephoned him late in the night to help Bernard who suddenly screamed in pain, unable to move. We had come home from a wedding where Bernard did his usual exuberant Russian dancing of the *Kazatzka*. Neil diagnosed him with disc pain and gave him medication.

"We are so grateful to you and very sorry to have woken you."

"No problem, I am glad to help. I am used to being called in the night. I open my eyes, start moving and a few minutes later my brain clicks in and tells me that I am awake," he said in stride, and left.

Neil never stated his reason for the visit and after some additional chitchat he stood up.

"Thanks for the coffee," he said.

I felt relieved when he left.

While the children were outdoors playing, Neil and Laura volunteered that they smoked marijuana and took Quaaludes to increase their sexual appetite and response.

"Do you use it?" they asked us, "if not, you should. What a difference!"

"Once I wanted to take aspirin and took Quaaludes by mistake," Laura said. "I overdosed and luckily Neil found me, but he couldn't figure out what happened to me. He finally did after he looked at the medicine cabinet. I had to be hospitalized and have my stomach pumped," she continued in an untroubled manner.

We went out together as couples after they moved to New Jersey. Laura became bone thin and happy about her new skeletal appearance. I had difficulty recognizing her. Her face took on an angular shape and her hair was short and edgy. Used to the roundness of her multiple pregnancies and her long shiny dark hair that she often wore in a ponytail, this skittish new Laura made me uncomfortable. "I have to lie down on the bed to get into my jeans," she said as we descended in the elevator to the parking structure. I looked at Neil to see his reaction. I wondered if he was pleased with this new thin Laura. He stood rigid, faced straight ahead with a serious expression puffing on his cigarette. Their aloof manner, trendy dress, and bluster about his success in the medical practice, made the evening with them awkward.

We exited the elevator to the parking structure. "You know you are a handsome couple and I expected all your sons to be good looking," she blurted. "You did succeed with the second." How rude, I thought but did not respond. I knew I wouldn't be seeing them again socially. I subsequently heard rumors about Laura from other neighbors and later from Neil that she was addicted to drugs.

I received a call from Laura telling me that they were leaving for California. She hated New Jersey and although Neil had done well financially, he had difficulty with the partners who refused to pay money owed to him. "Anyway," she said, "we can't stand living in this community and I want to move to a warmer climate. We've been here two years and I need a total change from this dreary area." I wished her luck and told her to keep in touch.

A few years after my conversation with Laura, I answered the phone one day and heard a familiar voice.

"Hi, this is Neil. How are you doing?"

"Fine," I said.

"I am in Queens, visiting my parents. I brought the children with me for their summer break and I thought our kids could get together and play. I come here for a month. It's a challenge to keep them busy."

"Where's Laura?"

"Laura and I are getting a divorce."

"Bernard and I are getting a divorce too. I live in Great Neck now."

"Do you want to get together?"

"Sure, you can come over the day after tomorrow."

He brought his four children ranging in ages from six to eleven. My sons were two, five and a half, and seven. Neil looked much trimmer than when I last saw him in his hospital garb with short hair. Dressed in jeans and a plaid shirt, his curly blond hair shaped in a large afro, he looked quite different.

"Your afro, how long have you had that style?" I asked.

"Since I moved to California."

Neil organized many games and kept the children busy and entertained while I served snacks. His warmth and playfulness with his kids and mine impressed me. I had not seen him in this fatherly role. After a few hours, it became more difficult to keep the children's attention. He decided it was time to leave. "We've had so little time to talk, why don't we get together for dinner and catch up?" I agreed and the children followed him out like ducks in a row.

We went out the following evening for dinner in a local restaurant.

"What happened to you and Laura after you moved to California?"

"We moved to California because Laura was so unhappy

in New Jersey. She gave me an ultimatum that we either move together or she and the children would move there without me. She suffered from serious emotional problems. She abused drugs and attempted suicide. She had to be hospitalized after that and went into rehab. I love my children too much to be separated from them. She chose Long Beach to live although we didn't know anyone there. I couldn't start a medical practice or get hired in someone else's practice. It was really tough to become accredited there. I worked in emergency rooms and covered for physicians. It required a lot of driving. I drove long distances on freeways and I'd catch myself falling asleep at the wheel. One time I did fall asleep, drove into the cement divider on the freeway and totaled my beautiful Mercedes sports car. Luckily I survived with no injuries. After this accident, we decided to move closer to the West side of Los Angeles where the work seemed to be. We sold the house at a loss. I may be the only person who lost money on real estate in California when real estate was booming."

"Why did you sell so low?"

"I got a position in West Los Angeles in a group practice and I didn't want to mess up the chance. Long Beach was not that desirable and we took the first offer we received. We rented a house in Bel Air and used the money from the sale of the Long Beach house to buy cars and furnishings. Laura loved the California lifestyle. She liked the weather and the beach, and spent her time shopping and socializing. She managed to buy herself a gold trinket every week. We dined out often and gave parties. The kids were not her priority. Whatever I earned was not enough to satisfy her appetite for luxuries. I found out she had male friends she went drinking with. When I pressed her, she admitted having an affair, but she was not contrite. She had a dismissive air about it as though it made no difference. I told her that if she couldn't be loyal to me we should get divorced. She ignored me."

He continued to tell me about Laura's excessive drinking, drugs and affairs culminating in his filing for divorce and moving out. Through legal proceedings they worked out a custody arrangement.

"You've really had a rough time," I said. "It's hard to believe that Laura has turned into this other person. She loved having the kids and being a homebody; a doctor's wife and all that."

"It's one thing to give birth to them and another thing to raise them. She didn't like the raising part. Drinking and drugs got the better of her. It changed her. Once I moved out, she implored me to come back. She told me no one satisfied her sexually like I did."

We talked about our marriage and divorce problems and I realized the Neil I knew before was different. I had not been attracted to him previously, but now I looked at him as an appealing man, not as Laura's husband. During his remaining two weeks in New York, we saw each other frequently. We dined at good restaurants, and had much to talk about as we faced imminent divorces and all the problems with our soon to be ex-spouses. "She's on a mission to have me return to her. That's not going to happen," he said emphatically.

To my surprise, after a few dates, I let my guard down and enjoyed his company. On parallel courses, we buoyed each other up during these tremulous times. We became intimate and he exhibited extraordinary sexual passion. Totally enraptured and consumed in sexual ardor we plunged into a relationship.

When we returned from a romantic overnight stay at the scenic coastal town of Nantucket, where we ate sweet meaty lobster like I have never tasted before, he introduced me to his parents who took care of his children while we were away. I received a chilling reception. His father, a short man with graying hair combed to the side, gave me a sleazy look and smirked, as his eyes roamed over my body. His mother and aunt, the mother's sister who lived with them, greeted me in a curt manner. They stood together, joined at the hip like Siamese twins. His mother's round spectacled face and curly blond hair contrasted with her sister, whose pointy nose and mournful look implied a life of sadness. I couldn't wait to leave. We only stayed a few minutes and he drove me back to my house.

"Why are your parents behaving that way?"

"They're not happy about the divorce. They feel sorry for their grandkids. I am their only child. I don't know what stories Laura has been feeding them."

Neil returned to California assuring me that he would return in two to three weeks and that we would speak every day. We expressed our love for each other. I was sad to see him go.

He telephoned me daily. I continued to live in the attic room. One evening as I lay in bed I received a phone call from Laura.

"I heard that you were dating my husband when he was New York. How long has this been going on?"

"He told me he's filing for divorce. Coincidently I am also. We're free to date."

"Have you two been seeing each other before? Are you the reason he's divorcing me?"

"We've never dated each other until these past few weeks. I don't know what you're insinuating."

"Well, I don't know how involved you are with him, but let me tell you that he has many problems. He's an alcoholic and a drug user. He's the one who got me hooked on drugs. Before I met him, I never used drugs. Over time he introduced me to one after another."

I didn't believe her story. It was the opposite of what I had been told. How could he be an alcoholic and drug abuser if he was a practicing doctor? I thought people with such habits languished somewhere on the street. Brought up at a time when the medical profession was revered, the fact that Neil was a doctor elevated his status and pleased me.

After the divorce Neil and I dated openly. We flew cross-country to see each other every month and when we weren't together we communicated by phone every evening. When I heard his voice, I was excited and relieved. His daily calls reassured me of his love. A delayed call brought on that old pang of doubt.

His parents continued to reject me in both subtle and open ways. One evening, we all went to a seafood restaurant his parents enjoyed. Neil's father, a retired shoe salesman and manufacturer routinely dined there with clients. "The lobster is really great," he said. "It's the best restaurant in Queens for fresh lobster." Neil, his father and I, at Neil's bidding, each ordered large lobsters accompanied by drinks and wine. Neil's mother and aunt heeded kosher laws that forbade the eating of shellfish. "I'll have white fish," his mother said. "Please sear it without oil, and make sure it is well done and dry." His aunt always requested the same. Since they did not eat non-kosher meat, their order never varied no matter where we dined.

I sat between Neil and his father. The conversation progressed cordially. At the end of the meal the waiter presented the bill to Neil's father. "Look at the cost of the lobster," his father said with disdain. He looked at me as if the high price was my fault. Neil quickly grabbed the check. "I'll get this," he said.

During our bi-coastal courtship, when Neil travelled to New York for a weekend, we stayed at a hotel rather than my home because of my children. He always advised his parents when he planned a trip to New York. They were delighted to see him, but not delighted that we were together. When I travelled to California, I stayed at Neil's apartment as his children lived with their mother.

I decided to consult with a past law school acquaintance, Arlene Schwartz, who specialized in family law in California. I needed information about my separate property and how to deal with our future earnings. Arlene however, had represented Neil during one of his court battles for additional child support brought on by Laura. To avoid conflict of interest issues, I had to obtain Neil's consent to meet with her for counsel. It had been ten years since our admittance to the New York bar, but she was still the dark haired vivacious woman I remembered, although considerably heavier. We were happy to see each other. After offering me guidance on the legal issues, she looked at me.

"Why are you marrying him? He has four children, a wife who will be after him for money and he has nothing to his name? The last time I represented him he fell asleep while standing against the wall waiting for his case to be called." I heard her, but I was not deterred. I simply continued on my course. The feeling of apprehension lasted only the few minutes it took for me to leave her office and rejoin Neil in his car.

Bella and Jonas, two of my closest friends in New York invited us to their home for dinner. They also warned me against marrying him. That afternoon, while in our hotel room, Neil smoked. He inhaled the cigarette in an exaggerated manner.

"What are you smoking?" I said.

"I'm smoking pot just to relax a bit."

I had never smoked pot. Unaware how much he smoked, or the effects it would have on him, I could not anticipate Neil's strange behavior that evening. After we arrived at my friends' apartment we sat on a flowered sofa. Bella had laid out a platter of hors d'oeuvres on the dark wood coffee table in front of us. Neil sat with his legs spread apart bending forward and quickly scarfed down all the food looking at us with a goofy smile. Normally a good conversationalist, he was distracted and his comments made no sense. I had looked forward to the evening and wanted to impress Bella. Instead, I was disappointed with his unexpected behavior. The next day I called to thank her.

"What do you see in him? You need someone more sophisticated. He's not the man for you," she said bluntly in her Hungarian accent.

"He generally doesn't behave like this."

"What's so special about him?" she continued.

"We are incredibly attracted to each other. He's intelligent and kind and a great lover. I just can't walk away."

"How can you throw everything away like that? You could do much better."

On an evening flight to California, my plane took off in a heavy downpour with poor visibility. Minutes into the plane's ascent the pilot came on the intercom and announced that the landing gear would not retract. "We have to return to the airport, but I have to jettison the fuel over the ocean before attempting the landing," he said.

The pilot then maintained his silence while flying the plane. I sat clutching my hands into fists and hardly breathing. I looked out the window splattered with rain into the black night as we flew through the storm. All the passengers remained quiet; our attention focused only on the sound of the engines, attentive for any changes. We circled around the airport over the turbulent ocean as we waited for reassurance from the pilot, but it never came. We finally hit the runway with a thud and skidded to a stop. Overwhelming applause erupted and everyone hurried to get off, feeling blessed that we had landed safely.

Later we were transferred to another plane flown by the same captain. An hour into the second flight, the captain emerged from the cockpit and sat in the lounge across from me looking somber. I asked him whether he could have given us more information during that harried part of the flight. I expected polite conversation and the usual calmness I associate with pilots. "Would you have preferred me to speak or to fly the plane?" he said brusquely. I felt foolish and said no more. We arrived in Los Angeles in the middle of the night, hours after the original flight was scheduled to land. Neil hugged me, relieved that I finally arrived safely.

During four months of dating we saw each other infrequently, but the time we spent together was intense. On seeing each other we couldn't wait to touch and meld our bodies together. His graceful walk, tall trim body, blond curly hair, and sensual gaze aroused me. An irresistible attraction possessed both of us. Entering our hotel room we clung to each other with desire leading to heated and erotic lovemaking until physically spent. Then we would lie in bed and gaze ardently into each other's eyes. During these loving times we talked about our future and how to resolve living on opposite coasts.

"I adore you. I want to marry you," he said.

"I love you too. We have so much to work out."

"We'll figure it out." He shifted his weight to his elbow. "You know, you're the love of my life. I have been in love with you since the first time I saw you. I couldn't take my eyes off you."

"I never suspected," I said, turning my head toward him.

"Sweetie, don't you remember when I came to visit you in your apartment? I wanted to say something, but lost my courage. I didn't think you were interested, so I left."

"I remember. It puzzled me." I sat up and covered myself with the sheet.

When separated we spoke to each other every evening and attempted to work out the best solution for our seven children logistically and financially. For us to live together in

California, my children would be separated from their father. If we chose New York, his children would be separated from their mother.

"Once I get serious with my practice money won't be a problem. You won't have to work. I have great earning potential. I am licensed here. I am not motivated to work full time because Laura keeps dragging me into court for more money."

I am fine with working, I thought.

"Bernard will be furious if I move." I shifted the phone to my other ear.

"I really need to be with my children. I love them so much," he pleaded.

"I know you do."

"I can't be separated from them. I can't trust Laura. My parents would go crazy. They warn me that if I move the kids won't have a father and they'll grow up to be juvenile delinquents."

"That's a strange thing to say."

"My mother sent me a letter ordering me not to move. They can't understand why I'm marrying someone with three kids."

I had been warned of the difficulty of finding another husband who would take on the responsibility of three children. We discussed the issue back and forth but we were both fervently in love. We decided that the best solution would be for me to move to California with my children, instead of him moving to the East coast alone.

During his short trips to New York, Neil displayed affection for my sons. He made hot chocolate when they returned from school, played ball with them and appeared comfortable in the role of stepfather. Sometime after our decision we sat across from each other at a casual restaurant in New York under the bright lights of faux Tiffany shaded lamps.

"Have you seriously considered the responsibility of taking on three more children? Shouldn't we discuss this more thoroughly?"

"It's not a problem," he said. "I'm good with children."

I held my breath as he responded, afraid that he would renege or rethink his position. Relieved to hear his response, I didn't pursue it. But I kept thinking there ought to be more discussion for such a weighty decision.

A week later as I sat at my desk in the office, I received a phone call from Bernard.

"Are you and Neil becoming serious?"

"I am seeing him as well as others," I answered, afraid to admit the truth and divulge my plans.

"The children tell me he's flying in from California often. You know how I feel about him. I don't like him. The time we spent with Laura and him, I was not impressed with either one of them. I am concerned that if you get serious you'll move there and I'll lose my kids. We just got divorced. Don't jump into anything, especially with him. Give yourself a chance. There are many available men in New York."

I sensed his concern and wanted to put him off guard. I mislead him into believing that my relationship with Neil was not serious. That evening I relayed the conversation to Neil.

"That must have been tough for you, honey." He exhaled deeply and I imagined the stream of cigarette smoke wafting from his mouth.

"I can't move to California with the children unless we're married first. I know that Bernard will go to court and bring a custody action when I tell him of our decision. That's going to be a difficult fight. He'll have to convince the court that I am an unfit mother." I sat down at the table and crossed my legs.

"There's no way he can do that. Why don't you fly here? We'll marry in a civil ceremony. That is the quickest way. You know how much I love you."

I was deeply in love with Neil. The divorce had emotionally drained me of any residue of feelings or sympathy for Bernard. I looked forward to putting some distance between us. So focused on my feelings for Neil, I scarcely thought about my children's separation from their father and lack of frequent access to him. The enormity of my choice never entered my head.

We married at the Culver City Courthouse in Los Angeles on November 24, 1978 three months after both of our divorces became final. We were wed in front of two witnesses, a married couple, Marion and Harold. They had been childhood friends of Neil. Having had an abysmal relationship with Laura, they were happy to welcome me as Neil's wife. I felt elated and proud to be married to him.

I learned to keep my trips to California a secret. I didn't want Neil's kids to inform Laura of my presence. During my last visit, she created a shocking scene just outside the apartment complex where Neil lived. I had been at the pool area with two of his children when his son told me that his mother called and would be arriving shortly to pick them up. Knowing how vindictive and spiteful she had become toward me, I quickly ushered Neil's children up the stairs and into his apartment. Right after I closed the door, I heard Laura screaming up to the window at me. "You stole my husband and you're a whore." Unnerved and frightened by this out of control woman, I telephoned Neil. He told me to let the children go to her and lock the door behind them.

A month after the civil ceremony, we decided to have a religious ceremony officiated by a Rabbi as was the custom. Neil's parents, more observant than we were, would not have recognized the civil marriage. Bernard refused to grant me the Jewish *get*, which according to Jewish law must be presented by the husband to his wife to affect the divorce. The essential text of the *get* states, "You are hereby permitted to all men." The wife is no longer a married woman and the laws of adultery no longer apply. The *get* also returns to the wife her legal rights held by the husband for her during the marriage. Without the *get*, a conservative Rabbi would not marry us. Neil found a reformed Rabbi who agreed to perform the ceremony.

During the time Neil and I dated, Neil's parents and aunt invited me to go shopping. At the store, Neil's mother suggested that she buy me a brassiere. I thought it was strange, but was flattered she wanted to buy something for me, so I agreed. The saleswoman picked out a few items and Neil's mother followed us into the dressing room. Being small breasted, particularly after losing weight during the divorce and going down four sizes, I could scarcely fill out a small cup. I looked at his mother who had a derisive smile on her face. She stepped out as I put my blouse back on. When I left the fitting room and approached them it was obvious she had been discussing me. Apparently she had described to her sister and husband how underdeveloped I was and they had a good laugh at my expense.

Two weeks before the scheduled Jewish ceremony with a feeling of elation, I telephoned Neil's mother.

"Do you want to fly in together to the wedding?"

"What wedding?"

Stunned that she did not know, I told her Neil and I were having a religious ceremony on December 24.

"Didn't Neil speak to you about it?"

"No, he hasn't said anything to us. We don't know what is going on and certainly nothing about a wedding."

I hung up confused and incredulous. She sounded so distant and I felt I had done something wrong. I left a message for Neil and couldn't wait to speak to him. Did he change his mind? How could his parents not be informed of such an important event? Later that evening he phoned me.

"Why did you call my parents?"

"I just thought they would enjoy flying in together for our wedding, but they didn't know anything about it."

"You shouldn't have called them," he said, not sounding like the tactful Neil I knew. "You should have left it to me. I know how to deal with them."

"Why didn't they know we were getting married? When were you going to tell them?"

"After we arrived in California. I had no intention of telling them until then. The way I would have dealt with them would have been to fly them in ostensibly for a holiday together. A day or so before the wedding I would have told them. They've been calling me and they're upset. I wouldn't have to go through all that if you left it to me."

It all sounded so bewildering. I became anxious that I had upset our plans.

"Are we getting married?"

"Yes, I don't want you to worry," his voice took on a warm

cadence assuring me we were back on track. "Just let me deal with my parents in the future." I agreed and hung up the phone relieved and completely baffled.

We had the religious ceremony as planned at University Temple off Sunset Boulevard. Neil's parents, his children and aunt, Martin, and Marcia attended as well as Neil's friends, Marion and Harold. I didn't feel comfortable with the thought of bringing my children to the ceremony. Having them witness me marrying another man would make me appear like a traitor to their father and I was not sure how they would react. It would have also entailed flying them to the West Coast and taking care of them. Their young ages spanning from four to just under nine would have made it impossible for me to relax and enjoy this important weekend. I did not tell them of my wedding plans or explain to them why I was not taking them along. I reasoned that at the time we needed to move, it would all come together. As to Martin, he came to see his grandchildren frequently and was unhappy that my marriage to Bernard did not work out. He had developed a close relationship with Bernard and enjoyed conversing with him, especially about politics, one of Martin's favorite topics. He had met Neil during one of the weekends that Neil flew in to New York. It was one of the rare times that Neil did not announce his plans to be in New York to his parents. He stayed at Martin's house.

"I like him," Martin said. He was impressed that he was a doctor and very inquisitive of his specialty.

"Do you only treat men?" he asked Neil.

"I also treat women for urological problems."

Martin looked at Neil with fascination. One morning Martin came to visit at my home to see the children.

"I have decided to move to California."

"That will be very difficult for me, not to see you and the children. Except for Marcia, you're all I have." His eyes welled up in tears. It never occurred to me to take his feelings into account. His display of emotion surprised me. He hugged me and shortly after he left the house head bowed, walking slowly.

The ceremony took place in the courtyard of the modern synagogue under the chuppah with the Rabbi clothed in a black robe. Neil dressed in a light blue suit, white shirt, and blue tie. I wore a pale, beige silk long sleeved blouse and a matching ankle length skirt. I carried a small bouquet of white orchards presented to me by Neil's mother. Surrounded by our relatives, Neil's children, and friends, we took our vows bathed in the warm late morning sunlight. Neil broke the glass and then placed a gold wedding ring on my finger sculpted in a contiguous bamboo cane design. He had picked it out for me at Tiffany.

We had our wedding reception in a fashionable, upscale restaurant in Hollywood specializing in seafood that satisfied the kosher requirements for Neil's aunt and mother. The horseshoe shape setting of the table allowed us to see each other. Before going to the restaurant Martin made it known that he intended to pay for the reception, as traditionally it was the bride's father who paid for the wedding. As we were getting ready to be seated at the table I saw Neil speaking to his mother. He looked miffed.

"What was that about?" I inquired.

"My mother asked me whether I didn't mind you being so small breasted." I looked at him in disbelief.

"I told her that's just the way I like you."

We returned to Neil's apartment in Marina Del Rey. We spent the rest of the day socializing. I asked Marcia whether she enjoyed the reception. "I hate fish. It's my least favorite food." I waited for a sign of acceptance from Neil's parents such as a gift, something symbolic of our union. I showed his mother my cherished collection of jewelry, a few pieces given to me by Uncle David when I visited him in Paris as a single girl. She looked at them and smiled, but made no response. Neil later asked me why I had shown my jewelry to his mother. "She has so much jewelry and I thought she would appreciate it."

CALIFORNIA

1980 - 1998

WHEN I returned from Los Angeles, I filed my request with the court to move to California with my children as I wished to join my husband. Bernard immediately responded to the court requesting sole custody and set out to prove that I was an unfit mother. He began to intrude and demand access to the children beyond the scheduled visitation. He left work early and took the children out. He accompanied them to the dentist and doctor appointments. He filed a complaint with Social Services claiming that I lacked maternal affection toward our youngest son. He described me to the caseworker as materialistic and decked out in jewelry. The woman in charge of the case visited my home one afternoon unannounced. She spoke to my older sons and wanted to know their feelings about moving away from their father. My middle son barely seven, shy and unwilling to communicate with her, flung himself on his bed. He placed his legs on the wall and refused to make eye contact or speak to her. When she was ready to leave, my youngest son called for me.

When I picked him up he wrapped himself around me, laid his face in the crook of my neck and held on. As she observed this I could see that she was now satisfied with our connection and convinced of my maternal affection.

We also had to go through psychological evaluation by a court psychiatrist. During my session with Dr. Wainston we reviewed the importance of clarity in describing why I would be the better parent. I was to explain my grievances and discontent with Bernard as a father and husband. It was all very clear to me until I sat in front of this stranger seated in his upholstered chair, cross-legged, holding pen and pad in his hand. I said some relevant things and observed his expression of disapproval when I brought up the matter of our loss of intimacy. I walked out feeling humiliated, puzzled and angry with myself. What could have possessed me to say that at this interview?

"Didn't we go over what you had to emphasize?" Dr. Wainston asked. "This is about custody of the children. What saved you is that he was not impressed with either one of you as parents."

A battle ensued between us to obtain statements from those who knew us lauding our parental skills and demeaning the other's.

My housekeeper was caught up in the melee. She gave Bernard a declaration to the effect that he was the better parent, more attentive to the children. Stunned and furious when

I received a copy of her statement, I went home to confront her. She stood at the sink in her blue uniform washing the dishes.

"Why did you do this Violet? Why did you write this?"

"I'm sorry, he told me I had to and if I didn't help him he would fire me." Her Jamaican accent emphasized her words.

"He's not the one who hired you or pays your salary. I do!"

"I didn't know that. I believed him." She lowered her head.

"I'm sorry you got involved in this. I can't trust you anymore. You have to go."

Bernard hired a renowned attorney with a reputation for being ruthless. His attorney put me on the stand and asked me how I interacted with the children and what it meant to me to be a good mother. I answered from my gut. No rehearsal of testimony was needed. I described my daily activities with them and besides the obvious demonstration of love and duties of feeding, bathing, clothing, story telling, supervising homework, buying toys and playing with them, I detailed sewing on patches, buttons, cutting their nails, baking cookies and how I took care of them when they were sick. I related one particular event on a late evening when Bernard was not at home. I always took my middle son to the bathroom after he slept a few hours. One night when I gently pulled him out of bed to stand him on his feet, I heard his labored breathing. Frightened, I called the pediatrician and told him the symptoms.

"I think he has the croup. It's been going around. Run hot water in the shower and let him breathe the steamy air."

Holding him in my arms, I ran to the shower and turned on the hot water. Not long after, I called the doctor, "There isn't any change. He's not breathing better. It seems to be getting worse. He's collapsing and not standing on his own."

"All right, I'll call the police to drive you to my office," he said.

Within a few minutes the bell rang. I ran to the door holding my son. Dressed in my bathrobe, the housekeeper rushed to my side with shoes which I slipped into. A terse police officer took us to his car with lights flashing. He asked me for directions. Driving along dark wooded streets, I prayed for the presence of mind to direct him to the doctor's office. When we arrived, the doctor examined him. "He has severe swelling in the throat. We have to rush him to the hospital. Let's go in my car. Open the window and keep his head out as much as you can." At the hospital he was immediately placed in an oxygen tent. He recovered the following day.

The young pediatrician who had recently opened his office appeared as nervous as I was, and later as relieved. "I had called a specialist to be on standby to do an endotracheal intubation. I am so happy that it was not necessary." After I arrived at the hospital, I telephoned Bernard. There was no answer. I telephoned a few times, then left a message. I stayed overnight at the hospital and he appeared the next day looking harried. He apparently hadn't come home that night and did not receive the messages. The excuse he gave for his absence was forgettable. The next day and thereafter, when asked of his whereabouts, he said that he arrived at the hospital shortly after my son was admitted and stuck to his fabricated version.

Before the court adjourned after the first day of testimony, I was asked by his attorney to provide information on where I planned to live, what schools I had researched for the boys' education, the location of libraries in the neighborhood, and the recreational activities available for the children. "I am looking forward to specific information on these issues when you return to testify tomorrow," said his attorney.

Neil was not in New York during the custody trial. I telephoned him when I returned to the house.

"I have to provide information about schools, libraries and recreational activities in your area. Can you help me with that?" My heart pounded as I had no idea how I would answer these questions in court.

"I don't know honey, but I'll find some information for you and call you early in the morning."

The more I thought about answering the attorney's questions, the more I realized that it might be a trap. Doing research at this late date and coming into court with lists of schools and libraries would look calculated and prepared overnight just for the trial. I returned to court the following day and took the stand. His attorney repeated the questions and asked me what information I had and what choices I had made for the children's education. "I have decided to do thorough research when I move there. I have not had an opportunity and have not spent enough time in California to make the important decisions."

The attorney looked at me surprised. It was such a reasonable and guileless answer that it thwarted his prepared line of questioning. The judge was satisfied with my answer. I looked at Bernard and saw his frustration and disappointment. I might as well have said checkmate!

Another surprise awaited me. Bernard had decided to subpoena Mr. Alberti, the attorney who had handled my reparation case against the German Government. I had not seen him for many years. Alberti had no choice but to come to the courthouse and bring my entire reparations file. It contained the report prepared by Dr. Hertz, the German psychiatrist who had interviewed me in my early twenties, including my psychological profile as a persecuted child of the Holocaust with all the deleterious effects on my personality. It also contained the reports and billings from Dr. Wainston, the psychiatrist who treated me since my nervous breakdown in law school. We had filed a claim against the German Government for reimbursement of the psychiatric bills amounting to approximately $60,000. They had declined payment. Mr. Alberti's assistant had failed to appeal the case by a specified date. It was definitely legal malpractice. They had admitted their mistake and were willing to pay an appropriate amount, but I declined their offer. I didn't feel comfortable taking his money.

Throughout my years of psychoanalysis I submitted bills to the German government under their program of Wiedergutmachung (Compensation) at the Saarburg office in Germany, which performs like a bureaucracy on steroids. Their file contains all my childhood and subsequent information. Instead of giving me the benefit of doubt, I have to submit layers of documentation proving my need for therapy and that there is no insurance coverage in the United States. Very recently they have allowed some reimbursement.

It was a cold snowy day when I met Mr. Alberti at the railroad station to accompany him to the courthouse. A white haired man in his late seventies, he walked toward me supported by a cane. He wore a dark winter coat with a grey scarf wrapped securely around his neck. Taken aback to see him so aged, I slowly guided him to my car and drove to the courthouse. As we entered, his appearance had an effect on the courtroom. It was apparent that this elder gentleman had travelled a long distance on this cold bleak day at some risk to his health. The attorney requested my file be placed in evidence.

"This file contains confidential information that I cannot release without my client's consent," said Mr. Alberti, quietly but firmly.

"Is there a motion you wish to make to the court?"

I leaned towards my attorney and whispered.

"Request the court to deny Bernard's motion to introduce my file into evidence. I don't want my medical records to be disclosed."

"My client has the right to confidentiality," my attorney said.

Bernard's attorney recognized the judge's resolve not to admit the file into evidence.

"We withdraw the motion," he said.

The favorable ruling allowed Mr. Alberti to leave the courtroom with my file. As he did, he wished me luck. That was the last time I saw Mr. Alberti.

Bernard later felt contrite about his legal maneuver to use the Holocaust file against me. "I was desperate. I had to keep my kids," he confessed. Bernard's attorney issued a subpoena for the children to appear in court. I anticipated that he might want to put the children on the witness stand and had probably prepared them to testify against moving to California. Although they were too young for the court to question their preference as to which parent they wanted to live with, I didn't want them to be subjected to this courtroom drama.

"Your Honor, we subpoenaed the children and I see that they are not in the courtroom," said Bernard's attorney.

"The children are in school and they are underage to testify. I therefore saw no reason for their attendance," I said.

Bernard appeared irritated, but I won on this point as well. The judge granted me custody of the children and the right to move to California. But the issue of child support also had to be resolved. In the judge's chambers, Bernard argued strenuously on this matter. He convinced the court that once the children left the state he would incur costly travel and hotel expenses. He argued that flying the children in for all major holidays and two months in the summer, during which time he'd have to take care of all their needs, warranted considerably lower payments. The judge sympathized with his separation from the children and reduced his child support. It was not enough to sustain one child, let alone three. "Don't let the money influence you. We'll manage. I've always told you that," Neil said, when I told him of the situation. I accepted the lesser amount. It was over and I was free to move with my children.

After the court order, I didn't waste any time listing the house for sale. I began to sort out what to take with me, and what to leave behind including a basement full of toys and memories. I went through our personal items and started packing. Things I would never miss again were relegated to large plastic bags heaped together outside the garage either for pick-up by charities or in large piles for the garbage truck. The heavy items, furniture, kitchen items, bedding and towels were packed, shipped and put in storage until I was settled. Sorting, discarding, segregating, and packing demanded a lot of me, mentally and physically. I went through this arduous task and focused on starting anew with Neil.

I didn't think about all the connections I was about to break with family and friends, nor did I think about losing my financial independence. This was to be my grand escape from depression and the old problems that still haunted me. I would begin a new life where all would be idyllic. "Don't rush, take your time. I'm not going anywhere. I'll be here for you whenever you're ready," Neil repeated nightly on the phone. Unsure whether his words were meant to bolster me, or whether he just needed time to deal with our arrival, the reality was fast approaching. To the chagrin of my neighbors, I sold the house at a low price to the first serious bidder, a middle-aged couple.

One of the neighbors confronted me. "You've brought the value of the neighborhood down. Why couldn't you wait for a higher offer?" Embarrassed by his attack, I knew he was right. I did sell too low, but I couldn't wait for a better offer.

The buyer came by from time to time to see the progress of my packing and offer his help. One morning when he came over for one of his inspections, I was wearing a flowered silk bathrobe. I carried a heavily filled garbage bag. As he spoke, he looked me up and down brazenly. I must have appeared an alluring figure to him, a divorcee who needed a tumble in bed.

When the time came, I dreaded the boys having to say good-bye to Bernard. They hugged each other and cried. Bernard assured them he would be visiting within a week or two. Finally, they unlocked themselves from him and we moved ahead to the plane, leaving their dejected father behind. We took our seats and settled into the flight that would take us to a new beginning on the opposite coast. My youngest son fell asleep immediately on take off. My other sons appeared thoughtful and unaware of the gigantic leap we were taking. I eagerly anticipated our arrival, seeing Neil smiling and welcoming us at the arrival gate. When we disembarked from the plane I searched for him, but he was nowhere in sight. We gathered our luggage and waited.

"Where is he? Is he coming?" asked one of the boys.

"Of course he is," I replied, sure he would come, but annoyed that he was late at such an important time. Fifteen minutes later, Neil rushed through the doors, breathless and happy to see us. "So sorry, I had a problem with a patient. How is everybody? How was your flight?" He hugged and kissed me, then the boys. We took our luggage and followed him to the car. We all squeezed in and drove to his apartment building in Marina Del Rey. He rented a two-bedroom apartment on the second floor where I had stayed with him during my earlier visits to the West coast.

The balcony overlooked the street and provided a glimpse of the ocean in the distance. The functional apartment had a master bedroom with its own private bathroom tiled in light green, and a second bedroom that opened into the living room where my children slept. We lined up a double and single mattress on the shag rug so they would have more room. Being accustomed to their own rooms, this close physical arrangement was an open invitation for the boys to fool around, pull the blanket away from each other, giggle and laugh out loud. "Keep quiet and settle down," we shouted repeatedly. One night they didn't stop, Neil went into their room and I followed. His face contorted in anger as he bent down and grabbed my middle son's leg and squeezed it roughly. My son looked surprised and upset. It was the first time I witnessed Neil so infuriated at my children, particularly at my middle son James. I shuddered with a sense of foreboding, but didn't say anything, not wanting a confrontation about this isolated event.

We settled Jonathan and James, nine and seven into the neighborhood public school. Finding a preschool for my four-year-old son Judson proved more difficult and he stayed home with me for sometime. Being in unfamiliar territory made me dependent on Neil to drive us around Los Angeles. I kept looking for the skyscrapers, the hustle and bustle of the city. Disappointed at seeing the same monotonous suburban landscape, I missed the familiarity of New York with its electrically charged pace. I had lived there since I was ten.

I missed being in a spacious house with my children. The large apartment complex where we were living temporarily did have some redeeming features. It had a large pond with colorful, patterned koi. A long wooden path led to a bridge over the pond, and to various shops and a grocery store that provided all the necessities for the single occupant. It also had a swimming pool and Jacuzzi at each end of the complex. The kids loved running down the paths and were enlivened each time they passed the pond stopping to admire the fish.

While the two older boys were in school, I walked to the beach daily with my young son. We enjoyed seeing the vast Marina with its lineup of blue and white boats. Being so young he wasn't sure where he was.

"Is this California?" he would ask.

"Yes," I said.

If we went to a different area of Los Angeles he would say, "Are we still in California?"

Six months later when we moved to a house north of Sunset, he asked,

"Is this the new California and where we used to live the old California?"

We took my sons to the beach often. They loved playing in the sand, digging with their shovels, building castles and jumping over the rolling waves. Sometimes Neil would join them to play or throw a frizbee. I loved seeing them together and happy. Other times Neil lay on the blanket, and looked into the distance as he puffed on a cigarette. He was most engaged when his children were with us. His three sons and daughter visited often. Older than my sons by two to three years, they were more mature and street-wise. With seven children in the apartment, the tension and jealousy his children displayed and the discontent at having their father live with other children percolated, and prevented the friendships from developing.

Neil's ex-wife Laura incited the children, especially Eric, who was closest to her and most reactive. Neil's daughter Toby clung to him emotionally and physically. At those times Neil's presence was important to control the situation especially when Eric, aged ten, bullied, tripped or pushed James. They regarded my four-year-old son Judson as a baby. They played with him and left him alone. They reasoned that he was too young to be picked on and not at fault for taking their father away. Neil's parents behaved similarly.

Jonathan possessed a charming and quick-witted personality that helped him navigate the hostile situation. Most of the wrath was directed at James. I had to come to his defense to protect him, which further cultivated the grievance that he was my favorite; a gripe that my sons held against me later on. All three had different personalities, but I felt James was most sensitive and vulnerable.

In spite of my asking Neil not to leave on a particular Sunday when all the children were together, he succumbed to his son Eric's entreaty to pick something up for his school project. "I won't be long," he said. As I anticipated, in Neil's absence Eric started fighting with James and hit him. Neil finally returned two hours later.

"Why would you leave me for such a long time with all the kids? You know how unruly Eric is."

"I'm sorry, I had to do this for the kid. He needs it tomorrow."

"Where did you go?"

"I picked up a sheet of plywood. I had to drive slowly, maybe five miles an hour because it didn't fit in the car."

"What did you do?"

"I stuck it on top of the roof and had to use my left hand to hold it down."

"You're a surgeon. Why would you take the risk of hurting your arm and hand just to bring back plywood?"

"I was careful."

I seethed at hearing about his foolish and irresponsible behavior.

Bernard came to visit a few weeks after we moved. The children were delighted to see him for the weekend. They enjoyed the beach together. At the end of his stay Bernard complained of the pain and desolation he felt. "I'm very lonely without them. It tears my heart apart, but it's a long trip and I can't see myself flying out every weekend as I thought I would," he said.

After six months of living in the Marina, Neil and I found a house in the Mandeville Canyon area large enough for all of us and in the right price range. I used most of my savings including the money I had from the sale of my house in Great Neck, New York for the down payment.

Located two miles north of Sunset, up a winding paved road, the house had a beautiful view of an uninhabited canyon. Situated in a neighborhood with a variety of ranch houses on streets branching out of the main thoroughfare, our house contained four bedrooms, a large living room, and kitchen with a separate eating area.

"I need to have the house in my name." I said. "The down payment for it came from my money and I want the financial security."

"Yes, but I will be making the monthly payments," Neil countered.

"If the title was in both our names as community property, you can depend on Laura coming after you. She will assume that you had money hidden from her. Let's see what happens in the future. We can always change the title."

We went back and forth and he eventually agreed. We made some improvements, added a guest bathroom, and changed the carpeting in the bedrooms. Although we had enough rooms for my sons to each have their own room, Neil demanded that one bedroom be his study. I couldn't persuade him otherwise. "My kids don't have their own bedrooms," he said. "How will they feel when they visit? Your kids have to share two bedrooms." It turned out he never used the bedroom as a study. He wanted a guest room for his parents when they came to stay. Neil also insisted that we put in a swimming pool. As I paid for all the improvements, I didn't want to finance the pool as well.

"I've spent so much money, let's not do this right now."

"This is California. It's important to have a pool for the

kids. It also enhances the value of the property," he said as he lay on the bed.

"You agreed that we would build a pool. I wouldn't have gotten into this house had I known you would delay this."

I could tell how passionate he was about it, and how despondent he became when I resisted the idea, so I relented.

A pool salesman came over and gave us an estimate for the pool with all the specifics. Neil dealt with him in a confrontational and demeaning manner. He behaved so rudely that the salesman turned bright red and became speechless from the shock of the verbal assault. On another occasion, Neil spoke to one of the workers in the same way. I had not seen this side of him before. At the end of the interview, we said goodbye to the stunned pool man and Neil dashed out to his car.

"How dare you behave in such a rude manner? Don't you ever do that again!" I shouted as I followed him out.

"He's stupid, he's just a salesman."

"Not everyone can be a refined, intelligent surgeon and behave like you."

I surmised that his behavior had something to do with his father being a salesman. In spite of the unpleasant beginning, the pool turned out to be a welcome addition. It served as a focal point for entertaining and for the children's enjoyment.

Being a cosmopolitan woman from New York, I found it unnerving to live within visiting and hearing range of wailing coyotes, rattlesnakes and other wildlife in the canyons. I had not expected this. I was petrified when a baby rattler was found in our swimming pool. Could the mother be close behind? Neil trapped the baby snake with a stick and flung it down the canyon. The boys were fascinated as they watched with curiosity and delight. I called animal control to obtain statistics on snakebites. As months passed without incident and with the reassurance of neighbors, I calmed down. "It's California. It's part of canyon living. Just make sure you don't have small pets. They disappear quickly," I was told.

My fear of canyon life was overshadowed by the uncontrollable rage of Laura pursuing her revenge against Neil. Our having settled into a home exacerbated her anger. On one occasion, while her children visited us, she appeared at the door after Eric called her. He had told her that I had eavesdropped on his phone calls to her.

She ordered her children to leave our house and they all ran toward her car. Neil ran after them while he and Laura screamed at each other. I stayed out of the fracas, huddled in the house with my sons, embarrassed that our neighbors witnessed this scene. Neil returned a few minutes later,

"Laura attacked me. She hit me," he claimed.

"This is crazy, we can't live like this! Every time your kids are over there's a scene. She incites them and then there's fighting. I think you should take a break from visitation."

Within a week Neil was served with a summons alleging

that he had assaulted Laura. She had filed charges with the District Attorney's office. In a written statement she accused Neil of hitting her. She denigrated his fitness as a father saying he referred to the children as "kids" rather than "children."

"Didn't you tell me that Laura hit you? Why is she alleging the opposite?"

"She's lying. She just wants to stir up trouble. I promise you that I didn't hit her."

I started investigating. Having a criminal complaint filed against Neil and going to trial could be devastating to our lives and his career. The neighbor, who lived in the house across the street, spent a lot of time on the front terrace, when not at his office selling insurance. Of Armenian descent, he was a friendly middle-aged grey haired man raising two adopted children and a baby born to his adopted daughter. He and his wife Mary, an avid tennis player, also adopted their daughter's baby. When I saw him in front of his house the next day, I approached him.

"Did you see what happened between Neil and his ex-wife?"

"That was quite a scuffle," he said. "A lot of screaming and hitting."

"She's filed a complaint against him for hitting her."

"I saw the woman taking swipes at him, but didn't see Neil hit back."

"Thank you. Can I count on you for a written statement if it comes to that?"

"Yes, sure," he agreed.

I went to the office of the D.A. named in the complaint and asked to see her. I waited while people behind their desks conducted their business with the public. Finally, I was called up to the counter and explained the situation to the young woman in charge.

"My husband's ex-wife is making life miserable for us. She's the one who came to our home and started a brawl in front of her children. This is not the first time she's been rowdy and vulgar. We're newly married and just trying to live a quiet life. I am an attorney admitted to the New York Bar and I will be studying this summer for the California Bar. I need some peace to accomplish this. The allegation that we are disrespectful to the children by referring to them as "kids" is ridiculous. We're not insensitive to them. A neighbor who saw the fight will swear that the ex-wife hit my husband."

"You're studying for the California Bar?" she asked as she observed me.

"Yes."

"I will have the complaint dismissed," she said.

Overwhelmed with relief, I thanked her. I left feeling a huge weight lifted and that my life could continue forward.

Neil decided to curtail his visitation. I could see the effect it had on him. He missed his children and brooded, but the alternative was chaos and the probability of another physical confrontation. He couldn't take the chance, but his separation from them caused undercurrents of hostility and resentment. When sitting with my children, a woman remarked how handsome my boys were. I smiled and thanked her while Neil just sat there looking unmoved.

My son James became the target of his ill will. We had been invited to dinner with my boys to Bill and Jane's, a couple we knew in New York. Neil and Bill had done their residency together at New York University Hospital. My children and their two boys were close in age. In their Beverly Hills home, a white colonial with front columns, we sat together with the children in the dinning room at a large table eating Jane's tasty cooking. She complimented the boys. "James has such a beautiful face, such perfect features," she remarked. After we arrived home we put the boys in bed.

"You know James has such a good looking face I wouldn't be surprised if he grew up to be gay," Neil blurted out later when we were about to go to sleep.

"How dare you say that? Have you had too much to drink? Don't you ever say that again!"

Concerned that his voice carried to the boys' rooms, I lay in bed confused and sad that he would speak with such unkindness and make disparaging remarks about my son. The next morning he was to take James fishing with his son Eric. He woke up early and started dressing to leave.

"Aren't you going to wake James so he can get ready?"

"I'm not taking him."

"How can you disappoint him like that? He's just a child. He hasn't done anything to you?"

"I've made up my mind and that's that." He turned and left. I walked into my son's room. He lay on the top bunk bed and cried into his pillow. "Why didn't he take me fishing? He promised he would." I tried to console him as best I could. Although Neil apologized after he returned, I found it difficult to forgive him.

Not long after that occurrence, on a sunny Sunday afternoon, we rode bicycles on the Santa Monica Beach bike path. A dog ran across the lane in front of James' bike. He slammed on his brake. The bike skidded forward throwing him over and he hit the ground with his head. He lay still for a few minutes, dazed and unresponsive. Frightened that he might have suffered a concussion I wanted to go home right away. As James recovered from his stupor, Neil demanded that he get on his bike again, but James refused. I was reluctant to get into the middle of it, but seeing how unsteady James looked, I insisted that we return home. Neil became testy but took us back.

"I should call a doctor," I said timidly after observing James' dazed state. I sat him on a comfortable chair in the living room, where he remained quiet and listless. In the past when I suggested calling another physician, I sensed that Neil took offense and felt slighted, as he was a doctor. "It's not necessary. He just has to be watched and kept from falling asleep. He may throw up, but he'll be okay," He said this in a matter of fact way as he stood at the other end of the living room. He showed no compassion for James. His manner had a chilling effect on me and on my response to James. I didn't feel free to react to my sons with motherly concern and affection. I feared I would offend Neil by showing a preference for my boys over him.

My New York friend Maxine, a good looking, buxom and vivacious woman was visiting us at the time of the bicycle incident. We had made dinner plans and Neil still urged us to go out.

"I don't think it's a good idea to leave James," I said. "I'm not sure he's recovered."

"I'll take Maxine out," he replied. "She doesn't have to stay home on her vacation."

"Why don't you come? He'll be fine," Maxine tried to smooth it over.

I was uneasy, but decided to go with them. I couldn't wait for dinner to be over. They were enjoying themselves wining and dining, whereas I remained quiet, worried, feeling guilty. I should have stayed home, I thought. Why could I not be more assertive about my feelings?

The boys travelled to New York to be with Bernard during Christmas and Thanksgiving holidays, and their summer breaks from school. Sometimes Bernard flew to the West coast to spend a long weekend or a short holiday with them in

Laguna Beach. After these visits with their father, the children suffered from the separation, particularly James. He cried from loneliness. Neil resented James' display of gloom and isolation. James took to his bed crying, wanting to talk to his father on the phone to be cheered up. At times I resented his sadness, because his return home wouldn't dispel his loneliness. The other two boys did not react with such emotion and resumed their lives without a heavy heart.

The dislike, almost hatred, that Neil displayed toward James bordered on paranoia. We had a serious quarrel when he refused to take James fishing. On another occasion, and after another dispute, I had made plans to have an evening outing to a concert with a girlfriend. When I told him I was going out with a friend he suspected that I had a date and behaved in an agitated manner. When I came home, it was obvious that he had been drinking. He sniffed around me like a dog attempting to pick up the scent of sex. As I walked to the bathroom, he followed me demanding to look at my underwear. I saw that my closet door, which I kept locked, had been taken off its hinges. He had tried to unlock the door and having failed, he took the door off. It had fallen and dented the silver venetian blinds that covered the bathroom window. The bathroom was a disaster.

"What did you do here? How dare you invade my privacy and remove the closet door? What did you think you'd find?

"Did you have sex?"

"I did no such thing. What is wrong with you? You're drunk. Get away from me. Did you dent the blinds? What is going on?"

"I didn't dent the blinds," he argued.

"How can you lie to me like that? When I left there was nothing wrong with them and now they're dented. You know the door fell against them when you removed it."

"I don't know how it happened, but I didn't do it," he insisted.

I didn't speak to him the following day. In the evening he called me into the den. I found him standing imperiously at the fireplace wearing a bathrobe, holding a glass of wine. I sat on the sofa while he spoke to me like a teacher lecturing a student.

"You know that all our problems have to do with your son James. You'll do anything to protect and cover him. You favor him over me."

"I don't know what you're talking about. You're blaming the problems we have in our marriage on James? How absurd. Even if I do feel close and protective of him, how is that different from the way you and Laura react to Eric?"

This conversation increased the mistrust I felt. I refused to speak to him. I regretted my decision to have married him.

What could I do at this point? I had invested all my money in the house. Where could I go now? I had sold my house in New York and I wasn't working. If I stayed in Los Angeles I would need to put my house up for sale. How could I make the payments in the meantime if I asked Neil to leave? Wouldn't Bernard demand custody if I returned to New York defeated? I had to make it work. I couldn't bear losing the children. This was my second marriage and I couldn't admit another failure. This impasse between us lasted a few weeks. Finally he came home and apologized.

"I'm so sorry. I spoke to my mother. She heard how miserable I sounded and gave me good advice."

"What advice?"

"That true love is never easy. The more you love someone, the more it hurts and you just have to forgive each other."

My feelings softened at hearing this, especially his reference to his mother who I regarded as my archenemy. If she recognized her son's love for me and advised him to apologize and make amends, it was an encouraging sign.

⤳

The acrimony between Neil and Paul continued. Howard, their oldest son, became a Bar Mitzvah. On this important occasion, a son becomes a full-fledged member of the Jewish community and is eligible to be called to read from the Torah, the totality of Jewish teaching and practice. Family members and particularly the parents are called to recite from the Torah and say the Aliyah, meaning to rise and ascend, and say a blessing. The parents stand at the Torah with their son, who after much tutelage, recites the Torah portion in Hebrew and discusses the Torah section. Not only breaking with tradition, but with the express purpose of humiliating Neil, Laura and her son denied him any recognition as the father. In the customary speech of thanks to the parents, Howard thanked only his mother and grandparents. Neil was not called up to recite the Aliyah from the Torah. This was the ultimate rejection.

I sat next to Neil with my children in an audience packed with people dressed for the occasion. Among the congregants were family members, friends and professional associates. Neil's face expressed incredulity and pain. Having been with the family the day before the ceremony for rehearsal and included in the rituals, this came as a complete surprise. Before the end of the ceremony, and in full view of the audience, he walked out of the synagogue belittled and embarrassed.

For the luncheon celebration set up in the synagogue community room, Neil and I sat with his parents. The children were seated at separate tables. The sun shone through the window and brightened our white linen table setting and added sparkle to the glasses, but our mood remained dark. We talked about Howard's shameful behavior and speculated on the reasons behind his angry and manipulative actions. Neil's father Dan, dressed in a dark suit, white haired and sporting a mustache, sat with us at the table.

"He's always had a loving and friendly relationship with his father," Dan said.

"He's influenced by his mother, she's so bitter," said Aunt

Edna with the usual look of sadness imprinted on her face. "How can she encourage her son to do such a shameful thing?"

Startled by screaming voices halfway through our meal, I looked up and saw Laura triumphantly pouring a pitcher of cold water over Dan's head. I was speechless. I had never witnessed such behavior. After emptying the entire contents, she quickly walked away. People around us sat stunned.

"This crazy woman is up to her nutty behavior," said Dan. He wiped his head and suit with napkins hastily given to him by everyone at the table.

"Let's leave. I've had enough of this."

Neil rose from the table and helped his parents and aunt out of the room. I rounded up my children and we drove back to the house.

I fabricated an explanation to the children when they asked why we were leaving so soon. After we reached home, we settled down in the living room and attempted to shake off the events of the unnerving day over coffee and tea. "This in not the first time that Laura spilled water over my head." said Dan. "She's done it at other family gatherings. She's out of her mind, what can I say? I feel sorry for the children." I started thinking they were all insane.

As irrational as Laura was, Neil too expressed his anger with a childish tantrum on many occasions after I confronted him about his rude behavior. One time we gave a lift to a couple related to an older attorney I knew in New York. During the ride Neil kept interrupting our conversation and denigrating my intelligence. I could see the couple's stunned expression.

On another occasion, I invited Neil to join me for lunch with the Russian parents of a friend of my son James. Neil said he would be late and when he arrived everyone at the table was engaged in conversation. He didn't respond to the couple when they greeted him. He just sat down, casually spread his legs apart and leaned on the table. Had it been a doctor and his wife, he would have been much more respectful. We had ordered lobster for lunch before Neil's arrival. When I turned my head I saw Neil holding a lobster shell up to his face like a mask. I seethed with anger at this childish, insulting behavior. My friend gestured to me to keep quiet and let it go. When we arrived home I told him I would not allow him to humiliate me like that again. He walked out of the room and went into the kitchen. He returned with a glass of water in his hand. I thought he must have just been thirsty, so I resumed the discussion where we had left off. With that, he flung the water in my face!

Within the next three years Paul and Eric, Neil's other sons and later his daughter Toby, celebrated their Bar/Bat Mitzvah without the offensive display that accompanied Howard's. Neil was given his fatherly recognition and called up to the Torah. I remained on guard for Laura's theatrics as she and her children projected angry stares at my sons and me. We attended the celebration out of respect for Neil. Not to attend would have given Laura the power to separate us as a family.

⌒

The next year 1983, Jonathan was to celebrate his coming of age. I chose an elegant hotel, the menu, and musicians for the celebration. We belonged to a synagogue where Jonathan and the other boys attended Hebrew school and he prepared to recite his Torah portion.

My relationship with Bernard continued on a rough course. His anger at me for leaving with the children had not abated. His only source of power was money and he made sure that I did not receive a penny more than the insufficient sum ordered by the court. Neil and I paid for the Hebrew studies and the Bar Mitzvah. I did however send an invitation to Bernard. I believed it was the right thing to do even though he planned to have a full celebration for Jonathan in New York for his family and friends. He accepted but his attendance complicated matters. I had to figure out how to position Neil and Bernard on stage with Jonathan and me during the ceremony to make sure that neither was slighted. I discussed the matter with the Rabbi, letting him know the delicate situation. "Please do not tell Neil that I mentioned this to you. As far as he's concerned we're just here for rehearsals." The Rabbi agreed.

The day before the services Bernard, Neil and I met with the Rabbi at his office in a contemporary style synagogue. I introduced Bernard who approached him holding out his hand.

"I am Jonathan's father," he said in a strong voice.

"Congratulations to you all on this upcoming happy occasion. How can I help you?"

"As Jonathan's father I want to stand next to Jonathan during the services."

"He lives with me and I am paying for this Bar Mitzvah," Neil said irritably.

Seeing the direction this was going, the Rabbi, a tall man with peppered grey hair and short beard moved between them and held out his arms in a welcoming gesture.

"We can resolve this to everybody's satisfaction. Please follow me to the assembly room." We walked through a passage leading from his office to the stage facing an empty auditorium. Behind us the Torah scrolls were housed in the ark, or ornamental closet made of light shaded wooden doors embellished with colorful mosaic stones. They stood out as the focal point of the large assembly room. During the day, light shining through the tall stained glass windows illuminated the room. The Torah ark would be opened the next day at the Bar Mitzvah service. The Rabbi spoke. "Bernard, why don't you stay with Jonathan at the podium when he recites his Torah portion, and Neil please stay a short distance to the side. When Jonathan has finished reading his portion, Bernard, you may step down and sit next to your other sons in the front row. Neil, you remain onstage until the services are over." This arrangement satisfied both of them and we thanked the Rabbi.

Everything went smoothly at the services the next day. Bernard and Neil kept their rivalry and acrimony in check. Neil stood stiff backed in a grey suit, his arms hanging and hands folded. Bernard dressed in navy stood next to Jonathan who wore a dark suit with a white *kippah* (head covering) during his Torah reading. Neil joined me at the podium after Bernard stepped down. We said our Aliyah, Torah blessings, along with other relatives and close friends who were called up to the Torah.

I wish I had been able to express my deep love, pride and well wishes to my son on this important occasion as is customary for parents. I wish I had been able to relate how bright, intelligent and humorous he was, and the amusing and memorable events we shared together up to that time. As always the paralysis and fear of speaking in front of people in groups, large and small, held me back. I did my best to stay calm, but inwardly I shook at being the center of attention. I knew what I should do, but could not.

The day of James' Bar Mitzvah the stylist cut and did my hair in a stiff and unnatural way. I watched him as he fussed with my hair feeling dissatisfied with the progress. I kept my emotions in and left feeling self-conscious. When the time came, we dressed to go to temple for the services. James put on his new dark suit, white shirt and yellow speckled tie. He could not find the new shoes we bought for the occasion. The night before at the dress rehearsal we had everything in order. We searched for his shoes everywhere. "Neil, have you seen James' shoes?" He didn't answer. My housekeeper, Reyna, searched all the rooms and closets, including the back yard, in case Neil had found them in the den and thrown them out. The children had a habit of taking their shoes off in the den when watching television. They often went to their bedrooms and left their shoes behind. I reminded them to take up their shoes but at times they forget. It irritated Neil, particularly when he came across James' shoes. He would grab them, open the door and throw them into the backyard.

It was getting late so James put on his old tight fitting dress shoes and we left. Just before he went on to the podium my housekeeper, Reyna, came running in with James' new shoes.

"Where did you find them?

"I find them in the back of the closet in the hall. They were all the way in there behind the doctor's things," she said with an air of satisfaction.

I felt grateful to her, but so upset at Neil's deceitful and outlandish behavior. James' recited his Torah portion beautifully and no problem arose with positioning Bernard and Neil. The enormous tension before the services, coupled with my fear of speaking caused me to stand at the podium like a frozen statue. When James and others came up to recite their blessing, I just looked down at the Torah. I could not express all the love and admiration I had for him or acknowledge his sensitivity, openness, and caring. That evening we had a celebration at the same hotel as Jonathan's Bar Mitzvah party. My sons took off their jackets and loosened their ties. They danced with school friends and ran around playfully. Balloons served as the centerpieces to their tables. We danced to the fast and slow rhythms of the band between courses of delicious food. I danced with James and will always remember in my heart the way he held me so lovingly. This beautiful boy with braces on his teeth reached just above my shoulders. Later he would grow to be 6'4". A large birthday cake with two pyramid shaped candelabra holding seven candles was brought out for the ceremonial lighting. Each candle was lit one at a time by relatives and close friends. As all the candles glimmered, the still childish faces of my sons were revealed so softly and tenderly, one following the other in celebration of their not too distant manhood.

Not long after James' Bar Mitzvah, I decided it would be the last one I would organize. The stress at Jonathan and James Bar Mitzvah's affected my health and enjoyment of the occasion. I didn't want to deal with Bernard's hostility and Neil's antics. When it was Judson's turn, I told Bernard that I didn't see the point of each of our sons having two celebrations. "I won't be making a Bar Mitzvah for Judson and I will not pay for his studies as I have with our other sons. This time it is your responsibility," I said.

He fought my decision, but ultimately had no choice. I refused to participate in any way. He contacted a Hebrew teacher in Los Angeles at our local synagogue and Judson learned his Torah portion for his New York Bar Mitzvah. Bernard did invite me and I attended with Neil. When we walked down the red-carpeted stairs to the synagogue, we met Bernard who frowned and muttered something rude to Neil. My son James, who was in hearing distance, later complimented me on my restraint.

The Bar Mitzvah was held at a small synagogue, resembling the ancient Portuguese style synagogue in Amsterdam where Sephardic Jews migrated when expelled from Portugal. The Bimah, the table from which the Torah is read, located in the center of the sanctuary was surrounded by white wooden fence around which the congregants were seated. Shiny brass chandeliers added light and warmth. I felt awkward being with Bernard's family, as did Neil, who soon lost any feelings of discomfort as he downed one drink after another at the reception. On our way out, we passed Bernard's sister.

"You should get varicose vein treatment for your legs before the condition gets worse," Neil said.

"How can you say that, you don't even know her?"

We returned to our hotel in the afternoon and Neil immediately fell asleep. Angered at his excessive drinking, lack of tact and embarrassed by his behavior at the Bar Mitzvah, I didn't wake him on time for a family wedding scheduled for that evening. His parents and aunt had flown in from Los Angeles to celebrate their family member's wedding in Long Island to which we were also invited. We were all staying in

Manhattan so we planned to drive there. When the phone rang in our room, I answered. It was his mother.

"We are waiting for you, where are you? We're supposed to be driving out together." The rain pelted the windows. I handed the phone to Neil.

"Here, your mother is calling,"

"Why didn't you wake me?" he said after a brief conversation with her.

"It's not my responsibility and not my family's wedding. You're the one who was drunk and overslept."

During the very slow drive I remained mute, seething with anger. I sat with his parents and aunt thinking surely they must know he was a drunk.

After some reflection, I decided to take Judson to Paris at the end of August as his Bar Mitzvah gift in lieu of having made a celebration for him in L.A. We stayed with Huguette and her husband Ben who provided levity to our trip. We spent a lot of time with them visiting the beautiful parks of Paris and the museums including the Musee d'Orsay, Pompidou and the Louvre. We sailed on the Bateau Mouche and spent time at Montparnasse. Judson fell in love with the Eiffel Tower. Regine invited us out to dinner one evening with her husband and their son and daughter. It turned out to be a good bonding experience and fun for both of us.

Neil and I took several trips to Europe. We often travelled during holidays while the kids were with Bernard. At those times Neil was more relaxed having me all to himself. I revisited the places I lived in Paris looking for shadows of my former existence. But I always returned from trips disappointed and empty.

I had returned to Paris many times to visit Uncle David when I was a young single woman. Uncle David died after Bernard and I divorced. When I came to stay with him in France as a child from war ravaged Poland, I had no family and no possessions. He too had very little. When they fled from the Nazis they left everything behind and sought refuge in the south of France. They hid in small villages like Pau, near Nice and Grenoble. Regine went to school at a Catholic convent and even learned the prayers like I had. When it became too dangerous for the convent to hide her, the mother superior had to ask her to leave. "Even though we changed villages many times, I did not feel afraid or insecure," Regine said, "I had my parents, aunts and uncles around me."

Within a few years after the war, Uncle David succeeded in getting back on his feet. After I left France, and after years of hard work, he became very successful. When I returned to visit him, more than ten years later, his affluent lifestyle and that of his relatives impressed me. The wife of Jenna's nephew, Huguette, an attractive, vivacious woman, particularly influenced me. A teenager during the war, the Nazis miraculously overlooked her and her family during the roundups. They knocked on their apartment door but their name was not on the list. Another family in the building where they lived who had the same last name were deported.

Huguette walked around the streets of Paris with the Jewish star sewn on her clothes, yet managed to evade deportation. She was called in by the French Police but saved because she had been born in France. In an attempt to make up for those years of deprivation and the loss of her girlhood, she loved dressing in the latest fashion, and wore expensive jewels and furs. Glamorous and full of joie de vivre, she dined at fashionable restaurants and drank champagne with her husband and friends until the early morning. I longed for the same lifestyle. Her husband's family, born in Biala Podlaska, and my Uncle David, had succeeded in building profitable businesses in men's and women's clothing and textiles.

When I traveled to France with Neil, we stayed with Huguette. She knew me as a child after the war when I lived in Paris, and in Queens, New York when I was a teenager and a woman. She and her husband David lived close to us in Queens for one year in order for David to maintain his American citizenship that he acquired by serving in the American army during the war. Soon after they spent a year in Queens the law changed, and residency in the United States was waived. Huguette returned to Paris, and raised a family of three. When her children were older, she often came back to New York and stayed with us for a month or two at a time. She loved the United States and the shopping. "I feel so free here," she said.

When Hilda passed away, she flew from Paris to attend the funeral. She continued to stay in contact with Martin, Marcia and me after Hilda's death.

Huguette's apartment in Paris reflected her creativity. She had a passion for needlepoint. A large wall tapestry custom designed for her, petit rugs, and upholstered chair seats were all her hand done work. Her colorful needlepoint pillows that adorned the sofas caught one's eye on entering the spacious living room. They depicted a variety of scenes including still life, animals, landscapes, and women dressed in forties fashion. When in France, I called her place home.

I loved the French language and I made sure to brush up on it before each trip. A devotee of French cuisine, from a ham and cheese baguette or croissant to luscious haute cuisine, Neil and I dined in the restaurants of the latest renowned chefs. We would walk for hours on end along the colorful winding streets admiring the spectacular architecture of Paris. When we travelled in other parts of France, we stayed at boutique hotels and converted chateaux scattered throughout the countryside, often part of the Relais & Chateaux collection.

In July 1987, Neil and I went on a trip to Italy while my sons were with their father in New York. Since we moved to California they spent the summers in New York with him, in addition to other holidays. At times the summer dragged on and being separated from the boys brought on feelings of detachment. They were enmeshed with their father and his family as well as Rudy who owned the house in West Hampton with Bernard. They had their grandparents, uncles, aunts, and cousins; an extended family that I could not provide.

I had previously seen a psychiatrist Dr. Norman Lachman for therapy as I constantly struggled with depression. When the boys were with Bernard and his family, Dr. Lachman helped me sort out my feelings regarding my role in their life.

I enjoyed the therapy sessions with him as he was helpful and had a sense of humor. When my sons were home, I knew they would benefit from talking to him about the separation from their father, and life with their new stepfather. James in particular closed off his feelings. During the sessions with Dr. Lachman he began to open up until Bernard warned him about speaking too much and revealing his emotions. "I don't want to talk to you about family matters," James said to Dr. Lachman. "It's private."

From then on James just sat like a stone in his office and would not speak. He appeared proud to be doing his father's bidding. Judson and Jonathan were more responsive to Dr. Lachman. The children were covered under Bernard's medical insurance but as he did not approve of the therapy, he refused to submit psychiatry bills to his insurance company and so the sessions ended.

When the children were with Bernard, I sought Dr. Lachman's advice. "Do you think I should call them? Do you think that my being away for a month in Australia without speaking to them would be upsetting to them? "Of course you should call them," he reassured me. "They'll be happy to hear from you. They miss you when they're away."

⤜⤚

Toward the end of the summer I received a phone call from James. He said he had decided to attend high school in New York and did not plan to return to Los Angeles.

"How can you do that?" I asked in alarm. "We never spoke about it? When did you make that decision?" He said he and his brothers had made a promise to Bernard that they would live with him during their high school years.

"We knew you wouldn't agree and we wanted to avoid a fight," he said. "I'll be the first to stay with Dad for high school since Jonathan is still in junior high school."

I couldn't just say O.K. I treaded water hoping for a lifeline.

"Will you return to Los Angeles before you start school in New York? I haven't seen you the whole summer. If you're just beginning high school you won't be able to come back for some time. Please come for a week or so. It's so important to me."

After much negotiation with Bernard in the background, he returned to the phone. "You have to promise you will let

me leave and return to New York for school if I come back."
So eager to see him, I promised I would and sent him a ticket.

When he arrived home I was so happy to see him. Tall and
lean, he had shot up to 6'4" so quickly his muscles and fat had
not caught up with his height. We enjoyed our time together
and had many good talks, but I could not dissuade him from
moving. He was set on living with his father in New York.

When the time came for him to leave, I couldn't keep
my promise. At the end of his stay after much talking and
entreating, I just couldn't let him go. I saw his pain and the
conflict, and the burden I placed on him. He lay on the floor
and thrashed his body around. "Are you sure you won't change
your mind," he pleaded, "because I'll go anyway?" He had torn
up his California high school schedule, ID card and closed his
bank account.

That Friday evening while the rest of us slept, he took
my car and drove to LAX. He called from the airport to say
his father had reserved a flight for him. He told me where he
parked the car and the location of the keys. I blamed Bernard
for putting him in that difficult position. I felt empty, betrayed
and lost.

The following day, he called and left a message on the
answering machine. "Hi mom, are you feeling better?" Conflicted and filled with grief, I thought that if I admonished him,
I would drive him away. He didn't deserve that. His message
sounded so concerned and genuine. I couldn't distress him further. I realized the enormity of the step he took. He deserved to

be in an environment with a male figure, his father, who showed pride and boundless love for him. When I finally could speak to him, I said he would always have me and he could return home anytime. I missed him terribly.

As a mother, the hurt was deep and long lasting. I masked my feelings with the distrust, anger and harshness I showed to the world. I wore an impenetrable, hard shell. I did not sense or comprehend that my sons saw this side of me or that because I didn't express my love they took it as the absence of love. I didn't know how to reveal my vulnerability. I sensed that there was danger in exposing my emotions. I continued my therapy with Dr. Lachman to arrive at the root of the visceral pain.

"You're reacting to your childhood experiences of such deep, deep loss," he counseled. "It always comes back to that."

Later I realized that I totally misread James' resolve and his need to get away.

⌐

In early 1988, against my wishes, Neil bought himself a Maserati sports car. One Sunday, after he left for the hospital, I received a call from a doctor at the Brotman Medical Center informing me that Neil had been in an accident. He had sped around a curve and smashed into a van. The faulty seatbelt in the Maserati came apart on impact. Neil broke both his legs and sustained other injuries. He had asked the police not to call and scare me. He also persuaded them to wait for an ambulance to take him to Brotman Hospital where he practiced rather than another facility. He spent a week in the hospital and when he came home he had to stay in a room on the ground floor in a hospital bed. When he began to recover he used a wheel chair to get around. In the six months he was out of work I became seriously depressed having to take care of him.

On a few other occasions Neil drank and drove even with the kids in the car. A few years before, his son Eric and my sons were returning from a ski trip. We stopped for dinner and when we left the restaurant we got into our SUV. I had just buckled Judson into the front middle seat. No sooner had we started moving than Neil crashed into a car making a left turn. Fortunately no one had major injuries but Neil's main concern was for his son's well being.

On August 10, I took James and Jonathan on a trip to Hawaii. When they went off on their own to participate in water sports, I read books while I watched them from the beach. We enjoyed being together. After the summer James left for New York. He had a particularly difficult time being torn from one parent to go to the other. We both had to deal with the sadness and pain of separation every time he left L.A. and returned to New York.

When it came time for Jonathan to leave for high school in the fall of 1988, I had prepared myself in advance for the difficult feelings. I was much stronger emotionally having explored with Dr. Lachman the deep meaning of separation from loved ones. I dealt with Jonathan's leaving in a much healthier way than I did when James left. As a superb athlete, I had confidence that Jonathan would find basketball an outlet for the rage and despair he buried inside after the divorce. When it was Judson's turn to go off to school like his brothers, things didn't work out as well for him. He hated the school and didn't enjoy the experience of living in New York. He decided to return to L.A. where he felt more comfortable.

In 1989 Neil and I toured the south of France and drove to Provence, the Cote D'Azur, Normandy and the Western parts of the country. While driving through the pastoral French countryside, one of us might say, "Let's stop here for lunch," on our way to a well-planned evening destination. On one of our trips, we stopped at Blois where Joan of Arc made her base of operations, and spent the night in a luxurious suite of rooms at the Domaine Haute de Loire where we dined on a delicious wild duck dinner. The next day we drove to Tours and arrived in the Perigueux region, at Moulin de L'Abbaye, located in a romantic market town situated on the banks of the River Dronne known as the Venice of the Perigord.

We had reservations for two nights. The first night's dinner consisted of a lamb cooked with beans and grapes, a delicious regional dish of the area. Neil became sick and unable to finish his food. He was feverish, with hot and cold chills. He took the antibiotics he always carried on trips and after the second day the fever subsided, but this was not an isolated occurrence. When this had happened before I asked, "Why are you getting these infections?" He said that he was clumsy and bumped into things in the operating room where he picked up a staff infection. His legs had many red puncture bruises. We're in France, I thought, how is that related to the operating room?

The next day, Neil stayed in bed. I walked around the romantic market village by myself looking at the abundant fresh vegetables and fruits displayed on tables set up by the local farmers. Villagers surrounded the tables dressed in an array of patterned clothes. Customers filled up their baskets with brilliant colored produce for the week accompanied by the clamor of good-natured banter. In the evening, I sat alone at the dinner table forlornly looking at the other couples engaged in conversation.

The next day we drove to Les Pres D'Eugenie, a spa where the creative chef, Michel Girard, prepared meals of unsurpassed taste, texture and flavor. On other trips to France we toured Avignon, Arles, Gordes, Roussillon, Grasse and the spectacular coastline cities of Toulon, St. Tropez, Cannes, Nice and Monte Carlo. We also visited other parts of France such as Bordeaux, Toulouse, Carcassone, Nimes and Normandy in the north. In one of the galleries in Cannes, I fell in love with a large painting of an emerald green sided sail boat gliding on an ocean of light greens and blues against a yellow green sky, with smaller fishing boats visible in the background. Painted with a palette knife, the colors and composition captivated me.

"I love this painting Neil, don't you? I'd love to buy it."

"That is really unattractive and not worth the price. I can't see it hanging in our house. It just doesn't fit. It's a fishing ship for God's sake!" We left the gallery and drove on for a few hours not speaking to each other.

"If you really love it so much, we can turn back," he said after a while, in a voice that meant, "I'd rather not."

"Never mind," I said, anticipating a long drive back. But I was perplexed. Did I really want the painting? Was it worth driving all the way back?

Morose and sullen at dinner, we sat in silence as he consumed an excessive of wine, more than his nightly routine. When we returned to our room, he grabbed his suitcase and started packing.

"This is a ridiculous vacation. I am going home. You can stay here by yourself."

"What are you doing?" I said, shocked at the abruptness of his behavior.

He picked up his suitcase and slammed the door. On other occasions he had acted paranoid and unpredictable, behaving in an angry and rude manner. I lay awake in bed totally confused. Should I remain by myself? Should I catch a plane home tomorrow? He returned about an hour later and apologized. Relieved to see him, we made up and continued our trip.

When I returned home, I obsessed about the painting. I asked Huguette's husband David to buy the painting on my behalf and have it shipped to my home. He did and I paid him for it later. The painting arrived and Neil did not say a word. That was his usual way of behaving. On other occasions when we travelled, I'd see something that I liked, but didn't buy it. Whatever the object, I obsessed over it until I found a way to have it.

Wine was always our companion. At dinner, I drank one glass to Neil's two bottles. He poured a second glass for me. After one sip I left the rest untouched.

"Aren't you going to finish your wine?"

"That's all I want to drink," I replied.

"I can't leave the table when there is unfinished wine. I have to finish it." He always drank the remains of my wine.

"Why do you have to drink such expensive wines? Two bottles cost over one hundred dollars at times?"

"Why not? I like it." I saw it as a waste. He equated it to eating expensive food.

Most evenings after a day of touring I went to bed early and he stayed awake in another part of the suite. Sometimes he'd stay on the balcony or in the bathroom smoking and drinking a few nightcaps. No matter where he hid, eventually the smell of the smoke permeated the room and upset me.

"Why don't you come to bed?" I asked repeatedly.

"I will soon, go to sleep."

Frequently he lay next to me, reading and scratching my back until I fell asleep. I would wake up in an empty bed. I smelled the cigarette smoke. I pulled the blanket over my head feeling despondent and disheartened.

Always on the lookout for a liquor store, he became annoyed when I resented searching for one at our various travel destinations.

"Are you an alcoholic? Why do you need to drink so often?" I asked him.

"Of course not. I just need to relax at the end of the day," he responded irritably.

Neil loved to drive and had a good sense of direction. In that area I depended on him but his drinking continued to escalate. One day he got in a row over a parking space after drinking too much. He behaved erratically and lost control.

⌒

Neil's heavy drinking would begin when we arrived at the airport.

"The airport is a trigger for me," he later told me. During the flight he drank one double after another until he passed out.

On one of our domestic flights, having drunk at the airport before boarding, he got very upset when seated in the center between two heavy men. One of the fat men overflowed into

Neil's space. "You are spilling onto my seat," Neil yelled. "I paid for one seat and I want it to myself."The flight attendant suggested Neil move to one of the open seats. He refused and continued to rant. The flight took off and he kept on arguing with the man. He would not stop no matter how many times the flight attendant warned him. The captain announced that we were returning to the airport. We landed and the police came on board to remove him. By that point he was fast asleep. They woke him up to take him off the plane. He appeared dazed. "Why are you taking me off? I was sleeping. How can I be unruly if I was sleeping?"They took him down the aisle in handcuffs. He passed my row and I acted as though I had no connection to him. We were on the way to his daughter's college graduation. The plane was delayed and it had been announced at the incoming airport that the delay was due to a passenger having to be removed. I exited the plane and saw Neil's daughter waiting at the gate. "Was it my father who was thrown off the plane?" she said despondently, "I had a feeling it was." He arrived hours later.

Our vacations overseas usually lasted about three weeks. We always dined at the best places and did our share of touring and visiting museums. I loved shopping. I bought all types of apparel, jewelry, shoes and bags for myself, as well as sets of china from different countries, glassware, art, furniture and a beautiful chandelier in Italy for our house. Unless I could acquire goods, I remained unfulfilled. For many years

I felt uncomfortable and anxious when asked what I wanted. I thought I didn't deserve to have things. Now, I could buy whatever suited my fancy and I did. Sometimes Neil was enthusiastic, other times he sat on a chair waiting patiently as though in another world, or slept.

At home, most evenings Neil was called out by the hospital or by a patient. There were times I noticed he set off his own beeper so that he could escape the house. He even did this when we were at an event. On vacation there was no beeper and no escape. In the evenings, while traveling, we sat at a table and waited for one course to be served after another, which at times in France would take as much as three hours and turn into a trial of patience. He developed an annoying habit of putting his legs up on a spare seat at our table. He would sit at an angle and watch the other people. He drank in between and I felt restless and bored. After a while our conversation ceased. Something would trigger an argument and I would become withdrawn, angry and silent. He would resort to more drinking and crazy outbursts.

⤶

Neil had a successful surgical practice in Los Angeles, but he wanted more. He was supporting his ex-wife, four children and with my help our household with three children. In 1994, an opportunity to make more money presented itself. A marketer approached him with the idea of doing male cosmetic surgery. Neil did the research and decided he would be comfortable doing the procedure. He set up an outpatient surgery center and the marketer promoted the technique by advertising and utilizing a sales staff located in various cities to bring a large number of patients to Neil's clinic. The practice took off.

Neil was under pressure to perform eight or more surgeries per day. I worked in his office to help with the paper work. After each surgery, I noticed that Neil ran into his private bathroom to smoke and take phone calls. He would then rush to the operating room to perform another surgery. His day would routinely go through these cycles. By the time he came home, he was exhausted and couldn't wait to drink. The stress of all the new surgeries exacerbated his drinking. He drank a large bottle of Vodka a day, sometimes more. He sat at the dining table glassy eyed, with the crazed look of an opium addict. Many times I spoke to him about his increasing habit. I hid the vodka bottles, but he was always a step ahead of me. He had bottles hidden in places I was unaware of, so I tried another tactic. I poured half of the vodka out and replaced it with water. He drank the whole evening while he sat and stared into space. His drinking made no sense.

"Neil, what are you doing to yourself? Your drinking is out of control."

"I'm handling it," he said. "I'm just going to do this surgery for a few years and then I'll retire."

It fueled my anger to see him drunk, so I requested he sleep in another bedroom. We ceased living together as husband and wife.

He became a celebrity with the novel surgery. He was asked to speak on radio talk shows and gave interviews for newspapers. His image appeared on the covers of national and foreign magazines. His ego became so inflated that he spoke of expanding internationally.

"This business can really take off," he said one day, as he stood shaving at the sink. "I can see hiring doctors in Europe and Asia. It will be a multi million dollar business."

"Be careful Neil. You may get your fifteen minutes of fame, then you will crash," I said. I was pessimistic about all the surgeries, the publicity and the disdain of other physicians.

"They're just jealous of the money I am making," he argued. "Regular medical fees are down. They read newspapers that exaggerate my income."

Neil continued to perform a large number of surgeries, but some patients were dissatisfied. Some suffered from infection, others had not had their expectations met. One afternoon during a surgery, Neil was suddenly overcome with chills and a high fever. His teeth chattered and he shook violently. After a dose of antibiotics the symptoms subsided. This began to happen more frequently and I became alarmed. In his private bathroom, I searched his purse and found a vile of medication. I tracked the number on the vile on a daily basis. Each day the vile had a different serial number. I knew that it was not a medication he prescribed for his patients. I asked a female doctor friend.

"What kind of medication is this?"

"Synthetic morphine," she replied.

It was a shocking discovery. All these years he had lied to me. The needles he used to inject himself caused the ulcerous marks on his legs, and the sudden violent infections. His erratic behavior and unpredictable outbursts were caused by his drug use. I thought about how he secluded himself in private bathrooms, in the office and on our travels, and realized he had been facilitating his drug habit. This revelation outraged me.

After a year of working together, the marketer wanted a higher percentage of the profit and more control of the medical practice. Neil disagreed with him and would not renew the contract. In retaliation, the marketer who had knowledge of the patients' information and knew which patients were dissatisfied with the result, counseled them to consult with malpractice attorneys and file complaints with the Medical Board.

A disgruntled nurse and a small percentage of the patients did complain to the Medical Board. Based on their written testimony, the Board closed down Neil's practice without notice. Everyone was sent home and a sign was placed on the office door. It was suddenly over. This left unpaid bank debts to creditors and money owing to patients who had paid for surgeries in advance and were entitled to full refunds. After compensating his patients, Neil's medical practice did not have the money to pay his other obligations.

I never imagined that his moral and ethical behavior would deteriorate to such an extent and that the endgame would be so agonizing. There was an avalanche of lawsuits by banks, creditors, patients through malpractice attorneys, bankruptcies, and a suit by the Medical Board to suspend his license. I lost over 20 pounds. I suffered major anxiety and depression and had to be medicated. I was afraid to open the door for fear of being served with a legal summons. I had to navigate through all the lawsuits. I hired my own attorney and was advised how best to protect myself.

It was two years of hell. Our relationship, previously on the brink was now in full descent. His drinking was out of hand. I had to get away from him. His erratic moods frightened me. I researched the substance abuser's personality. I was afraid of violence. I had no idea when I married him that he was an alcoholic and a drug addict. He was a functioning surgeon. How could he be an alcoholic? Weren't all alcoholics homeless and living on the street, not running a medical practice and holding high positions on hospital boards? Neil was at a dark stage in his life, particularly after the closing of his practice. Advised by a therapist to protect myself, I asked him to move out of the house. He did eventually and I changed the locks. I put all his things into the garage and watched with sadness and relief as he and his son carted them out to his son's truck.

"Why are you doing this?" he cried on the phone after he left. "You know how much I love you. I adore you. I'd do anything for you."

I cried too. I felt sorry for him. It was a wrenching experience. I knew that there was goodness and generosity in him, but I could no longer trust him after all the years of lying and duplicity. He continued to deny being an alcoholic and drug abuser.

"You need to go to a detox clinic," I said to him many times.

"I am not an addict, but I'll go to the Betty Ford Clinic," he said after he moved out. Astonished by his denial, I soon learned this behavior was the norm for a substance abuser.

His daughter opened up to me. "He was so devastated that you changed the locks and security code that he agreed to go to the clinic," she said. "I told him to take responsibility for his addictions." She became more responsive and our relationship improved. One of his sons confessed, "I've known that my father was a drug abuser since I was a child. My mother would take us away so that we would not see him shooting up."

The following day, at the attorney's office Neil denied that he agreed to attend the clinic and refused to go.

"I will only go if you agree that if I go and get detoxed you will remain committed to me," he said.

"I can't take anything you say seriously anymore," I replied.

I went home, exhausted from all the back and forth emotional conversations. I just wanted a good night's sleep. He kept insisting that I call him. I refused. What if he detoxed for a while and soon went back to his old habits? He'd been doing it throughout his adult life. He admitted to me during a rare introspective moment that he was also addicted to needles. "That's part of the addiction," he confessed.

⌒

I heard Neil speak highly of a doctor, Mike Klein. Dr. Klein had been an alcoholic and drug user, but had been sober for many years. He now counseled other addicts.

"Can you assure me that you will consult with him and place yourself in his care?" I asked. He finally agreed.

"You need to separate yourself completely from him," my attorney advised me. "Separate your property, close all joint credit cards and do not give him any money."

My therapist, an elderly, slim, white haired woman, renowned in her field, agreed that I had to separate myself from him no matter how emotionally difficult. The thought of being alone devastated me. I didn't know if I could survive.

"Unless he detoxes and stays clean for at least one year and gets therapy, you cannot trust him," she said in her Austrian accent, at one of my weekly sessions.

Neil and I went to see Dr. Klein. A tall slender man with brown curly hair, he welcomed us into his small office. I brought a two-pint vodka bottle to the meeting to show him that Neil drank three to four of these bottles per week. After one half hour of conversation Dr. Klein asked me to remove the bottle from his desk.

"After all the years of being sober, seeing the bottle in front of me is too much of a reminder of the addiction," he declared. I was stunned.

"It's futile for you to use logic with Neil. He's completely in denial and under the control of the alcohol and compulsion of the substance. The more he uses it, the more denial sets in. What he needs is intensive treatment and counseling," Dr. Klein said. "In the sixties, my wife and I got into it," he related. "She was able to give it up, but I couldn't. I was depressed and suicidal and continued to use substances to counter the depression and suicidal thoughts. I had low self-esteem and lacked self worth. The radio station in my head was always tuned to K-FUCK, but I was finally able to deal with it and haven't used anything for over fourteen years."

He described the blackouts, memory loss, and grey areas waking up and not being sure what plans he and his wife had made for the day. "Not everyone reaches a bottom from which they cry out for help. For some people death is the bottom. Nothing you do and say to him will make a difference. It is up to Neil. Don't speak to him anymore about treatment. He has to know that only his actions count and not words. Leave all legal matters until after he detoxes. He can't control his ego, nor can he make rational judgments. His moral and ethical behavior has deteriorated."

I found Dr. Klein knowledgeable and articulate. At least I knew the situation and had confidence in the steps I needed to take. "You need to examine what it is about your personality which is acting as an enabler and co-conspirator." I took that to heart and thought about the negative aspects of continuing the relationship with him. First, I didn't want my children to be subjected to his rage and immaturity with his corny and goofy attitude and laughter. I had put up with his behavior because of my own fears and insecurity, particularly since this was my second marriage. Although I knew there were problems from the beginning, I believed that I had burned my bridges and could not go back to New York. I was so afraid of rejection that I wouldn't speak about my feelings. Neil's non-communicative nature made it easy for me to avoid talking. I had not been exposed to discussions of feelings, but rather to sharp attacks and rejection from my adoptive father. I could not open up.

For the most part I rationalized that his drinking was under control. There were isolated incidents of his outrageous behavior. During one of our visits to New York I had made plans to dine with my friends and for us to go to the theatre after dinner with James and his girlfriend Kricken. I looked forward to this evening. I hadn't seen my friends, nor James and Kricken for a while. Neil behaved restlessly as he waited for my friends to arrive at the restaurant. They were about ten minutes late. On their arrival Neil yelled, "Can't you manage to be on time? We've been waiting here for ten minutes!" I sensed that his rage would not abate that evening. He disliked the table we were seated at and criticized the noisiness of the place. He got up a few times during the meal and left the restaurant. I carried on a polite conversation with my friends, but it was obvious to them how unnerved I felt.

At the end of dinner, Neil refused to go to the theatre.

"I have tickets for the four of us. You know I made plans for us to go to the theatre with James and Kricken," I said.

"I don't want you to go to the theatre. I want you to go back to the hotel with me," he declared.

I stood my ground and refused to go back with him. I sat at the theatre with James and Kricken, but could not enjoy the comedy although I laughed with much exaggerated gusto trying to release the tension I felt. At the end of the evening I returned to the hotel by taxi and attempted to enter our room. The door was double locked with the chain in a locked position. I knocked several times. Finally he let me in and I went to my room. I removed my shoes and was about to get undressed when he came in, obviously drunk, hardly able to walk straight. Glassy eyed and red faced, he pulled me and forced me out the door.

"What are you doing?" I said. "You're drunk. You don't know what you're doing. Let go of me."

"If you loved me you would have returned to the hotel with me. Your son is more important than I am to you. I have all your jewelry, your money and the airline tickets." He slammed the door and left me in the hallway, shoeless and bewildered. I knew that I had to ask for his forgiveness and declare my unconditional love to get back into the hotel room. I kept knocking at the door and told him many times how sorry I was and how much I loved him. He finally opened the door and hugged and kissed me. "Here are your things and airline ticket," he said after retrieving them from his room.

We slept in our separate rooms. I finally managed to go to sleep, but fear of being with him crept in. This was the first time I had experienced such anger and physical behavior toward me. I attempted to speak to him about it the next morning. "I don't remember anything that happened last night," he said.

One day he asked me to help him out in Small Claims Court. I agreed and then discovered that at the end of his case he had arranged to have a process server serve me. Another time he invited me to lunch with his mother and aunt. While at my home getting ready for lunch a Marshall rang the bell repeatedly. I didn't answer the door. He was there to serve me with process. At lunch I turned to Neil. "I don't understand why a Marshall was ringing my door bell. Who would want to serve me?" He just looked at me. Later I found out he had arranged it.

I stayed in the marriage because of convenience. He was away most of the time so I had my independence. I did and bought whatever I wanted. Negative thinking took over. I believed that either I didn't deserve better or this was as good as it got being married. There was no perfect marriage. I day-dreamed that eventually it would be over. I didn't know when or how it would happen, but I sensed in my gut that it had to end. I didn't see myself married in the future. My marriages were a continuation of the pattern of my past relationships, the longest one with my adopted parents. I didn't know how to deal with the ups and downs of a relationship or how to handle disagreements without assuming it was the ultimate rejection of me. I didn't know how to maintain the harmony and balance of a good relationship, and most importantly, what qualities to look for in a person.

I should have left Neil early on when I saw his hostility and emotional mistreatment of my children especially of James. I should have seen the warning signs when his strange, pathetic parents and aunt subjected Neil to "roasting" and enjoyed mak-ing him feel inadequate. I should have reacted to their obvious rejection of me. I should have been alerted when his ex-wife tormented me and turned her children against me. I ignored so many signs. My greatest regret is that I was so insecure, fright-ened and dependent that I allowed my children's well being to be compromised. At great emotional and financial cost to me, I ended the marriage in 1997 although that didn't stop his lawsuits against me. After ten years the lawsuits finally ceased, but only by court order.

Part II
1984 – 2013

A Time to Discover:
Pieces of My Past

Restless and unsettled, I have always searched for clues to understand my loss and find that missing love. Inspired by a longing to find a place I belonged I had a constant desire to travel. During my marriage to Neil we travelled all over the world. We visited China, Japan, Africa, Hong Kong, France (many times), Italy, Switzerland, Czechoslovakia, Hungary, the Baltic region, Australia, Poland, and Israel. Attached to these trips were many dramatic and disturbing events. I also made discoveries that would begin to change my life.

AUSTRALIA

1984

IN 1984, I travelled to Australia with Neil to see the Polish woman who had played such a pivotal role early in my life and had composed the letters full of details of my childhood. I wanted to meet Ida and her family after all those years. Elated that we were coming to visit for two weeks, she suggested we extend our time so that we could also see some of the country.

If you could come to Melbourne around 24 December, my husband and I can arrange holidays as the week before the 24th is our busiest. While in Melbourne we can plan day trips and spend as much time together as you like...

We took her advice and toured before going to Melbourne. We marveled at being "down under", thrilled to see the exotic wildlife, rain forests and the rainbow colors of the coral barrier reef.

In anticipation of reuniting with Ida, I wondered how I would feel, and how I would react when we met. We landed in Melbourne on December 27 and were greeted by Ida and her family. As I had no real memory of her, I did not recognize the woman at the airport walking toward me. I had only seen her photographs. She sent one taken in 1970 in response to my first letter. On the back she wrote, "To Gita and Bernard, Love Family Koper, October 1969." In the photograph Ida and her daughter Isabel sit on a green lounge chair on a grassy area surrounded by rose bushes and trees. Salek and Alex stand behind them. Ida and Isabel are wearing summer dresses. Salek is in a short-sleeved shirt and Alex wears a suit and tie.

The second photograph was taken in Lodz after the war to send to my Uncle David in Paris to assure him that I was well taken care of. It is a posed portrait of both of us when Ida was thirty and I was eight. She looks glamorous with bright blue eyes, wavy blond hair, and a radiant smile. Studio lights illuminate our faces placed close to each other. I have a serious expression.

In another photograph, I have a dreamy look as I lay my face affectionately on Ida's shoulder. A large white bow is fastened in my hair, a common style for little girls at that time that compliments my white sailor blouse with blue trim.

As we walked toward the people waving, I tried to pick out Ida's face from my memory of the photographs. An elderly blond woman approached and I recognized her blue eyes and facial structure. Short in stature, I bent down to hug and kiss her. We clung to each other. My eyes welled up with tears, yet I felt disconnected. What did I expect? How much of our past connection could be recalled and expressed in a fleeting embrace.

"I am so happy to see you," said Ida. With outstretched arms we looked at each other, our faces filled with emotion.

"I can't believe that we are finally meeting," I said. "This means so much to me."

"Let me introduce you to my family. We are all so excited." She introduced me to her husband Salek, a thin man with dark rimmed glasses, and then to her daughter, Isabel, and her son Alex, both fair with light eyes.

"This is such a historic moment," said Alex. "I should have notified a newspaper. They would have been interested in this story. I'm sorry I didn't think of it in time."

After the introductions, we gathered our luggage and made our way out of the airport. I invited Ida and her family to come with us to the hotel so that we could relax and get acquainted, but only Ida and Salek were able to join us. "We will drive with you to your hotel," said Ida.

When we arrived at the hotel tea, mini sandwiches and pastries were being served in the lobby.

"Please join us for tea," I said. "I am sure we can all use some refreshments."

We sat at a table and enjoyed the afternoon tea served in the British tradition with sterling silver tea service and fine china. Ida and Salek were interested in our lives, our careers, and our children.

"Your children are beautiful," she said. "I was so happy to receive their photos." We studied each other as we talked. At times I strained to understand her Australian accent. I felt withdrawn and sensed that she too felt uncomfortable. In spite of our past, at that moment we were strangers.

Incredulous that we were together, I wanted to learn as much as I could about my life during the war and after. We had lived through a time when we were hunted simply because we were born into the Jewish religion. Only Ida could describe the circumstances of where I was hidden and under what conditions. I hoped she could give me more information about my parents and brother and what they had endured. I hoped that there was more to tell than what she wrote in her letters. I wanted there to be so much more.

We spent five days in Melbourne. I learned that Ida and Salek had a small stall in an outdoor market where they sold jackets and sweaters. It was not a lucrative business. They had a hard life, but had managed to eke out a living and support their two children until they were grown. Her son became a pharmacist and her daughter and husband owned a small knitwear manufacturing business.

Ida invited her two sisters, their husbands, children, extended family and friends to dinners at her home. Some were war survivors from Biala Podlaska. They arrived at Ida's house with flowers and greeted me with warmth and jubilation. We sat at the long dinning room table where we spent hours eating and getting acquainted. The room wallpapered in a light grey geometric design had a mahogany credenza that contained knick-knacks, dishes and family photos behind glass doors. Ida and her daughter Isabel helped serve Ida's delicious Jewish cooking. I realized how much effort she put into the preparation from the variety of dishes she served.

Each time her friends and family saw me, they showed their amazement and happiness. I was living proof of Ida's courageous deed. Never at a loss to entertain, his glass frequently filled with wine, Neil took center stage at the table amusing everyone with his repertoire of jokes and tales. He also kept a bottle of wine or liquor in the hotel room. "Let's take everyone out for New Year's Eve," he offered. We brought in 1985 together wearing colorful shiny hats and making toasts with champagne to our health and our next trip back to Melbourne.

When we found the time to be alone together, Neil and I sat with Ida in her living room and listened to her vivid and spirited descriptions of life during the war. She retold the story written in her letters to me about the events that led up to her taking me out of the orphanage. As I listened, the courage and determination still rang in her voice. I no longer saw the older Ida sitting in her armchair, but the young woman whose resolve and perseverance accomplished this dangerous mission. If Ida had not undertaken this courageous mission I might never have discovered my Jewish identity.

After Neil and I returned home to California, I received a letter from Ida on February 25, 1985.

Dear Gita,

Meeting you face to face after all these years was an unfor-gettable experience for me, one that I will always treasure. I had always hoped that we would meet one day and recall the past in more detail. Maybe someday you could return for another visit to Australia.

Love Ida

Back row left to right: Alex and Salek / *Front row left to right:* Isabel and Ida Melbourne, Australia 1969. (This photo was enclosed in Ida's 1969 letter--the first one I received from her.)

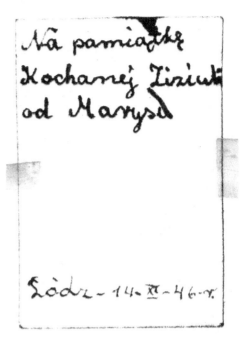

Gitta, Lodz, Poland, November 14, 1946

Back of left photo: In memory of past friendship to beloved Zizuli (my name for Ida) Marysia

Gitta, Lodz, Poland

POLAND

May, 1990

FIVE YEARS later, in 1990 Neil and I decided to travel to Poland. This trip would prove to be the beginning of many discoveries.

I knew very little about the location of my birthplace Biala Podlaska, only that it was close to Warsaw and the Russian border. When younger, I found it difficult to accept being born in such a strange sounding place and shameful to admit being from there. I wanted to be an American.

I had a strong desire to see the orphanage where I had spent those early years. "Why don't we invite Ida and Salek to travel with us to Poland?" I said to Neil. "I think Ida would appreciate seeing her old town and would be so helpful in reconstructing the events exactly where they happened." Neil agreed and I wrote to Ida extending the invitation.

Ida's daughter Isabel answered my letter. She said that Salek, her father was ailing. He suffered from persistent heart problems and a trip of that distance would be too much of a strain on him. She was also concerned that the trip might take an emotional toll on her mother. After reading her letter we decided that we did not want to endanger their health. The trip was not as important to them as for me, so Neil and I decided to tour Poland on our own.

Because of the importance of the trip I didn't want to leave anything to chance. I needed all the arrangements to run smoothly, so I booked all our flights and hotel reservations through a travel agent I had used many times. We were to fly to Paris, stay overnight and fly to Poland the following day. We allowed plenty of time to get to the airport in the morning after a lovely dinner and evening in Paris. We arrived at Orly International Airport ready to board the flight. I had not been to Poland since I left at the age of seven. Filled with excitement, yet nervous as to what I would find and how I would react, I handed the tickets to the agent at the counter.

"I'm sorry, but you are at the wrong airport," she said. Your flight leaves from Charles de Gaulle Airport at the other end of the city."

"You must be mistaken," I said. "How can this be?" Anxious and breathless, I showed her the itinerary. "The printout says that we leave from this airport." She called LOT airlines and confirmed that our flight did indeed leave from Charles de Gaulle Airport but there was a chance we might make it, so we hurried out and grabbed the nearest taxi. The driver took what seemed an interminable route. We remained tense as we sat in the back seat winding our way through the early morning

Paris traffic in the rain. We rushed into the airport hoping to make the flight, only to be told we had just missed it. The next flight to Warsaw was not until the following morning. The Air France agent apologized profusely and arranged to put us up at a utilitarian IBIS hotel near the airport. Our room had a double bed almost wall to wall, and a sink with a pull out faucet that extended into the open shower, but we made do. I called my travel agent and she responded to my hysterical voice by saying that she merely followed the Air France printed schedule. I also contacted my client in Los Angeles to inform her of the mix-up. Her sister Anna had already departed for the airport to pick us up in Warsaw, but she assured us that Anna would be there the following day. When we finally arrived a day late, Anna, a cheerful, young blonde woman met us. She would serve as our translator. She took us to her in laws for our first dinner in Poland.

During my first night in Warsaw I burst into tears overwhelmed by being in the country where such tragic events had caused my life to splinter as a child. I had come to visit Biala and to see the orphanage, but unprepared to probe deep wounds. Our guide Anna was not up to the task of exploring for information, but in reality, neither was I.

On a warm, sunny day with clear blue skies, we drove from Warsaw to Biala Podlaska in the chauffeur's old model car that could barely exceed thirty miles per hour. Biala is a picturesque city of two story structures with a park in the center of the town that forms the town square. I have a photo of my father with my brother on a tricycle taken in that park. A variety of small shops line the narrow cobblestone streets. A burly woman wearing a headscarf and pumping water from a well jolted me back in time.

We walked to the building where my parents had lived at 8 Grabanowska Street. Anna spoke to one of the tenants in Polish, "Can we go inside?" He agreed and we entered the shabby building with peeling paint and climbed up a few flights of stairs. "Were there changes made to the building since the war?" she asked.

"Yes, the building was divided into many small apartments under Communism." The man opened the door to his apartment and left us to look around. His apartment was small and narrow. There were primitive appliances in the tiny kitchen situated against a wall in the living space. Only the exterior resembled where we once lived. The interior was in disrepair. I looked around hoping to see the apartment as it was when my family was alive and we were living there. I wanted to see the living area, the bedrooms, and the kitchen where all the Sabbath and family meals were prepared. I expected to see lace curtains, decorative objects, furniture and silver candlesticks in my previous home. I had hoped to see my past. What I saw alienated and depressed me. Overcome by a feeling of aversion and claustrophobia, I had an urge to run away and panicked. "I can't stay. There's nothing for me here." I turned, ran down the stairs and left through the unkempt yard in the back, where weeds grew and junk had been thrown to the side.

Biala looked poor and lacked character. Nothing remained to indicate that Jews had lived there. The cemetery near the town had been dug up and only one monument of a 1953 burial remained. Even after all these years, being in Poland frightened me.

We visited the site of the orphanage in Sitnik. The building no longer exists. A school and a church now stand in its place. The surrounding fields are reminiscent of vague memories. Neighboring farmers told us that the orphanage was taken down and that it may be now located in another town. Curiosity brought people out to see us. They appeared to be poor with few articles of clothing. The priest from the nearby church dressed in his black attire, white collar and black hat walked over to greet us. Although forthcoming and open, he unfortunately had no further information. We gave him some money. Most appreciative, he told us he would use the money to have the church painted and also see what he could research for us. We followed the trail given to us to a nearby town, Janow Podlaska still looking to find some connection to the original orphanage.

I had travelled all the way from the United States hoping to find some answers, but was sadly disappointed that I could not see the physical structure of the orphanage. I had expected that the experience of looking at the building and walking through the interior might bring back some memories and I would recall events of my childhood. Discouraged and disheartened, I left realizing that there were some pieces of my past that I would never be able to retrieve.

We continued on to Warsaw where we went to the Jewish cemetery and the Warsaw Ghetto Memorial. We also visited the beautiful Jewish synagogue with its well maintained white interior and balcony that overlooks the main prayer chamber. The seventy-eight year old caretaker told us there were only 5,000 Jews left in Poland. He also said the thirty synagogues in Warsaw were all destroyed but because this one had been used as a stable for horses, it had survived. As there were no festivities, weddings or Bar Mitzvahs, he believed the synagogue would eventually become a museum.

On May 16, we went to Krakow and visited the run down Jewish section and the buildings that served as synagogues and Talmudic school. Piles of dusty old prayer books were stacked against the wall.

A few days later we toured Auschwitz. I never thought that I would ever visit this place of horror. It looked antiseptic except for the piles of human hair, eyeglass frames, suitcases, and prosthetics. On a sunny day in such a picturesque part of Poland it was difficult to imagine the atrocities that had occurred there. It is beyond comprehension. I elected not to visit Birkenau, the killing site of Auschwitz.

When I returned home I sent photos of our trip to Ida. She wrote back on July 30, 1990.

Dear Gita,

The photos of your parents' house on 8 Grabanowska shot from different angles made an impact on me. There is very little difference between how the scene looks now compared to my memories of it in 1942. It took me back in time and evoked much emotion. I can remember all of the activity in the ghetto at that time and the fear and apprehension we experienced during that traumatic period of our lives. I lived only a few blocks away from where you lived. I can still see the little girl running around the streets and playing with other children, not comprehending what was going on around her. I often replay those times inadvertently in my sleep, but the photos make those events at that time in my life even more vivid than I can imagine... It must be strange for you to realize that you spoke the language, which is foreign to you now. You will be interested in the three photos that I am enclosing of you as a little girl. Two of them are originals with your writing on the back of one of them and the third is a photo I enlarged and copied that shows your writing on the back...you write Lizuli, which was the nickname that only you called me. From the name Ida, you changed it to Idula, then Lizula. The writing translates:

For remembrance, Love to Lizuli from Marysia.
Love Ida

I was so grateful to receive the photographs with my writing in Polish. I often wondered whether I did speak the language and if so, how fluently, as I have no memory of it.

NEW YORK

1991 / Hidden Child Conference

Only 7 percent of all Jewish children in Nazi-dominated European countries survived. If we add the escapees aided by youth aliyah (moving to Israel), as well as the children sent to safety just before war broke out, the total numbers of Jewish child survivors still does not exceed 10 percent. Nine out of 10 of us were murdered.

– ROBERT KRELL

IN THE February 25, 1991 edition of *New York Magazine*, I read an article on an upcoming conference that profiled poignant stories of five women who were Hidden Children of the Holocaust. The conference to be held on May 26 and 27 at the Marriott Marquis Hotel in New York would be the first

International gathering of children hidden during World War II. It would bring together renowned psychologists and survivors to "enable us to recall the past, to understand how our experiences shaped our present and future lives and to help one another recall and share events some of us were too young to remember." Conceived by Myriam Abramowicz, this forum came about as a response to her film *Comme Si C'etait Hier* (*As if it Were Yesterday*) documenting the experience of Belgian children in hiding and non-Jewish people who risked their lives to save them. I decided I would attend.

This unique generation of Hidden Children came together at the conference to participate in workshops, discussions, films, press conferences and other events to share a legacy.

Speakers included:
- Abraham H. Foxman, National Director of the Anti-Defamation League of B'nai B'rith
- Yaffa Eliach, Professor of Judaic Studies, Brooklyn College
- Robert Krell, Professor of Psychiatry, University of British Columbia
- Mordecai Paldiel, Director, Department for the Righteous Among Nations, Yad Vashem
- Serge Klarsfeld, President, des Fils et Filles Deportes Juifs, France
- Ellie Wiesel, Professor and Political Activist, Nobel Prize winner and author of 57 books including *Night*

Topics ranged from:
- "On the Threshhold Between Childhood Memories and Historical Documentation"
- "The Psychological Impact of Being Hidden as a Child"
- "Why We Are Here"
- "To Hide No More"
- "What Motivated the Rescuers?"

Workshops topics included:
- I Never Said Goodbye
- Fear of Relationships
- Abandonment
- I Never Told My Story
- Where Was God?
- The Guilt of Surviving
- Who am I, Christian or Jew?
- What Have We Learned?
- Where Do We Go From Here?

I chose to explore the topics of Abandonment, Identity Crisis, Trust and Relationships. We sat in a circle around the facilitator. Participants gave a short introduction to the group of 10 to 12 people. They each shared where they had spent their years as a Hidden Child and what happened to their family after the war. I could hardly get through the first three sentences. I choked up. When it came to saying that my whole family was killed, I cried uncontrollably.

Even though I could barely get through the introduction and made very little progress in expressing myself, I learned so much. The similarity of emotions and experiences of other Hidden Children gave me a sense of belonging and safety. For the first time I shared the same feelings with the 1600 people who attended from the United States and many other parts of the world including Australia, Belgium, Canada, France, Germany, Greece, the Netherlands, Israel, and Korea.

In his speech *Hiding During and After the War: The Fate of Children Who Survived the Holocaust,* Canadian psychiatrist, Robert Krell talked about the consequences for children of being told not to speak. For them, it was a life and death situation. I had never made this simple connection. I spoke Yiddish and as a child I knew I had to keep silent so as not to give myself away and be killed by the Germans. Krell's words made a tremendous impact on me. He articulated and illuminated what I had never put together:

> "Of all voices from the Holocaust we have been the most silent and the least noticed. For good reason, many of us were raised in silence, enveloped in silence. A child not noticed might survive. We could not draw attention to ourselves - not in that world. In this world too, silence remains a companion of

sorts. After the war we were discouraged to speak of it. In the interest of our future, mostly well-meaning persons unintentionally silenced us.

Silence became a child's most valuable ally. Those children who were able to control normal complaints, suppressed cries or laughter, ignore the playfulness of childhood, they stood a better chance to survive. Within the framework of silence, the child's chameleon like ability to adapt to every changing situation was required. It helped to be quick to learn languages and adopt the trappings of religion in order to blend with new surroundings. Child survivors became adept at reading signals without verbal communication. And it is common to hear them say that an intuitive response at a crucial moment saved their life. It is no wonder that one of the psychological aftereffects of hiding is further hiding. Silence served so well that it remained the mainstay of existence for many of us...

Memory has to be experienced in a sequence that makes sense or it becomes disorienting and destructive. The coexistence of silence with an ambivalent identity results in the diminishing of personal power. To be uncertain of one's self leads to powerlessness, it prevents us from speaking up for our rights. Sometimes it prevents us from speaking at all."

I reveled in this new knowledge and understanding of the panic and terror that gripped me all these years. It didn't suddenly change like a magical Hollywood ending, but my nightmares began to dissipate and my fears slowly subsided. I found comfort knowing where they came from.

Elie Wiesel, author of his memoir *Night*, spoke on the topic of "Hidden Memories." He began with a condemnation of Hitler's war crimes and then cited the story of the first hidden child in Jewish history to establish a precedent. *Moses too was abandoned by his parents simply because Moses was in danger as all other children, male children then were, and his parents abandoned him simply because they wanted to save him... and so one day Batya (a Gentile), daughter of Pharaoh went for a walk at the Nile River and heard a child weep and...she understood according to the Bible that he was a Jewish child.*

Wiesel focused on how we had been robbed of our childhood and how the enemy had succeeded in replacing it with one that was not meant for us. It was as if his questions were meant for me.

"What have you felt at the moment your father or mother left you? What took place in your still fragile but already wounded subconscious? A rejection, a betrayal, perhaps? How long did it take you before you grasped the full meaning of what your parents had to do on your behalf? How long did it take you to overcome the anger...you might have felt, could have felt, towards your parents as you held them responsible for your separation? When exactly did you understand this fathomless strength they needed to give you up to strangers in order to spare you their own destiny? On the brink of death they tore themselves away from you so as to tear you away from death. Since perish they must, they chose to go toward the flames without you, faraway from you… How did you manage to grow up so fast? How did you manage to so quickly learn terrible and grave ways of keeping alive? How have you managed to hide and or forget so many things in order to hide the Jewish child in you? And how have you managed to vanquish fear and loneliness resulting from your parents being absent from your life? How have you managed to overcome suspicion and not see an enemy in every passer by? How did you manage not to respond when your Jewish name was called? How did you manage all of a sudden to behave as if you were someone else? How did you manage to fall asleep without being caressed by your mother, be reassured by your father?"

Wiesel encouraged us to not only face our memories but to share them "… from now on you should speak aloud for even when you whisper your whisper will be a loud whisper and things happening in the world must be affected by your whispers or by your shouts or by your testimony." His words had a profound and lasting effect on me.

I began to confront the questions he discussed about the events of my childhood: how I dealt with the abrupt separation from my parents and how I replaced my childhood with a false one. I had been terrified to speak. "One careless word, one wrong gesture and it was the end. One frightened look, one sigh poorly suppressed, one prayer poorly remembered, one cloud of sadness on your face and you were discovered and thrown away again and separated again, this time for good." But discovered as what? Did I know what I was not supposed to be? Why I was hidden? I knew I was different, but how? I knew I was supposed to be silent, not to draw attention to myself, become adept at making changes, reading signals, or the slightest change of mood. Be quick to learn other languages. Did I think that my parents would come back for me? When did I grasp the meaning of what it took for my parents to tear themselves away knowing they would never see me again, so that I could escape death?

One and a half million children were murdered. Hitler's Germany "...sought to deprive us as a people of our right to a future and of our childhood memories. In forcing hunger and despair upon Jewish children Hitler's Germany sought to eliminate laughter and joy from our entire lives." I came from a loving environment, with parents, grandparents, aunts, uncles, and cousins. How did I adapt to all these childhood changes that eliminated laughter, joy, security, and love from my young life and substituted it with despair, hunger, powerlessness, rejection, and betrayal?

Not until years later did I understand the fathomless strength it took for my parents to either hand me over to strangers or let me wander off in hope that I would be found. It took decades to comprehend the selfless courage of the nuns who hid me for those years at the risk of their own lives. Anti-Semitism was open and violent and the Nazis more cruel and brutal against the Poles than to the people of any other country in Europe. It took unimaginable fortitude to save Jews.

The Conference shed light on the lasting psychological ramifications of what had happened to me as a child. Until then I had no real comprehension of the effects the separation from my parents had on me. I referred to it as "being abandoned." Many times people asked me, "How did you get to the orphanage?" The words that immediately came to mind were always the same. "They gave me away." After the conference and many therapy groups, I stopped using the inappropriate and dismissive term "abandoned." I could finally discern the chasm between being given away as an unwanted child and being the recipient of a miraculous and courageous act of love.

It took a long time for my brain to excise the negative feelings of an unwanted child. I struggled to unearth a memory. Any memory no matter how painful would be better than nothing at all. Who left me? Where? What was I told? How did I react? Under what circumstances did I see my parents for the last time? Were they together? When did I last see my brother?

After the conference, I began for the first time to read history books about Treblinka and became riveted to foreign films, especially Polish and German ones portraying those times. I could imagine what it was like, the cobbled streets, the homes they lived in, their possessions, their jewelry and silver, all ripped away from them. I saw what the countryside, the trains, and the concentration camps looked like. I could envision what my parents went through. Before when people asked me questions, I always said,

"I don't remember."

"You were too young to remember," they would reply.

Abraham H. Foxman summed up the experience we shared at the conference. Foxman had been raised by a Christian nanny in Vilnius, Lithuania, from the age of two when his parents fled to escape the Nazis and survived. He too was a hidden child.

"There were thousands of us hiding during World War II. To this day some of us still do not know our true identity. We were hidden for years in basements, attics, sewers, and in convents. Many of us changed our names and our religion in order to survive.

For 48 years we tried to forget our war experiences as we build our lives in new places far from the destruction of our fragile lost childhood. It is now time to bear witness to our past.

We hope this Gathering in New York will help us to remember and share with one another. We want to understand the effect of this unprecedented happening upon our past, present and future lives. We want to honor our rescuers and celebrate our survival. We need to tell our stories. We need to clarify why we see the outside world the way we do. We need to tell our children and their children about our long-hidden secrets. Facing this together will start the process of healing our long buried wounds."

After this conference, I started attending others and eventually I learned to tell my story without choking up and crying.

I wrote about the conference to Ida. In my letter I asked if she had a recollection of the priest's character or could remember details about the nuns. I asked her about the teacher who was a nun. She replied to me on July 7, 1991.

Dear Gita,

I was pleased to read you attended the conference in New York for Hidden Jewish children. I read about it in the paper (the Australian Jewish News) and I was thinking about you. I thought that it would be a rewarding experience for you, but I understand that it must have also been quite difficult. I am also pleased that you were thinking of writing a memoir about your life. I would be very pleased to read it if you decide to do it. Unfortunately I cannot tell you in great detail about the people. As to your questions, the priest was a tall man in his 40's who had a stern nature, and a strong rule. I do not remember much about the teacher only that she wore a scarf over her head and appeared to be from the lower class. At the time that all of these events were occurring in our lives, I naturally did not realize that one day a recollection of all these would be of great interest to you and to me. I was concentrating naturally on what was happening and what needed to be done. Thank you so much for your kind invitation to visit with you and United States. Under normal circumstances 20 years earlier I would have loved to come. However, at this point in time considering my health and age I don't think it would be a great idea.

Love Ida

ISRAEL

1992

IN MAY 1992 Neil and I planned a trip to Israel so that I could attend a conference on *Child Survivors of the Holocaust*. I spent a few days in Paris en route and was to join him in Tel Aviv so he could meet my cousins Yudit and Eva. I stayed in Tel Aviv for a few days enjoying the time with my cousins and looking forward to introducing Neil to them. Instead, he called to say that he had gone to Jerusalem and that he had no recollection of our plans to meet in Tel Aviv. When I arrived in Jerusalem I found him asleep in our hotel room.

As part of the Conference itinerary, we spent an entire day at the Yad Vashem Museum. As we entered the Children's Memorial, we were plunged into darkness as thousands of candles flickered in the many mirrors and were reflected back like countless stars. At the same time, the names and ages of the murdered children were called out in different languages one at a time. I thought of my brother, a brother I do not remember, and how at the age of eight he was brutally killed. I looked at the photos of the children. With the murder of one and one half million children and over 90% of the Polish Jewish population, what were the chances that I survived?

I made progress in confronting my connection to the Holocaust by filling out Pages of Testimony listing my parents' and brother's names, place and date of birth for each family member, as well as how and where they were killed. Some time later, I completed Pages of Testimony for my grandparents and my aunt and uncle with photos attached.

We loved spending time in the historic city and seeing all of the well known sights. The day before the Conference we enjoyed lunch at the renowned King David Hotel.

The following evening we attended an outdoor ceremony commemorating the killing of six million Jewish lives. A choir of young children's beautiful voices accompanied the lighting of six flames to symbolize the horrific event.

Every year since the 1960s, on April 27 the day called Yom HaShoah, the sound of a siren stops traffic and pedestrians throughout Israel for two minutes of silent devotion at sundown, and once again at 11:00 am. To witness this awe inspiring event gave me chills. All radio and television programs on this day connect with the Jewish destiny in World War II, including personal interviews with survivors. Even the musical programs are adapted to the atmosphere of Yom HaShoah. There is no public entertainment; theaters, cinemas, pubs, and other public venues are closed. To experience Yom HaShoah in Israel was very special to me and gave even greater meaning to being a Jew.

We visited the Valley of Destroyed Communities of Europe, unfinished at the time. Chiseled in stone are the names of all of the locations where Jewish lives were destroyed. Nothing is built above ground. The site consists of 2.5 acres dug out of natural bedrock that houses a labyrinth of stone and rock. The names of over 5,000 destroyed Jewish communities are etched in Hebrew and English on the 107 walls. "It is as though what had been built on the surface of the earth over the course of millennium—a thousand years of Jewish communal life—was suddenly swallowed up."

We also toured an Absorption Center for Ethiopian Jews with David, our informative guide. "Solomon's Rescue" involved the liberation of 14,000 Ethiopian Jews in 72 hours. 747 aircraft used for the mission had the seats removed and carried 1000 passengers. These immigrants had no reading skills and it took them a long time to learn the language. They had large families and with the high rate of infant mortality, they had to confront the issue of family planning. Life expectancy was only 45 years of age. Quiet and polite, the dark skinned children were beautiful with large brown sparkling eyes and delicate features. They enjoyed eating a new diet of yogurt and vegetables.

On the other end of the spectrum, 400,000 Russian Jews were also assimilated. Educated in the arts, music, medicine and engineering, they studied Hebrew in the Ulpan method of total immersion for six months. The government paid their rent and gave them $8,000 for one year. The average Israeli earned $12,000 a year.

As our trip came to an end, I was grateful for the recognition and honor that the Israeli government representatives had bestowed on us. They treated us royally, but also delicately as they acknowledged our harrowing experiences. Honored to be a part of this Jewish community and Jewish country, I was happy to be there.

Child Holocaust Survivors Conference 1992, Tel Aviv, Israel (Gitta, top row, second from right)

AUSTRALIA

1992, 1995

I RETURNED to Australia to visit Ida in 1992 arriving in Melbourne on March 3. Salek had passed away in 1990. We were delighted to see each other again and enjoyed being with her family and friends. This time I was more comfortable talking about the past. Whenever Ida wrote about me or spoke about my experiences, I was captivated by the story, her description of me, what I said, and how I reacted. But I didn't feel like the character. That was some other little girl. I wasn't in her skin. I didn't own her story.

I brought a tape recorder to document Ida's memories. One of the recording sessions took place in a restaurant where she appeared relaxed not having to worry about food preparation and cleaning. She expanded on her recollections in the letters. After the war she returned to Biala Podlaska.

I recorded as Ida talked. Some of the information on Ida's tape is repeated in her letters, but contains facts and descriptions that were not in the letters. Rather than exclude the repetitive facts, I decided to transcribe the tape in its entirety.

Polka, a Polish lady told me, "You know I saw Rozencwajg's nice little girl in the excursion from the village." The children from the orphanage at times came to the city, on a church holiday for recreation and she recognized you among all the children.

"There are so many children, how could you be sure?"

"I saw her, I saw her. I know Rozencwajg's little girl," Polka claimed.

I went back to Lodz, a bigger city, where I was living. It was impossible to live in Biala Podlaska. The Polish bandits killed a lot of Jews; those who returned to their home town from the concentration camp. They went through such hell and still they were killed. Before the war there were 8,000 Jews in Biala. After the war, 30 returned from camps and hiding places and of the thirty, five were killed. The remaining Jews left Biala for larger cities. I came back to Biala a few times by train because I had a house to sell and to find gold money buried by my father before the war. Biala was the same, but it looked so horrible without the Jews. Everything cried out for the absence of Jews. You know it was a Jewish sector. There had been Jews everywhere and plenty of synagogues. It was all gone after the war. The houses remained, but at night everything was very black. No lights were on except in the Jewish homes where the Poles lived and have remained.

When Polka recognized you on the excursion to Biala from the orphanage, being a busy body, she started to find out things and she told me that you were named Czekanska. In the Catholic Church when you are christened you automatically take on the name of Maria after Santa Maria, so you were named Maria Czekanska.

I often questioned how you became Maria Czekanska. I assumed that on the transport of Jews from Biala to Miedzyrzec, wagons loaded with older people and children as the younger people walked, that in desperation your mother put you off the wagon and told you to run and hide knowing that they were going to the gas chambers whether the next day or in a week. She knew, they all knew. Even though they couldn't save themselves, she wanted to save her child. One thing is certain. You eventually came to this teacher. Somebody found you. There is a little village just 5 km from Biala. There is a school that can be seen from the road. The school is the first building and then there's a little village where the teacher of the school lived. There was only one teacher who taught everything and his name was Czekanski. You must have come to him or he found you. You asked me once if I knew exactly. No one knows exactly, but I think that a farmer found you and brought you to this teacher because in those times a teacher was considered a very intelligent man. I would like to have known more about this teacher Czekanski. I wanted to go to him, but he lived in Poznan, a large distant city. At that time I thought it was not so important, so I didn't make inquiries. For you now, it is important, really important. I too would like to know how you came to this Czekanski.

Polka also told me a farmer found you, kept you for a few days, afraid for himself and his family, and that he brought you to this teacher Czekanski. The teacher didn't know what to do with you, so he brought you to this orphanage and they christened you. When you came to me from the orphanage you told me that you remember being in a place with many children before the orphanage. I surmised that it was a school because the teacher could not have had such a large family. Czekanski placed you in an orphanage in another village called Sitnik approximately 25 kilometers outside of Biala. He got in touch with the priest there. The orphanage belonged to a church. He probably told the priest the truth, that he had a beautiful girl and she must be Jewish because what four year old child would wander around the woods. It was understood that you were Jewish because this transport was leaving for days with wagons.

I remember your mother as a beautiful woman. I remember your mother before she was married. She was elegantly dressed and lived in the Polish part of Biala. I was very young but I remember her, as I was her neighbor. After the war started all the Jews had to live in the ghetto, which was in the Jewish part of Biala. I again found myself a neighbor of your parents. We both lived on Grabanowska Street. I remember you as a young child running around with other children on the street not knowing that your world was crumbling.

The first time I went to Biala after the Committee in Lodz agreed to send me to have you released, I went to Polish police, the militia who I was told would do anything for money. I went to the chief of Police and showed him a letter from your family in Paris and the Jewish committee and asked him to help me and that he would be compensated if he agreed.

At the orphanage when the policeman asked the priest about you the priest replied, "You are a policeman and your job is police work. Do not interfere with the work of the church. We do not have any Jewish children here so go home and don't make any trouble."

During that first trip to Biala the committee gave 5,000 zloty to present to the church as a gift, which is a very substantial amount. I made a second trip to Biala and this time I was advised to follow a different lead. I took the letter from your uncle in Paris and went to Lublin, which is the head office in charge of the education department and orphanages. An attorney in Lublin advised me to get a letter from the Education department, which stated that if Maria Czekanska is identified by an independent witness as Gita Rosenzweig then the church had to release you.

I found a man who knew your father and worked with him in 1939. This was 1945 and of course he remembered your father but not you, as he hadn't seen you in years. I went to him and said, "Minska, you knew Usher Rosenzweig, well his little girl is in an orphanage in Sitniki and I need your help. I need a witness to identify her. You need to come to the orphanage and identify her so she can be released." I took him with me, as well as Polka, the letter from Paris translated into Polish, the letter from the Jewish committee, and the letter from the Department of Education from Lublin and went to Sitniki. We didn't go to the orphanage. We went directly to the church. The priest agreed to follow the instructions of the Department of Education. He made all the children line up for identification. I was very nervous as I stood with my two witnesses and a bag of lollies. As agitated and fearful as I was of not recognizing you, seeing all these Polish kids with blond hair and blue eyes and at that age having similar features and looking alike, I kept watching and watching and as each child came up I gave her a lolly and suddenly I saw you and after not seeing you since you were 3 ½ years old, I recognized you. You were painfully skinny and undernourished with legs like sticks and ribs sticking out. I nudged the witness and he said very convincingly, "My God, my God, that's her. She looks like her mother and father. She looks like both parents." Of course he didn't know you and he never divulged that to anyone. When you came up for the lolly I said to you that you can take another lolly and another one. You asked why you could have more than the others. I left the lollies with the teacher and told the priest that the girl who took 2 or 3 lollies was Gita Rosenzweig. I positively had identified you and so had an independent witness.

The priest knew that I had made the correct identification. He refused to speak about you. He was upset. He is Catholic and since you were baptized you too were a Catholic. To him I was taking out a Catholic child. I returned to the priest's office. Everything was legal. I had brought a witness, the letters from the family, and the instructions from Lublin. There was nothing more the priest could require except that he did impose one more condition. The priest demanded 100,000 zloty, which was a huge amount. I was shocked. I said that the church was given a generous gift of 5000 zloty and the priest said, "No lady, I want 100,000 zloty. This girl will be happier than the other children. She's going to a family to another world to a better life. Why not provide something for the other children?" The money was quickly raised from your uncle in Paris and from committees in Biala and Lodz. I made arrangements that the priest was to bring you to Biala. I didn't want to return to the orphanage, as it was too dangerous. Each time I returned from Sitniki I went to the synagogue and cried and was thankful to have returned alive. The Polish resistance groups were everywhere and they hated Jews. They killed many Jews after the war especially in the forests. My brother-in-law and another Jew came out of concentration camp after going through hell and they came to Biala after the war only to be killed by the Poles. That's why I hate the Poles. It was so dangerous for me to go to this village. I put on my cross, I had my Polish passport and sat between two Poles so that if they came out of the forest I would be protected.

It took two weeks to raise the money. Once I had the 100,000 zloty I made arrangements for the priest to bring you to Biala, as I would not return to Sitniki. It took a full day of traveling from Biala to Warsaw and from Warsaw to Lodz where I was given the money. When I got the money I returned to Warsaw and spent the night with a friend. In the morning I took a train to Biala. We waited at the outskirts of Biala and when the priest came I gave him the money. The priest counted the money. I also brought a friend who took pictures. I went to take you but you refused to go with me. You were frightened and kept running away. The Poles were looking and I was afraid that something would go wrong. The Polish lady who told me about you in the first place (Polka) also helped me during the war. She now helped me to quiet you down. She gave me one of her son's coats to keep you warm as it was a chilly autumn day and you had nothing on but a cotton dress. Polka's husband was a butcher in Biala and he made very tasty sausages and he gave me some. You loved the sausages. I was afraid to let you eat so much but you were very undernourished. When I came out I wanted to see you again and talk to you but you ran away. You appeared to be running for your life. At a later time you told me that the teacher said that the lady who brought you the lollies is a Jewess. "Don't go to her. Jews make Matzot from the blood of Christian children." We went by train to Warsaw and from Warsaw to Lodz. The trip took two days because we spent half the day at Polka's house in Biala and spent the night at a friend's house in Warsaw. On the way I kept buying you toys and food as I did in Biala. I telegraphed my family to advise them of the time of arrival. When we arrived my family came to greet us at the train station. Many came to see the Jewish girl who was christened and had survived. It was such a big event. During these two days of travel you started to trust me and were no longer afraid of me. They had told you in the orphanage that I was going to kill you. You told me that the Jews were going to put you in a barrel full of knives and make Matzot out of you. In Poland if a Christian child was lost it was believed that the Jews took the child and used the child's blood to make Matzot. You started to trust me and to lean on me when you saw that I was not so bad as you were told.

I learned many more details about my childhood experiences from this tape. With time I began to merge myself with that little girl and her story.

During one of our walks through the scenic wooded areas

of Melbourne with Ida's friends and family, I had an opportunity to speak to her friend. He told me that Melbourne served as the hub in Australia for survivors from Biala Podlaska. He had been in Biala Podlaska during the round ups. He told me that he saw my mother sitting with the rest of the people in Miedzyrzec about to be forced on the trains. She was alone without any family member. He ran away and hid.

On Saturday night Ida invited another friend to dinner who knew me when I lived in Lodz. She told me that the school I had attended was located in her building. She remembered me as being very shy and said I used to hide behind Ida's legs when I met new people. She also told me that I spoke Polish well.

Ida was very organized and she made three dinners for us during our stay. Each time her friends came they brought me flowers. I had four vases filled with bouquets in my hotel room. At the parting lunch we said goodbye to Ida and her family. We kissed and then she came back to kiss me once more and said, "I may not see you again." I assured her that I would come back.

It was difficult to say goodbye to her son in law David who was so generous and cheerful and to her daughter Isabel who was warm and kind. I felt like I was leaving family.

Ida was my only link to the past and it felt comfortable to listen to stories about myself. Only she could provide those details of my early years and describe my behavior at the time. In a sense she gave me a personality from her recollections, that I don't remember having before. I would never have known that I spoke fluent Polish, that I questioned her when she gave me more lollies than the other children at the orphanage, that I asked about my parents and being Jewish. And I would never have known how I reacted to her taking me out of the orphanage. In a photograph she gave me of the scene where I was transferred to her, I can see from my body language that I appear to be challenging the nun, trying to tell her that I didn't want to leave.

On this trip I gained so much valuable information from Ida and every detail was precious to me. When we departed from Melbourne, I left Ida the tape recorder and asked her to continue recording her recollections and mail it to me when she finished. Months later, I received a notice from the post office to pick up a package. The postal clerk handed me a brown envelope with Ida's return address. I immediately opened it and found the tape recorder and the tape. I drove back home and parked in my driveway. I couldn't wait to listen to more stories and began playing her words.

Do you know about a woman who came from Paris? No. You never heard? When you lived with me in Lodz, I often spoke to you about a man named Vjernick. He wanted you out of my house because he saw that you were too attached to me. He said it was better to put you in the Jewish orphanage in Lodz. After the war there were many kids found hiding in Polish homes. These kids were later sent to Israel. This orphanage was only for Jewish kids and he wanted to send you there so that he would be in charge of the situation and appear as the important one. Yes, he was staying in touch with your uncle in Paris. That's very important. As a matter of fact, I think your uncle knew him very well in Biala. They wrote to each other all the time. Vjernick was the type of person who lived off other people's charity. He didn't work. He must have thought that this was a good opportunity to ingratiate himself with your uncle. He called the meeting of the Biala committee members and (I was there too) and told them that it would be better if you were not staying with me. He thought you should be in the Jewish orphanage. I was very against it. I said, "No. I will not allow this child to go to another orphanage." All right, it had better conditions than the Catholic one, but it is still an orphanage for Jewish kids. He started to be suspicious and said, "Why are you not letting her go? She's not related to you." He must have started thinking that I had material reasons for not letting you go. I thought that it would be very cruel to put you in an orphanage again and especially when I saw that you liked me so very much. I was against that orphanage. When I told you that you will eventually go to your uncle, you said, "I don't want to go. I want to be with you."

A few weeks after, a lady came to us from Paris. She brought a letter from your uncle. She came to take you from Lodz to Paris to your uncle. We went to the committee meeting.

I asked, "How?"

"She's little, but she doesn't fit in your pocket. How will you take her?"

"Well," she said, "We will go to Warsaw and I will tell them this and that and with the letter I have from her uncle we will ask for a passport and we will do something."

The committee listened to her very loose plan and agreed to let her try. The three of us went to Warsaw. We managed to get a passport for you at the Polish consul, but the French embassy did not want to give you a visa. I don't remember why exactly. We were upset of course. I wasn't as upset as she was. She wanted more than anything in the world to bring you to Paris. Maybe your uncle promised her something. I don't know. We came back to the hotel and she said she was willing to take you without a visa. She said that since you have a Polish passport she would smuggle you in.

"She's a little girl," the woman said, "It will be all right."

I said, "No. Such business I won't make." I said. "Listen lady you go back and I will send her when the time comes."

When we were in Warsaw you were crying. You asked what was happening? What was going on? You understood that something was happening. I told you my dear Gita; you will have to go to your uncle. He's your mother's brother. You have to understand, you have to love him.

"But I don't know him," you said.

"You'll get to know him."

You didn't want to listen. You were a child. You had me now and you were holding on. After the orphanage, you came to me and you didn't want to change to something else. Maybe something else would be better, but you were always afraid. The woman from

Paris was angry with me. She wanted the passport in the worst way. I had the passport in my bag. She grabbed my bag and she wanted to take the passport by force. We started to struggle. It was in Warsaw in a room in a hotel and you were a little girl. You were shouting, "What's happening?" We were struggling and fighting. Once she had the passport she would be the boss. Anyhow she didn't get it. You and I came back to Lodz and she came back by herself. I told the committee no, it was not a suitable time and I will not send you. Weeks went by.

They called a Zionist organization HIAS that took care of all little Jewish kids that had been placed in Jewish orphanages in Poland. When they had 40 or 50 children, they sent them off to Israel. One evening a friend, not a good friend, but a friend of my husband had a sister who worked in this organization. He came to see us and said,

"If you want to send the little girl to Paris, it is a beautiful suitable time."

"What happened?" I asked.

He said, "This evening a whole group of children are going straight to Paris by train. Everything is paid. Everything is fixed. Everything, but one little girl became sick. She cannot go. Your little girl can go instead of the sick girl and use the other girl's name because the girl has a passport with a French visa and everything is legal."

So I didn't know what to do. It came so suddenly that I was furious. I was crying. Remember, I didn't know what to do because

— 321 —

I knew that if I sent you back, I would hurt you. I had to do something. This French woman would go back to your uncle and tell him that I am a witch and all kinds of stories about me. She would tell your uncle that I wouldn't let her take you. She was angry with me. She must have said terrible things to your uncle. That's why he never wrote a letter to me. As to Vjernick, he admitted that he said terrible things about me to your uncle. I understood that Vjernick talked to him about your eating potatoes and bread. He said something about eating food at my house like she was still in the orphanage. This gossip got around. What did happen was that one evening maybe on Hanukah, I don't remember, you and Carmella, both kids in the same school, came home and you didn't want to eat dinner because you ate something in school at the Hanukah party. I said, all right. Later in the evening you were a bit hungry and I said I would warm up some meat and potatoes. I warmed potatoes in the frying pan. Vjernick came to the house unannounced because he was with a Biala committee member and also a friend of Moshe Schneidman, my sister's husband. He looked at the table and saw you eating potatoes without vegetables. He wrote a letter to your uncle and said, "Look what she's doing to your niece. In the orphanage she ate only potatoes and now she's feeding her only potatoes too."

You see everything looked like I did not want to give you up. Vjernick wanted to take you to the Jewish orphanage and I didn't let him. The woman came from Paris and wanted to take you and I didn't let her. It looked like I was an awful person. At that moment I said why do I have to have so much trouble and I agreed to send you on this train. Of course I knew...that for a month or two you would be unhappy, but you were going to family. That was true. Everything came together in my mind. I had to react in a few hours. If I had more time I don't think I would have managed it. I would not have sent you alone. It was a matter of a few hours to get everything done. I took your best dress; you had a pink velvet dress, not pink a red one, so I thought I would put that one on. It was a cold day. You started to get very nervous when you saw me packing your things.

"Where am I going?" You kept repeating. "Where am I going?"

"To your uncle," I told you. "The time has come and you have to."

You said, "You're going too, if you are going then I will go."

So I had to tell a lie. I said, "Yes," I was going.

If it were normal times I would go with you to Paris. You wouldn't be so unhappy if I would go with you to your uncle. It would be different. That's the point. These were not normal times. Everything was unsettled after the war. I couldn't get a visa. They didn't let anyone leave. Jews from Poland were not allowed in any other country. That's important, if it was normal times it would be very advisable and very good to go with this little girl to Paris to your uncle. I would say here you are, this is your uncle and this and that. I would stay in Paris with you for a week or two and then go home.

It would have been really wonderful and you wouldn't have felt so bad. But these were different times, so I told you a lie that I was going with you. Salek, my fiancée, went to the station with us. I couldn't hide my tears. I knew it was going to be a terrible moment. You were very nervous and held my hand tightly. You wanted only one thing, for me to go with you. Yes, you had been so many times in your life left alone and sent somewhere foreign. You were afraid. We were sitting in a carriage, not a taxi, and holding my hand. You kept saying you are going too, you kept repeating you were going with me. When we came there you knew that you were leaving in a few minutes. And then came the moment. I told you Gita darling I have to go. I am not allowed to go with you. You started to cry and scream. You held on to me terrified of letting go. With the help of another woman she wrenched you from my neck. It was a terrible parting for you. Just like at the orphanage. You had been happy there. It was all you knew and you fought and cried not to leave.

I went back home. Your screams were in my head the whole evening and night. We kept hearing your voice, the shouting, for many nights after. I sent a cable to your uncle the same day with your new name so that he would have no trouble finding you. Everything was fixed so that you would not go to Israel with the other children. I was brokenhearted because I saw how unhappy you were. You were very happy in my home. Since then I haven't seen you and now I see you.

IDA'S STORY

IDA ALSO recounted pieces of her own story. I have spliced together the events of her escape from Poland and how she survived until she returned after the war.

Before my parents were married, Ida and my mother had lived in the same neighborhood, the Polish part of Biala. When the Germans invaded and eventually drove the Jews into a ghetto, my parents lived in a house inside its perimeter. Ida and her family, forced to relocate became neighbors again with my mother and family on Grabanowska Street. Ida and her family escaped the roundups of the Jews from Biala to the Miedzyrzec ghetto during Sukkot of 1942. They managed to hide during the turmoil, as the multitudes were being herded and crushed to exit the ghetto. They remained hidden in Biala for a week.

Ida scrounged for food with no possibility of a future if she stayed hidden. She decided that she had to get to a large city and Warsaw was her best option for surviving. She knew a Polish woman in Biala whose family lived in Warsaw. They came to Biala to visit her during the summer. Ida thought, "I will work for the family just to have a roof over my head and food." She approached the woman and asked for help but the Polish woman refused to take any chances. She told Ida that she was afraid to help, because she would suffer punishment or death letting in Jews and she wanted Ida out quickly. A young Polish man from Warsaw overheard Ida's conversation. When he heard that Ida wanted to go to Warsaw it presented an opportunity for him as he was convinced that all Jews were wealthy.

Ida remembered this young man, her senior, from high school as a rowdy boy who enjoyed playing tricks on other kids. He told her he would help her. "I have a girlfriend in Warsaw. I will come to Warsaw and rent a flat and we will live together."

Ida said he wanted her to pay for everything because this girl had an affair with him and was pregnant. As he came from a better home with a nice family, marriage was out of the question for him. He wanted to get rid of his girlfriend, but he wanted to leave her in good health. "I will rent a flat for you," he said," you will pay the money, she will live with you, she will have the child and then you will have the hiding place."

Ida was reluctant to agree, as this sounded much too complicated. "I was afraid, I was always afraid of Poles," she said. "They are not sincere and I thought maybe I could have trouble, but I didn't have another choice."

He gave Ida an address in Warsaw of his girlfriend's sister. "Tell her Mr. Gonikovsky will come and take care of you."

Ida didn't say whether this actually happened, but to leave Biala she needed money for the train and eventual lodging in Warsaw.

Before the deportation, Ida's father had gathered his frightened family together and said to his children, "Whoever will survive, this is where the money, gold coins and jewelry are hidden." He pointed to corners in a large cellar where he had dug and concealed his property. Other money and gold coins were hidden near a shed on the property dug ten feet into the ground. At that time nobody thought they would survive.

After a week of hiding Ida made her way into the family home down to the cellar and dug out some of the money and gold coins to buy her train ticket. It was equally dangerous for Ida to go to the Biala train station, but she felt confident about her appearance. "When I came to the station in Biala, I was young, I looked very good, I was speaking very good Polish."

Because of her Polish looks, she made her way without incident to Warsaw. Her sisters and mother followed soon after Ida used some of the hidden money to escape. Her father did not survive. Ida, her mother and sisters lived together in Warsaw during the war. Ida's mother only spoke Yiddish. She never left their flat and impersonated a deaf mute when a stranger knocked at the door. When she was safe in her bed, Ida or her sisters would open the door.

When Ida arrived in Warsaw, the city was new and unfamiliar to her. She set out to find employment. She decided that it was safest to work as a housekeeper because it would give her an opportunity to hide. Not knowing anyone, she read the help wanted ads in the Warsaw newspaper and went for some interviews. She came upon the Weber family. Mr. Weber was half Polish and half German. He liked Ida and asked her for references. "I never heard this work references. I didn't know what it is and I said no, I didn't work."

He replied, "So how can you be a housekeeper?"

Ida told the Webers she came to Warsaw to escape from

her village because the Germans took young people and sent them to Germany to work. "I want to work so I came here to work with Polish people."

Mr. Weber assured her that no one would touch her or send her to Germany, and he offered her the job. Mrs. Weber, not so sure, asked Ida whether she had experience cooking and cleaning. Ida said she did, but she actually had no experience. Being a young girl, her mother did all the cleaning and cooking. "Cleaning in a small town like Biala didn't compare to cleaning a large apartment in Warsaw. I came from a village, I was not a maid for a rich home. It's different, different cooking, even cleaning a house is different like you're cleaning on a farm or something."

Mrs. Weber then asked where she had her luggage as maids who applied for jobs came with two suitcases of clothing. Ida ran away from Biala with only the dress she was wearing and no coat. She hesitated and said she would bring her clothes later. "All right, we'll try it out for a few weeks," said Mrs. Weber just to please her husband.

Ida recounted with a light air how incapable she was as a housekeeper and how upset that made Mrs. Weber. She managed to peel vegetables and potatoes but when asked to kill and cook a chicken, Ida nearly fainted from fright. Her mother bought chickens at a Jewish butcher who performed a kosher ceremonial killing. Mrs. Weber in frustration and anger told Ida to hold the chicken legs while she killed the chicken. Ida was asked to remove all the feathers and that presented another challenge. As Ida started to pull out the feathers Mrs.

Weber screamed, "Aren't you going to put it in boiling water?" Ida complied. She had never seen the flicking of a chicken before. This only added to the list of ineptitudes Mrs. Weber had to deal with.

In the first few days Ida worked, the Webers had a party. "I had just come from Biala where I was starving and my stomach had shrunk. I saw all this food and tasted a little of every dish. I became sick to my stomach and I developed fever. At home, my mother and father would have given me an oil and lemon mixture to settle my stomach. I kept asking for that mixture knowing it would help me." Eventually when she didn't get better the Webers called a doctor who told them, "Madam Irina (Ida was called by her Polish name) has to stay in bed." To add to this predicament, Ida had also injured her leg. "Jesus Christ, what a maid I have. She comes here and she eats, gets sick, and now she has to be in bed," shrieked Mrs. Weber. This job lasted only two weeks.

These fragments of Ida's own story also showed me her courage and the will to survive. Ida goes on to say that her brother in law and sister left Poland and went to Sweden. Poland did not offer a life for Jewish people. Such a tragedy happened to our people that I don't know how Jews could live in such a country all those years. When I was in the presence of Germans I was nor afraid because the Germans would not recognize me as a Jew. Never. But Poles, yes. No matter how well I spoke Polish. I had a Polish passport and I looked good still they recognized me as a Jew.

Left: Ida and Gitta,
Melbourne, Australia
1992

Below: Ida in her home,
Melbourne, Australia,
1992

AUSTRALIA

1998

IN THE fourteen years since my first trip to Australia with Neil, I had accumulated some of the missing pieces of my past. By August of 1997 my marriage with Neil officially ended.

In December 1998, I made one last trip to Australia. I wanted Ida to meet my sons in person. I wanted her to see the next generation of Jewish children made possible by her courage and persistence in taking me out of the orphanage. Otherwise, I would have continued my life as a Catholic.

Jonathan and his friend, James and his fiancée Kricken travelled with me to visit her. Unfortunately Judson could not join us. Overjoyed at meeting my sons, Ida celebrated our being there with her friends and family. My sons towered over her. To take photos, we had Ida stand on telephone books and Jonathan and James stood beside her like giants.

While we were there, my sons investigated various activities for us. We toured the rainforest and snorkeled in the Coral Sea off the coast of Cairns. I passed on the invitation to go horseback riding on the beach as I panic when I am on top of a horse. I relate my fear to a mental image I have of the Nazis riding on the orphanage grounds, men in uniform with tall boots positioned in the stirrups.

Jonathan then suggested that we go skydiving. He and Kricken had tried it. James and I were not thrilled with the idea but after being playfully called "chicken" and persistently told what a great experience it would be, we relented. I was definitely nervous as was James and Jonathan's friend. After about an hour's drive we located the dwelling on the airfield and were told we could be the last on the schedule for the day.

We suited up and were given basic instructions. Each one of us would jump in tandem with an instructor strapped to our back. The instructor would pull the parachute at the right moment. The five of us, five instructors and the pilot squeezed into a small plane. What am I doing here? Do I have to prove I'm as foolish or as brave as my sons? Am I trying to impress them? Too late. The plane took off and I became more edgy and worried. Before I knew it we were flying at 14,000 feet.

"Who wants to go first?" asked one of the instructors. Jonathan volunteered and he and his instructor jumped out of the plane followed by James. Well, I might as well follow my sons. I jumped with the instructor on my back and we were free falling thousands of feet. He swirled me around so I could see the beautiful green mountainous scenery and the vast expanse of the terrain. My teeth chattered as we swooped down lower and lower. Finally he pulled open the parachute and it felt like we had come to a standstill. What a relief! We were gliding and floating in the air. "Remember," the instructor said, "keep your legs up, bend you knees just before we land so that I don't fall over you and one of us breaks a leg." My brain comprehended but my legs would not bend no matter how many times I commanded them to do so. We landed and thankfully no legs were broken. I was so relieved to be on terra firma.

As soon as I got to a standing position and took the straps off, I saw that James and the others were watching Kricken and her instructor up in the air. Their primary chute would not open but finally the backup chute did. Shortly after that the primary chute also opened and became tangled with the second one. She and her instructor were frantically pulling in one of the chutes and trying to avoid landing on the electric wires as they were off course. All ended well but could have been catastrophic. Kricken said she would never sky dive again.

The experience pumped up my confidence. It left me gratified and thrilled that I had the courage to go through with it. I thought if I could do that, I could do anything. That feeling of exhilaration lasted a few months. My sons were proud me. Jonathan loved telling his friends that I jumped from a plane at 14,000 feet.

Visiting Australia and having my sons meet Ida was a memorable and happy time for all of us. Sadly it was the last time I saw her. Born on September 25, 1915 in Biala Podlaska, Ida Rozenszajn Koper passed away on January 21, 2003.

Jonathan, Ida (standing on a phone book) and James
Melbourne, Australia, 1998

Suited up for Sky Diving
Left to right: Kricken, James, Gitta, Jonathan, Australia, 1998

PART III
2007 – 2013

*Heritage and
Jewish Roots*

ISRAEL

2007

IN 2007, I took my youngest son Judson to Israel with a group called *Stand With Us*, a non-profit pro Israeli education and advocacy organization. We visited the new Yad Vashem Holocaust Museum inaugurated in 2005. The plans for this commemoration project, a remembrance and education center, began in 1953. Designed in the shape of a prism that penetrates the mountain, it is divided into nine galleries. "The museum relates and demonstrates the stories of the Jewish communities before the Second World War and the series of events beginning from the rise of the Nazis to power, the pursuit of the Jews, their eviction to the ghettos and ending with *the Final Solution* and mass genocide."[3]

On this trip I was introduced to the Coordinator of the Memorial Cave Project, Pearl Weiss. In 1997, I had ordered a memorial stone for my mother, father and brother. I was married to Neil at that time and used my married name as well as my maiden name. I wanted my married name removed from the stone. When I came to the Yad Vashem Museum, Ms.

Weiss assured me that it would be taken care of. When I told her my background, she asked if I had any pictures and historical evidence that I could donate to the museum. I explained that I had donated most of my original photographs to the Holocaust Museum in Washington D.C. In fact, the Washington Museum used the photograph of me sitting on the lap of the Head Sister when I was taken out of the orphanage for their special exhibit called, "Life in Shadows, Hidden Children and the Holocaust." My photograph was on all the brochures and banners and prominently displayed outside the museum. I was the poster child for this exhibition that travelled to various cities in the United States. I visited the exhibition in Washington D.C. with my sons, and daughter-in-law, and my then only grandchild. I also went to the exhibition in New York. Visitors were both surprised and pleased when I was introduced as the person whose photograph appeared on all the written material. My experience and the experiences of the other hidden children were documented by photographs and written accounts.

Disappointed on discovering that I had donated all of this historical evidence to Washington instead of to the Yad Vashem, Ms. Weiss explained, "We are the main repository for collecting and documenting all the pieces of evidence of the Shoah." I said I would send her copies of all of the photographs, as well as any others I had not given to Washington. When I returned home I sent copies of the few photos I had of my family.

Poster for Life in Shadows exhibition, Holocaust Museum,
Washington, D.C., September 19, 2003 - May 12, 2004

LIFE IN SHADOWS
Hidden Children and the Holocaust

An exhibition organized and circulated by the United States Holocaust Memorial Museum.

When World War II ended in 1945, six million European Jews were dead, murdered in the Holocaust. A million and a half of the victims were children.

Thousands of children survived this brutal carnage, however, because they were hidden, many by Christian individuals and organizations. With identities disguised, often physically concealed from the outside world, these youngsters faced constant fear and danger. Theirs was a life in shadows, where a careless remark, a denunciation or a neighbor's suspicions could lead to discovery and death.

Photo courtesy of USHMM, gift of Gitto Rosenzweig.

Spertus Museum | March 20 – July 31, 2005

Poster for Life in Shadows exhibition, Spertus Museum, Chicago.
March 20 - July 31, 2005

POLAND

2010

MY TRIP to Poland in 1990 with Neil had proved disappointing and disturbing. I thought if I could visit the orphanage where I had been hidden and wander through the physical structure it might trigger forgotten memories and I might recall events that had long been erased.

For many years I searched for my identity. I hoped that one day I would find my birth record and records pertaining to my parents, brother and family, all killed during the Holocaust. I knew if there was ever a chance of locating this evidence I would have to travel to Biala Podlaska, Poland once again.

One evening in April of 2010, my son Jonathan and I were having dinner at my kitchen counter.

"You know mother, I'm planning to go to Europe. You and your family are from Poland. It is a country I've always wanted to see. I'd really like to go there and trace my roots."

"Why don't we go together?" I said surprised and delighted by his interest. I've been hoping to take you and your brothers to Poland."

"That's a great idea," he said.

I called James and Judson to see if they were also interested in going to Poland. They were both excited at the idea and said they would love to.

"Well, I'll start making plans then."

By October the arrangements were made and we travelled to Poland on the trip I had contemplated for so many years. Our collective mission was to trace my experiences as a Hidden Child in Poland during World War II. I also wanted my sons to be acquainted with the lives of their grandparents and family in Biala Podlaska. On a broader scale, I wanted them to learn about the horrific tragedy of the over three million Jews murdered in Poland out of a total of six million Jews throughout Europe and Russia, and to visit the sites in memory of those who lost their lives.

The excitement to obtain my family records intensified as our departure date approached. I knew so much in my early life had been fabricated to conceal my identity in order to survive as a child. I wondered about my birth name. Was it really Gitta Rosenzwieg? Was my birth date actually September 15, 1938? I never possessed my birth certificate, or the records of any of my immediate family.

In 1948 when Aunt Hilda went to France to obtain a visa for me, my birthplace was listed by the American Consul as Breslau, Germany, as no visas were available for Polish nationals. As a result of this, my French Identification and Travel

Document, my school records and my American citizenship certificate contain Breslau, Germany as my place of birth.

In 2000, I had requested and paid for a copy of my birth record from the Polish Consulate in Los Angeles. On the form I listed my birthplace as Biala Podlaska. A few months later the Consulate informed me by letter that they could not locate any record of my birth. Disappointed and frustrated, I later realized their computer search led them to Breslau, Germany.

As I put our trip together from the US, I managed to make contact with a knowledgeable guide in Poland, Tomasz Cebulski who specialized in Holocaust Studies and has since published his Ph.D. thesis on the subject. I emailed him with the details of our quest to locate family records and the places I most wanted to visit including Miedzyrzec Podlaski, Lodz, Wroclaw, and Sitnik.

We arrived in Warsaw at 9:30 am on October 11 and were greeted by Tomasz at the airport. We wanted to see as much as possible during our eight days in Poland, so we packed a lot into our itinerary. We decided not to spend a whole day in Warsaw in order to give us more time in Biala. It was more important to see what we could discover at the records center in Biala and have time to talk to some of the older people there, as well as visit the site of the orphanage in Sitnik. As Treblinka was only a two-hour drive from Warsaw in the direction of Biala, we decided to begin our journey by making the death camp our first stop.

TREBLINKA

"IN 1942 Sukkot fell between September 23 and October 2. The final deportation of the Jews from Biala Podlaska started on September 26 and ended on October 1st. Organizing the roundup of Jews on holy holidays was a common practice of the Nazis. They surrounded the ghetto by police and military units the night before September 26. In the morning they started to crowd thousands of Jews into the Main Market Square. Anybody resisting was shot on the spot. Brutality prevailed. There was bloodshed in the Jewish hospital. Some people with work permits were selected and sent to nearby labor camps. Thousand of others were put on horse drawn wagons or forced to walk to the Miedzyrzec railroad station. Miedzyrzec became an assembly point for local Jews of Podlasie before their deportation to Treblinka. It was a vestibule to hell. The German Police found it difficult to pronounce Polish Miedzyrzec and even more difficult to use the Yiddish pronunciation of Mezridge, so they coined the nickname Menschenschrek, meaning "men's horror." Most Biala Jews were gradually deported to the death camp of Treblinka until spring, 1943. Usher and Hudes were probably among this last group to leave Biala for Miedzyrzec and then to Treblinka."

—TOMASZ CEBULSKI

Treblinka was an extermination camp not a concentration camp like Auschwitz. No chance of survival existed. It has taken years for me to read about the death camp or even research it. I could not join the image of my mother's face to the horror of what Treblinka represented. Some survivors claim my father was shot when he refused to board the deportation train. He was not seen at Miedzyrzec ghetto with my mother. Ida's friend told me she was alone.

We arrived to the entrance of the Treblinka Death Camp, the final destination for my mother. A memorial built by the Poles at the site of the death camp consists of thousands of granite slabs of different sizes that memorialize the number of people killed in various towns and cities in Europe. Natural rock and stones scattered in random ways represent tiny villages next to larger ones.

My sons and I walked in silence through this area of stones, slabs and ashes. Buried deep inside us, our thoughts gave way to emotions and tears as we tried to accept the horrors of the past and live in the present. We hugged and shared these moments of searing pain in memory of the lives that were cut short so brutally leaving a void for generations to come.

We brought written messages from my grandchildren expressing their loss at never having known their grandparents, aunts, uncles and cousins. We placed their letters at the granite slab, resembling a tombstone, with the name Biala Podlaska chiseled on it.

BIALA PODLASKA

WE CONTINUED on and arrived in Biala later in the evening. We checked into our hotel tired from traveling and processing the horrific history of Treblinka. We were shown to our tiny dimly lit rooms eager for a good night's rest. The child size narrow beds, with mattresses that lacked support, were far too small to accommodate my over six foot tall sons. The steps leading in and out of the rooms posed a dangerous situation in the dark. We ran down to catch Tomasz before he left the hotel. "Tomasz, we have to check out and find rooms with larger beds!" He asked the clerk to check availability at another hotel. The sympathetic clerk reserved rooms for us at another location. We gathered the TV remotes given to us when we checked in, to return, and thankfully drove to the new lodgings with larger rooms and normal size beds. The tacky, garish decor of my new L shaped bedroom and living room inspired me to take many photos of the red velvet sofa, red accessories, carpet and paintings of veiled women, thick grey stucco walls, and plastic palm trees. This pseudo bordello atmosphere created some levity after a long, arduous day and night of travel from Los Angeles to New York to Warsaw, and finally to Biala Podlaska. The next day I discovered I still had the TV remote in my pocket. I left it at the second hotel.

The following morning, our first day in Biala Podlaska, Tomasz met us in the dining room for breakfast. We greeted each other and discussed our plans for the day. He said his preliminary research indicated that my birth month was April, not September. I found it almost comical. I didn't feel like an April person. All my life I assumed my birthday was in September. We considered this new information and left for our scheduled appointment at the Registry Office of Biala Podlaska in search of my birth certificate and whatever other documents we might be fortunate enough to obtain.

The Registry Office located on 27 Janowska Street is set back 50 feet from the sidewalk, surrounded by a lush lawn and verdant trees. Housed in a two story white building, with red tiled roof and skylights, the building is traditional and formidable compared to the other two story wooden structures in the city. The tall glass windows, with brown painted frames reveal drapes on the interior. At the front of the building is a circular concave glass awning on columns. Metal plaques of Polish writing attached to the wall describe the history and function of the building.

We climbed a few steps and entered through the front entrance with signs directing us to the records department. From the waiting area, we could see three female clerks through a door with the upper half framed in glass. Apprehensive and tense with expectation, I kept wondering if I would finally obtain my birth certificate. Would I see my name and date of birth and parents' names on an official document verifying my true identity?

Tomasz warned us not to have high expectations. Before we entered, he counseled us to be silent and just observe. He approached the clerk closest to the door and in a humble and respectful manner confirmed our appointment in Polish. He briefed her about the purpose of our visit, gave her a succinct history of my family, and stressed the importance of finding some records. He introduced us and wrote out the name ROZENCWAJG. The clerk in her early forties, dressed in a skirt and blouse, brown hair pinned back, in quick business like movements shook our hands, smiled and asked us to return to the waiting area.

With tense faces we complied. We slowly dispersed to look at the photos on the wall and made small talk with each other and Tomasz. We agreed it would be so amazing to find official records of me and of my parents—my sons' grandparents.

We marveled at the fact that we were here in this small town that contained so much history for us. My sons looked around and went outside to take photographs. I used the rest room. We waited. We breathed deeply. The tension and excitement palpable, we paced and looked at the clock. After twenty minutes the second clerk walked out from an interior room carrying two leather bound registry books, each approximately three inches thick. We looked at each other and let out deep breaths and smiled. The clerk opened the books to the place where she had marked the pages with paper inserts.

We were overjoyed to find such treasures. The pages contained hand written entries of my family's history. My birth certificate validated my actual date and place of birth September 15, 1938, Biala Podlaska. It bore the original signatures of my father and mother, who I knew only through photographs. We also found a birth certificate of my older brother Israel Itzchak, born five years before me. Other than this record and a few photographs, I have no memory of him. His recorded birth gave a description of our parents, stating their age and bearing their original signatures and those of other witnesses.

To our further amazement we found a beautifully hand written record of my parents' marriage certificate recorded on June 24, 1932 when my mother Hudes was 27 and my father Usher was 26, witnessed by their parents, my grandparents, and others. Astonished, we saw names in my family genealogy written in their own hand.

We also found a death certificate of my fraternal grandfather who died in February 1939, just seven months before the German invasion. I had mistakenly believed he was killed during the Holocaust and subsequently corrected this information on my Pages of Testimony. The names of his parents, unknown to me, were listed in this record. We also found the birth record of my father's youngest brother Yarichem, born November 19, 1919. He was thirteen years younger than my father.

The discovery of these records provided some relief to the sadness and grief that my family and I went through. We were given excerpts of the original entries signed and officially sealed by the Polish government. Finally I had my official birth record and gained closure to this life long pursuit of evidence.

SITNIK – THE ORPHANAGE

I WANTED to visit the orphanage at Sitnik once again. This time I was more prepared. I already knew the wood building that used to house the orphanage was no longer there. Devastated by its absence on my last trip, I had anticipated seeing the table where we ate, the room and beds we slept in, and the areas where we played and studied. I had hoped to reclaim some memories and gain some new insights.

According to Tomasz, during the war years when I was found, large posters hung by the Nazis on every city corner made it clear that providing any help or shelter to a Jewish person in occupied Poland meant the entire family would be executed. I had told him what I knew of my history from Ida and about the Czekanskis. He deduced the Czekanskis must have been aware that sheltering one girl, with restricted food rations for everybody was extremely risky. Even though a few people would be aware of the situation, it would only take one person to betray them. Therefore Tomasz surmised that Czekanski, a teacher, who protected me a for short time, found the orphanage run by the Catholic nuns in the nearby village of Sitnik, just 15 kilometers north of Biala to take me in. I believe the nuns baptized me Maria, and Ida concluded they gave me the teacher's last name, but with the feminine ending "a" instead of 'i'. This is most likely how I became Maria Czekanska but I was also sometimes called Marysia, a term of endearment for little girls.

I had brought a few photographs with me from the day Ida took me from the orphanage at the age of seven and a half. All that remains are the concrete steps that once led to the wood building and a little shrine devoted to the Holy Mary that stands on the edge of the village road. She had dutifully protected our orphanage during the war. A communist style school now sits on the plot of land, a square building devoid of any architectural interest. The stables that had once been part of the orphanage estate are the only other remaining structure.

Prior to our arrival, Tomasz researched and discovered the order of *The Congregation of the Daughters of the Holy Heart of Maria* active in Biala before the war who ran the orphanage. They wore ordinary clothes rather than habits as evidenced in the photo of me with the nun wearing a street dress. Aniela Szozdzinska, The Head of the Institution, chronicles details of the orphanage in her 1951 writing, *The Short Story of the Orphanage in Sitnik:*

In 1939 The Charity Society in Sitnik suggested that the Congregation of the Daughters of the Holy Heart of Maria take over the orphanage of Sitnik. This was accepted on August 1, 1939. Our work started in very hard conditions and circumstances. There were always around 50 orphans from 2-14 years old. The orphanage was located in a very picturesque rural area. The institution was co-educational—boys and girls were mostly from the area of Sitnik and its larger administrative district. The upkeep costs of the children, as well as some construction funds were raised due to the hard labor of the sisters as well as their personal savings. The sisters worked selflessly, not taking any payment. The constant in-flow of children caused the existing building to be too small, so a new addition was constructed from the internal funds. From 1946 the orphanage was named The Social Home of a Child and started to get the government subsidies granted to all such institutions in the country.

Taking into consideration the well being and skills of children the directorship of the Orphanage laid a great stress on versatile education of children, with an aim of upbringing useful members of the holy church and socially aware citizens of the beloved country of Poland. Our pupils after finishing the primary education were advancing to different schools in the region, which was often connected with changing the place of their residence. After being sent to other orphanages they would never lose contact with their home place in Sitnik. The contact with former pupils was constantly up kept through letters and meetings during summer and winter holidays.

From 1939 till the moment of the house liquidation, or rather the moment when we were fired because the house got nationalized on the 1st of August 1951, there were over 700 children-orphans who were given education and upbringing.

In Sitnik we spoke to some of the elder locals. One man, a teenager during those years, remembered some of the young pretty girls. He said the children walked in perfect lines in unison from the orphanage to church. On seeing the procession of children he made sure he was not mistaken for one of the orphans and included in the disciplined line overseen by the strict nuns. To substantiate my vague memories, I questioned whether he recalled bombings in this village close to the orphanage, but he said he did not.

We walked over to the nearby church and met the young priest, newly positioned in the area. He welcomed us, but couldn't provide any information about the orphanage except to offer that photos were taken at the orphanage on a yearly basis. He believed that an album of these photos remained with the sisters.

Tomasz had researched the present location of the *Congregation of the Daughters of Holy Heart of Maria* and found they lived in Nowe Miasto nad Pilica. He made contact with them, but they said they had no information about the orphanage at Sitnik, only a few pictures. Nevertheless he made an appointment for us to visit their offices and convent, but did not reveal that I was a Jewish child hidden by the sisters during the war.

We drove to the convent on our way to Lodz. We arrived late in the day and were welcomed into a small waiting room at the entrance of the building, but not in the convent itself. We were all very excited and respectful of the surroundings. To be with the order of nuns who had taken care of me during the war years felt like an enormous step to discovering who I was, and whether my vague memories about that time were grounded and not just imaginary. We were dependent on Tomasz to translate the sisters' Polish into English for us while we remained attentive to their facial expressions.

Two sisters, Maria and Theresa, women in their late fifties, dressed in street clothes, welcomed us in a formal manner.

"I am unsure how to approach them about your story," said Tomasz, as we sat in the waiting room. "I'm not sure whether to tell them that you were a Jewish girl hidden by the nuns in case they did not know their fellow sisters hid Jewish children." He decided not to say anything. He began the story of Marysia Czekanska and observed an increased interest in the sisters' faces. Once they realized I was one of the children from the orphanage, they hugged and kissed us, expressing genuine happiness and joy at our visit. They greeted me like a dear relative lost for over fifty years. Everyone had broad smiles on their faces while tears welled up in our eyes. We were escorted through the doors and courtyards of the convent into the interior where the nuns lived. We were led through a dim corridor into a large well-lit room with a long table in the center covered with a white lace tablecloth. An abundance of cakes, cookies and candies awaited us as well as a tea service. In the short conversation, we learned there was not much left of the Sitnik documents as the Communists nationalized the property in 1952. There were no sisters old enough to remember. They gave us an album of ten photographs taken at the orphanage before and after the war, of children in groups with the sisters and the priests. They were the same photographs that the priest had given us copies of at the orphanage. The wood building, concrete steps, and the small shrine of the Holy Mary were identical to those in the picture of me of sitting on the lap of one of the sisters. There was no doubt this was the right place. As we looked through the annual group photos of the children, we saw there were no pictures taken during the war years when I was there.

Both sisters showed compassion and understanding. Sister Mary was flushed and perspiring. Sister Teresa, the Head Mother of the entire convent in Poland, became more energized and remembered writing on the Jews in the orphanages during the war years. She put on her coat and wrapped a scarf around her neck and head to keep warm in the cold late afternoon weather. She proceeded though the courtyard to the archive room and disappeared for what seemed a very long time. She made this trip to the archives three times to retrieve one piece of writing after another.

On her first trip to the archives she brought back an article on a number of orphanages run by the convent during the war. Tomasz distilled the information in the article that described how Jewish children all over Poland had been hidden under false identities. Eleven children had been saved in Warsaw living at various addresses, two children had been saved in Nowe Miastro, two in Skozec, ten in Otwock, four in Swider, and a number of children were saved in Sitnik, Kolno, Janow Podlaski, Wilno and Pinsk. After the war most of the children were not identified. They were the only survivors and lived under their new identities. The article also referred to Sitnik and gave details about two boys who were given Christian names and surnames, and mentioned a few other Jewish children. There was also a brief note about a little girl named Marysia Czekanska saying it was difficult to hide her from the

Germans. After the war, a Jewish organization took her to join her family abroad.

On hearing the name Marysia Czekanska, I did not initially absorb the meaning of the words. Is this about me? Astounded, I became breathless when she read my name. I watched the look of delight on Tomasz' face as he took the article from the sister and read the paragraph with my name. Both he and I radiated with astonishment and joy at this discovery. I looked at my sons in sheer amazement. They were equally stunned and happy. We stood up, hugged and kissed each other with tearful emotions. This finding far exceeded our expectations. Tomasz recalls that I then submerged into traumatic memories of when I was taken away from the orphanage and the nuns. I described being hidden in the bunkers with the sisters and other children during bombardments as well as the harrowing memory of waking up in the middle of the night to the sight of a man aiming a rifle at one of the sisters in the doorway of our sleeping room. We ran to the Sister, surrounded her and prayed, cried and begged for her life. Overcome by the sight, the man retreated back into the night. I had no context for this memory, but as a child it evoked overwhelming primitive fear in me causing me to scream and stop breathing. At this point I managed to emerge from my traumatic memories and regain my sense of time and place.

When Tomasz asked Mother Teresa for the source of the article, she returned to the archives again. She rushed back filled with excitement and a bounce in her step, carrying a thick volume containing her Master of Arts dissertation. She started flipping through the pages, a chapter on the war, a chapter on helping the Jews from Sitnik, and then moved down to the reference section where she came upon the *Personal Diary of Sister Jadwiga Gozdek from Sitnik Orphanage*. She made her third disappearance to the archives bundled up in her coat and scarf. She returned with the hand written diary, the last of the puzzle pieces of my quest for information about my life at the orphanage in Sitnik.

From the diary of Sister Jadwiga Gozdek: *On the 25th of June 1943 I took my first convent vows and I was immediately directed to the orphanage in Sitnik—a village close to Biala Podlaska. I finally reached Siedlce, but I was deprived of my luggage. On the way to Biala Podlaska every few kilometers there were derailed and burned trains and twisted rail lines. This was the result of activity of the local partisans who were exploding the German trains. We were all constantly unsure if we would get there as those were the last months of occupation and the fights were getting more and more severe...In Sitnik the sisters welcomed me warmly, but they were also full of anxiety as the night before there had been a Ukrainian raid on the orphanage. They were looking for young nuns to have fun with. They threatened to shoot the head mother. She was saved by the children who refused to step away and begged for her life...The orphanage was located in two old houses without electricity or hygienic facilities. The sisters and girls lived in the larger house with a veranda. The larger room was changed into a canteen and day room for the children. The place was very packed. A few sisters had to share one room...Our Head Mother was Sister Aniela Szozdzinska, there were 7 sisters in total and around 40 children aged 3 to 19, boys and girls...There were 15 hectares (37 acres) of land, garden, orchard and bee hives. We had a few cows, horses, pigs and chickens. Work was extremely hard, as there were no tools and we did all the work manually with the help of older children...Children were mostly orphans and half-orphans due to the war. They arrived terribly dirty and insect ridden. Often we had to burn all of the children's belongings on their arrival. They were often brought to us naked and barefoot. Thanks be to God, we had enough food. Sometimes I watched with pain how our children were throwing away bread. I told them about people starving all over the country. The worst situation we had was with clothing and shoes. We were stitching new patches into the old ones...It was the worst with shoes. Father Edward Kowalik was an incredibly good man, devoted priest and a former teacher. The man with golden hands and heart, he spent all his spare time with the children. He was able to resolve any problem. He acquired some military tarpaulin, organized a shoemaker and was personally producing wooden soles...In this way we made shoes for the children...Winters 1944/45/46 were the hardest. Then we started to get some donations, but often we had to match two shoes that were different to give shoes to every child. Among our Polish children there were also Jewish children. Some of them had very characteristic Jewish features. We had a lot of anxiety and troubles connected with that, especially right after my arrival when part of our house was confiscated for the German police commando station. We had to constantly hide the children and do our best not to be betrayed, because we were aware that in such case we would all be killed on the spot...* **One particular girl was very beautiful and she stood out from all our children. She had a very pale and delicate complexion, blond, curly hair, blue eyes and for a long time she had a hard time to learn to speak clear Polish. The Germans were constantly asking who this child was and why she was so different from the others. We were all the time saying that this is a child of Polish nobility and for this reason she is so different and delicate. After the war some Jewish organization traced her. In spite of her resistance and great despair, because she became very bonded with the Sisters, she was taken away with force and taken abroad where she probably had some rich family. All of these children had Polish papers. The girl was named Marysia Czekanska,** *the boy was named Henryk Golubiak, deaf and dumb Andrezej Sitnicki, and others whose names I don't remember... In the summer of 1944 after the Germans retreated we were located in the middle of the front line. We spent a few hard days with children in the bomb shelters dug in the garden, because once Germans and once Soviets started the offensive. Next to the out house there was an explosion of inflammable bomb, but the trees sheltered the house from fire and sparks...The nearby village was completely bombed and devastated...God had saved us and the children, and after the war as* *a thanksgiving we placed a figurine of the Holy Lady in front of the house...The Germans have taken our horses...When the first time we noticed the Polish soldiers with white Polish eagle on their military caps we burst into tears of happiness...After Berlin was taken we had some Kosciusko Army (Communist Polish Army: TC) stationed at our place and they were very helpful with harvesting. They gave us horses. They were helping us with children and dreaming of their own families. Very soon they left to fight against the partisans in the forests. We were crying once we heard the machine guns in the forest against the partisans. The incredible pain as we knew and loved men on both sides of this fratricidal battle...*

After reading the diary, we looked at each other incredulously. At best, we had hoped to find a group photograph or any photo that I might be in to prove my connection to the orphanage. The discovery of this nun's diary that included not only my Polish name and a vivid description of me, but also details of events that corroborated some of my most frightening memories such as clinging to the Head Sister for protection from an armed intruder and hiding in a bomb shelter during a bombing was a miracle. Finally I had some written evidence of my time during those years.

I lived in constant fear at the orphanage knowing that I was being hidden. I didn't understand why I was concealed behind doors, in far away corners, out of sight when German men in boots approached, and or why I was always told to keep quiet.

I didn't realize that my Polish tainted by Yiddish, which was spoken at home and was undoubtedly my first language, was a death sentence. This led to my deep-rooted fear of speaking as an adult. At times, this fear caused me to panic and make irrational decisions if it involved public speaking. Being silenced during those early years profoundly affected my ability to communicate.

MIEDZYRZEC PODLASKA

THE FOLLOWING day we set off for Miedzyrzec Podlaska, the most difficult place for me to visit other than Treblinka. Located 15 miles from Biala, the Miedzyrzec ghetto is the last place my mother was seen alive. On August 25 and 26, 1942 the first mass of deportation of Jews from Miedzyrzec took place. Approximately 10,000 Jewish prisoners were forced onto 52 cattle cars (shipment #566 according to German inventory) and sent to Treblinka extermination camp. Two days later the Miedzyrzec Podlaski ghetto was established and two more mass deportations occurred. Of the 12,000 inhabitants of Miedzyrzec in the 1930s, three quarters were Jewish. By July 17, 1943, when the ghetto was officially liquidated only one percent of the Jewish population had survived the Nazi death camps and mass executions.

Here as tourists, we were alive, trying to reconcile the horrors of the past with our current existence. We walked around a beautiful park in the center of the city. The sunshine accentuated the colors of the shops and the awnings of the two story buildings surrounding the square. Shopkeepers and merchants sold their wares. We took photos of the monument erected in commemoration of the ghetto.

I struggled to imagine what my mother and thousands of other people went through as they stood in terror on these bloody streets. Watching and being the target of sadistic acts and killings, they waited to be herded onto a cattle car to Treblinka, knowing they were being sent to their death. How dark and evil the world must have appeared to them as they sat guarded by brutal men with frozen eyes, armed with guns, whips and dogs.

We looked around, paid our respects, and departed. We continued our journey to Majdanek and Auschwitz-Birkenau concentration camps, places as horrific as the human imagination can fathom.

MAJDANEK AND AUSCHWITZ-BIRKENAU

AS WE drove, Tomasz told us the history of these camps. Built in 1941 by 20,000 Jewish forced laborers, Majdanek located in the major city of Lublin, became operational in 1942. Many of the laborers died from typhus, the elements, or starvation.

It was initially used as a secondary storage and sorting depot for property and valuables taken from victims of Treblinka, Sobibor and Belzec. It was then turned into a killing center in order to kill a large Jewish population in southeastern Poland including Krakow, Lwow, Zomosc, and Warsaw. Victims were murdered by Zyklon-B gas or exhaust from tanks, as well as by mass shootings.

It was cold and grey when we arrived late in the afternoon. The camp occupies 670 acres of mostly bare land within the boundaries of Lublin and can be seen from the newly built high-rises.

The Russians had approached Lublin so rapidly on July 24, 1944, that the German staff only partially succeeded in destroying the crematoria, leaving Madjanek the best preserved camp of the Holocaust. The horrors discovered there were widely publicized.

We visited the Memorial at the entrance gate to the camp, a symbolic pylon intended to represent mangled bodies. Ashes of those murdered are strewn on the nearby walkway.

We also visited the Mausoleum erected in 1969 that contains the ashes and remains of cremated victims collected into a mound after the liberation of 1944.

We resumed our drive, stopping to visit Auschwitz-Birkenau on the way to Krakow. We saw more horrific sites including the railroad tracks that brought the cattle cars full of Jewish men, women and children to the crematoriums, and the repositories of tens of thousands of shoes, eyeglasses, prosthetic devices, suitcases, and other gruesome artifacts.

Only ashes remain of the millions of Jews who perished.

KRAKOW

WITH HEAVY hearts Tomasz drove us to Krakow. We decided to spend three days in this vibrant city that had escaped destruction. For centuries, Christian and Jewish cultures coexisted in the Jewish section of Kazimierz. Today Kazimierz is one of the major tourist attractions in Krakow and an important cultural center of the city.

Devoid of Jews for a period of time after the war, the communist authorities neglected Kazimierz. Since 1988, a popular annual Jewish Cultural Festival has drawn Cracovians back to the heart of the Jewish sector and re-introduced Jewish culture to a generation of Poles who have grown up without a traditional Jewish community.

In 1993 Steven Spielberg filmed many scenes of *Schindler's List* in Kazimierz even though very little of the action took place historically there. The filming drew international attention to the location. The restoration of important historic sites in Kazimierz has also fueled a growth in Jewish-themed restaurants, bars, bookstores and souvenir shops. Jews from Israel and America returning to Kazimierz have created a Jewish population boom in the city.

We arrived in Krakow in the evening and stayed at a beautiful hotel. I didn't have the energy for a night out and retired to my bedroom. My sons deserved some gaiety after the mournful sites we had visited. They decided to go out and enjoy the lively, historic city. At night, the streets are filled with young people walking by the open shops, restaurants and bars.

The next morning at breakfast, my sons told me they had gone to a club near the hotel and had a few drinks. They listened to the chanteuse, Magdalena, who they befriended. Jonathan caught her eye as she sang. He gestured to her to join them at the table by raising his glass. After her performance, she came and sat with them and chatted. Shortly after, Magdalena and Jonathan were left alone.

The next few days Tomas joined us briefly and pointed out some of the famous tourist attractions. We ate delicious traditional Jewish food served in Jewish style restaurants. Meanwhile, Jonathan kept receiving messages on the phone and making plans. "I met someone," he said. "She's really beautiful. We're going to have dinner together. Sorry Ma, I'll catch up with you tomorrow."

We saw less and less of Jonathan during the next three days. When we left Krakow to take the train to Warsaw to spend the night before our flight home to Los Angeles, Jonathan left word that Magdalena would be driving him to Warsaw.

Jonathan and Magdalena fell in love. After we returned to Los Angeles, he travelled back to Poland six times within nine months to be with her. During our trip he had endured a painful back problem that required surgery in the US. As soon as he recovered from the surgery, he returned to Poland.

Soon after, I filed a fiancée petition so that Magdalena could immigrate to the United States. It took nine months to finalize her permanent resident visa. Jonathan and Magdalena were married in 2011 in Los Angeles. A year later we returned to Poland for their Polish wedding with Magdalena's family and friends at an elegant renovated castle, Zamek Korzkiew, near Krakow. What an unexpected and joyful connection to the country of my birthplace and my family.

Entrance to Treblinka

Treblinka memorial stones

Above: Gitta at Treblinka

Opposite page top / left to right: James, Gitta, Jonathan, Judson, October 11, 2010, Treblinka

Opposite page bottom / left to right: Tomasz, Judson, James, Jonathan, Treblinka

Letters from grandchildren, Biala Podlaska memorial stone at Treblinka

Biala Podlaska

Registry office of Biala Podlaska

Entrance to Registry office, Biala Podlaska

Tomasz at the Registry office, Biala Podlaska

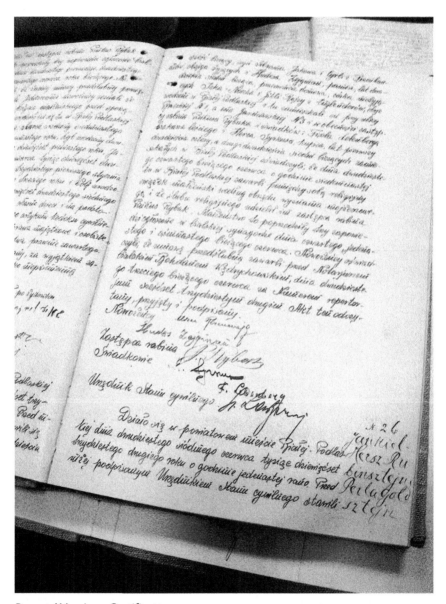

Parents' Marriage Certificate

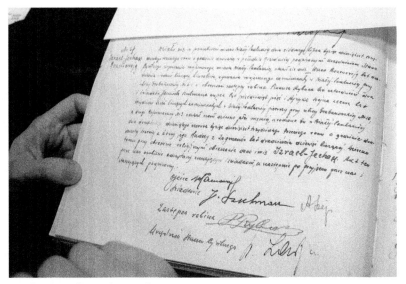

Brother Izrael's Birth Certificate

Birth Record, Father's youngest brother, Yarichem

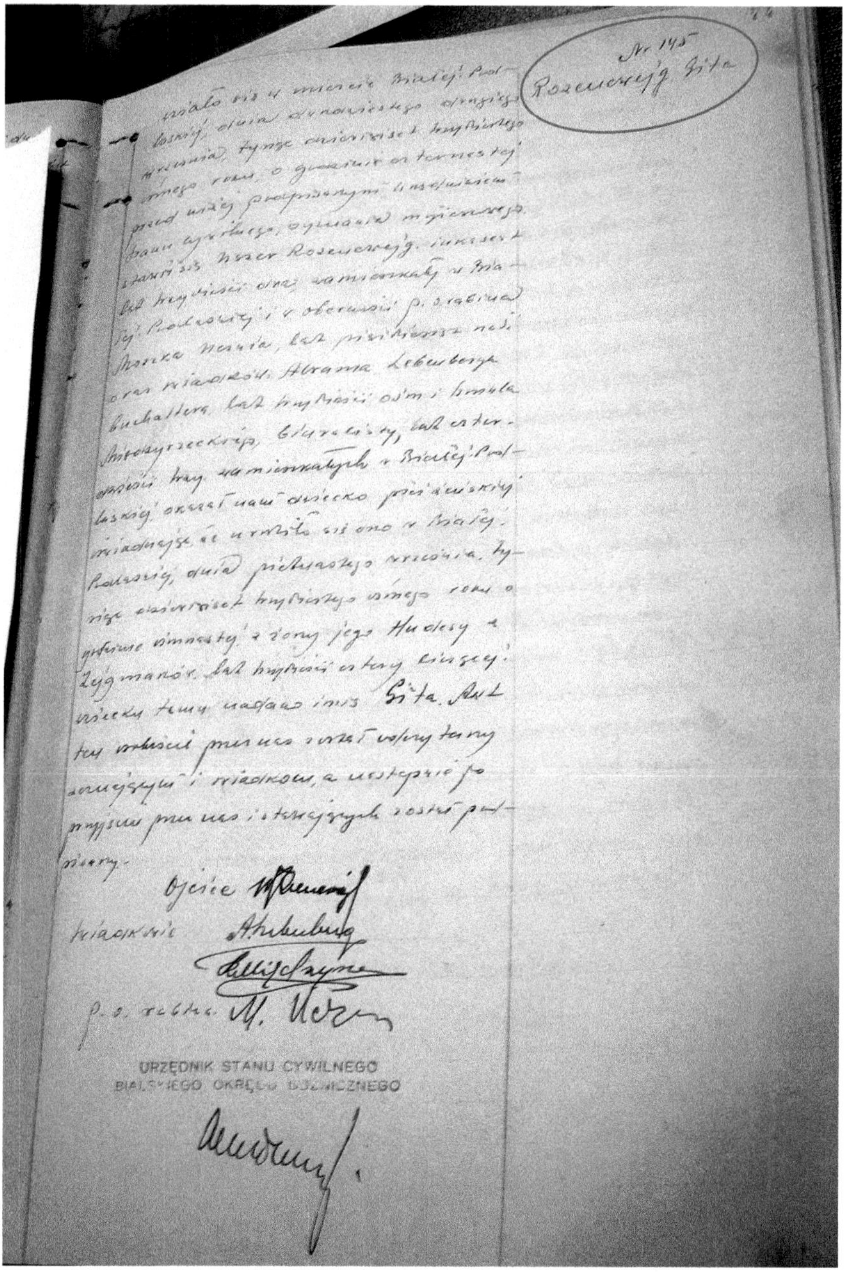

Gitta's Birth Record

Holy Mary statue, Orphanage, Sitnik, Poland

i dlatego takie inne, delikatne. Po wojnie organizacja żydowska odnalazła ją u nas i mimo jej oporów i ogromnej rozpaczy, gdyż przywiązała się bardzo do Sióstr, siłą ją nam odebrano i wywieziono za granicę, gdzie miała prawdopodobnie bogatą rodzinę. Wszystkie te dzieci miały polskie dokumenty. Dziewczynka nazywała się u nas Marysia Czekańska, chłopcy: Henryk Gołubiak, głuchoniemy Andrzej Silnicki i inni, których nazwiska zapomniałam.

Latem 1944 r. po wycofaniu się Niemców przeżyliśmy front wojenny. W schronach zrobionych w ogrodzie spędziliśmy z dziećmi kilka ciężkich dni, gdyż to Niemcy, to Rosjanie nacierali. Obok naszego drewnianego domu padła bomba zapalająca, ale stojące przy domu drzewa zatrzymały iskry i ogień. Bóg ocalił nas i dzieci, za co po wojnie wystawiliśmy figurę Matki Bożej przed domem, jako dziękczynienie za opiekę i pomoc, a w gorących modlitwach stawiliśmy Boga za dobroć i miłosierdzie. W okolicznej wiosce spaliło się kilka gospodarstw i mendle zboża na polu, były wielkie szkody. Nam Niemcy zabrali konie i gospodarza na podwody, gospodarz wrócił, ale bez koni. Ogromnie trudno było zebrać z pól przy pomocy rę-

Sister Jadwiga Gozkek's personal diary

Back row / left to right: Judson, Jonathan, James; *Front row / left to right:* Sister Maria, Gitta, Head Sister, Mother Teresa. Headquarters of Daughters of the Holy Mary Heart, Nowe Miastro, N. Pilica, Poland

Tomasz Cebulski, Polish guide, Treblinka

ISRAEL

2013

ON DECEMBER 21, 2013, I returned to Israel and visited the Yad Vashem Museum once again. I walked through the galleries as I listened intently to the audio recording of the personal experiences and feelings of the victims, and the stories of the Jewish communities before the Second World War. On display are photographs, films, newspapers, pamphlets, letters, works of art, personal items found in the camps and ghettos, and various reproductions that reveal the degradation and terrorization of the Jews in Germany and other countries. After more than a few hours of intent concentration listening to the narration and viewing displays of the horror, I was exhausted and emotionally drained.

The final part of the exhibition, the Hall of Names, consists of 600 photographs and fragments of Pages of Testimony submitted to the Yad Vashem from people who have known someone murdered during the Holocaust. They are powerfully displayed on the cone shaped ceiling that rises 10 meters high, skyward. At the entrance to the Hall is a quote from Benjamin Fondane, (Exodus) murdered at Auschwitz in 1944.

"Remember only that I was innocent and, just like you, mortal on that day. I too had a face marked by rage, by pity and joy, quite simply a human face."

As I entered this cone shaped gallery one particular photograph caught my attention as I walked past. I had to step back to take a closer look. Stunned, I recognized the portrait of my mother that I had donated to the Museum. Her hair is pulled back with one lock falling on her forehead by design. She is wearing a silk print blouse with a string of pearls around her neck. She looks to the side and smiles with warmth in her eyes, her mouth slightly open showing her teeth. It amazed me to see her photograph so prominently displayed there.

Initially happy to see her looking as glamorous as a movie star, I soon had the overwhelming realization that her photograph hung there because she was murdered in Treblinka. My mother, along with thousands of other ordinary innocent people, who after three years of fear, humiliation, terrorization, and days of hell, were herded into cattle cars and killed by forced inhalation of poisonous gas. No records exist from this barbaric place. The meticulous, bureaucratic Germans did not have time to write down the names of these victims. They literally went up in smoke.

FINAL DISCOVERY

2015

Yizkor Elohim – May God Remember

MANY YEARS ago Uncle Martin told me about books written in Yiddish that contained information about my family. In 2015 still hoping to find more answers, I began to research these books and with the help of a translator Hershl Hartman I found specific references to my family and even my father's words.

The Yizkor books compiled by survivors of the Holocaust serve as the communal memory of those who perished as a result of the persecution of the Jews. They derive from an ancient Jewish tradition to remember deceased relatives whose names are read aloud during Yom Kippur and on other important holidays. These Yizkor or remembrance books, of which there are hundreds, contain descriptions and history of a community, town or region as well as personal recollections of people and events before the war, biographies, and eyewitness accounts of life in the ghettos, deportations and mass murders. Often they include photographs, maps, and other memorabilia.

In the 1953 Yizkor book of Biala Podlaska written by M.J. Feigenbaum, a survivor who lived in Biala Podlaska, I discovered my father Usher Rozencwajg had been one of six librarians in the Tarbut Library, one of the first Zionist institutions in the city. In 1933 the library contained 2,385 books written in Yiddish, Hebrew and Polish. Drama and literature clubs also functioned in the library. I have a photograph of my mother in the drama club where she and Uncle David Zajgman participated. My mother attended the gymnasium or secondary school that prepared students for higher education.

During the war the library housed refugees and the books were hidden in the headquarters of the Judenrat, the Jewish Council appointed by the Nazis. After the liberation by the Soviet Army in 1944 no trace of the books remained. Feigenbaum speculates Polish traders took them for scrap.

In the 1961 Yizkor book, an article written by Nakhman Vaynberg (Nathan Weinberg), one of the organizers of the Zionist sport, cultural and political youth group founded in 1916 during the German occupation of World War I, I found a photograph of my father. He was a member of the Makabi football team. He is also in a group photograph of a fundraising for a charitable hospital organization.

Gordon Weinberg, the son of Nathan Weinberg, sent me a momentous book from Israel by M.J. Feigenbaum. Written in Yiddish in 1948 and later translated, *Podlaska in Extermination: Notes from Destruction* chronicles the events in Biala and

Miedzyrzec. In the chapter "Treblinka Revisited: The Ghetto in Miedzyrzec May 2, 1943, The Fifth Aktion," he describes chilling details.

"You see scenes all too familiar from previous aktions. A mother carries an infant in her arms. A father stands next to his weeping little daughter, who, having been rudely awakened from her sleep, can't seem to get control of herself and doesn't realize that tomorrow at this time she will have fallen into an eternal sleep in a mass grave at Treblinka...Mrs. Levenberg (Avraham Aharon's wife) from Biala is dragging her little grandson by the hand (the youngest of Matke Nortman who was taken to Treblinka on October 6, 1942) who was just learning to take his first wobbly steps. His mother is probably off somewhere looking for a hiding place."

In this book I also came across a reference to my aunt Haya, my father's sister.

"Mrs. Hayele Levenberg from Biala (nee Rosenzweig) goes by with her younger son. Their husband and father have in the meantime run off looking for a hideout for them. She anxiously looks in all directions to see if he has returned."

In another reference, he reports, "As rumors spread about Treblinka, hiding places became the first priority. Money was no obstacle for this purpose."

In one passage Feigenbaum describes a rare beautiful autumn evening. The sun illuminated from the western sky. And then I read my father's words:

"You see," said the Jewish policeman Asher Rozencwajg, "the sun that is setting so magnificently despite
everything—is setting in Biala for us Jews for the last
time."

On reading these words, my father came alive for me and
yet it filled me with overwhelming grief and heartbreak.
Until then I had not known that my father was a policeman. I also discovered a eulogizing reference to his police
service in the 1961 Yizkor book.

"The ghetto order service (police force) can also not
be accused of crimes, although some of them did not
always adhere to the highest principles. One cannot
say that the order service in Biala was beloved by the
population because who was then beloved if he held a
position of authority? Let it, however be stressed that
there were several order servicemen who were specifically beloved by the Jewish population, such as Usher
Rozentsvayg…"

The final piece of information comes from Feigenbaum's
chronology where he lists an event in February 1943, "Ten
Jewish Policemen Executed in Mezritch" (the Yiddish spelling
for Miedzyrzecz). This revelation haunts me. Is this the time
and place my father was killed? I am even more desolate for
not having known him, my mother, brother and family and
mourn for the loving life I would have had.

Above, bottom row, at left:
Mother at Drama Club, Biala
Podlaska

Right: Aunt Haya

Commemorating the Last Deportation during Sukot, from Biala Podlaska,
Lodz, Poland, 1942. (Gitta, first row, second from right)

EPILOGUE

"While it is possible to argue that the older survivor suffered more acutely due to their cognitive awareness of their suffering, their chances to rebuild were enhanced by their recall of a model to emulate. Children were considered to have suffered less by virtue of their assumed compromised ability to remember. This turns out to be wrong. Children have plenty of memories borne of severe trauma; however, they are fragmented and seldom sequential. But they may lack the memories that can serve as building blocks to a new life. As a consequence, child Holocaust survivors faced a series of obstacles not encountered by the adult survivors."

—ROBERT KRELL (The Resiliency of the Survivor: Views of a Child Holocaust Survivor/Psychiatrist)

Forced to be silent as a child so as not betray my presence, I learned not to speak. I also learned the fear that accompanies this silencing. Often hidden abruptly from the Nazi's, these unpredictable and terrifying episodes have had life long consequences for me.

I developed unnatural fears and a distrust of people at an early age. When told that Ida would steal my blood and make Matzot with it, I was terrified I would be killed if I went with her. The practice of blood libel originated by a monk in the 12th C required Christian blood in a secret Passover ritual. Without it, Jews would never be able to return to their ancestral land.

Until 1984 when I made my first trip to Australia to visit Ida, I had no real understanding of the events of my past or conclusive evidence of my experience during the war years. Until 1991 I had no realization of how the profound effects of being a hidden child had shaped my life. I couldn't make sense of my paralyzing fears.

Until 2010 when I returned to Poland with my three sons, I had no record of my birth or any other family records. I knew my parents and my older brother only through photographs.

As a child I was known by three different names: Gita, Marysia, and another anonymous child's name. I learned to practice two different religions: Judaism and Christianity, and repeatedly had been hidden from sight without explanation. I realized how perilous a situation the sisters at the orphanage faced by protecting the Jewish children from the Nazis. Until I read the words in the diary of Sister Jadwiga Gozdek, I had no knowledge that the German Police Commando confiscated and occupied part of the orphanage soon after she arrived. The sisters' heroism was even more courageous than I imagined. Being constantly on their guard, they must have experienced incredible tension, terrified that if the Nazi's discovered me, everyone's life would be in danger.

As an adult I experienced recurrent nightmares. In one, my jaw locked. In another one I chewed on gum that dissolved, but remained in a great mushy lump that couldn't be dislodged from my teeth. This pervasive gum nightmare prevented me from using my mouth. I had no context to explain this terror.

My fear of speaking caused me to leave law school two times as well as two government positions. I settled on legal work which was not emotionally demanding. I knew that I could not live up to my potential, but given all my childhood trauma, I am content to have accomplished as much as I did.

A similar experience occurred during a talk I was asked to give on basic immigration law before other attorneys. I started speaking from well-prepared notes. Barely into the presentation my mind went numb. I began to disintegrate, sweating profusely and speaking in what seemed like distant sounds from someone other than me. I glanced at the audience and saw some of the attorneys smiling in amusement. I don't know how I ended the presentation. I was so humiliated and ashamed that I never gave another one. Any public speaking engagement inevitably ended with disgrace. When asked to take on a new case, if I was unfamiliar with any procedure I was not willing to take the risk and make a mistake.

When I started driving, no matter how many times I went somewhere and took the same route, I worried that I would not find it again. I would never stroll around and explore a city. This fear deterred me from being adventurous. I wouldn't experiment by taking a different route. I was never sure if I would find my way home. If I had to detour from a known route and go on a different street, I panicked. I did whatever I needed to do to return to the familiar route. I even made U turns in dangerous places. I would break out in a sweat, my heart pounding, and become disoriented. Afraid of not getting to a safe place or to my destination, I had to force myself to focus and try to remain calm. I avoided going to ceremonious occasions such as a wedding of a dear friend for fear that I would get lost. I thought I would disappear, going around in circles, adrift in time and space. I often had nightmares of getting lost. I'd wake up breathless and soaked in perspiration. Each nightmare would be cast in a different context with the same underlying fear of not getting where I wanted to go. Strangers appeared to block me and other impediments got in my way.

I no longer harbor my fear of getting lost. Sometimes I even test myself and take an unknown route just to see how my mind and body will react and am amazed the symptoms no longer surface no matter how much I go out of my way. I can thank my new GPS technology.

At many points in my life I have tried to fill the void by acquiring material goods. Although deprived of the basic necessities as a child such as food and clothing, it was the emotional deprivation I continually needed to compensate for in a way that would provide me with an identity. During the war years money could make the difference between life or death for many Jews. People sewed jewels and money into their clothes and used valuables to purchase a slice of bread or pay for escape. Uncle Martin instilled in me that money is security, but denied me money when I needed it. Aunt Hilda bought me attractive clothes and I looked great, but inside I felt unattractive and empty.

The discoveries I made at the Hidden Child Conference in New York in 1990 had the most cosmic impact on me, particularly the words of Elie Wiesel and psychiatrist Robert Krell. It has been a long journey of discovery to excise the negative feelings of what I presumed to be an unwanted child given away.

Throughout my life, I have tried to find a way to make up for the absence of my mother by seeking a connection with various other women who might fill that void. I unconsciously sought to attach myself as an embryo to the womb. A few times I clung as a bud on a branch only to be quickly dislodged and dejected. I formed strong attachments to the sisters who not only nurtured me, but also risked their lives to hide me from the German demons, but then was taken away. I developed a deep affection for Ida who so courageously rescued me from the orphanage and reunited me with my family, but I was wrenched apart from her when I went to France. In Paris, I developed a fondness for Aunt Jenna who cared for me. When she died in childbirth, I lost her too.

When I visited my cousin Hildita, I saw the mother daughter bond she had with her mother Eva and envied the closeness and effortlessness of that relationship. I thought if I behaved like one of the daughters that I observed, that amorphous connection would be mine if only for a short time. When I imitated their mannerisms, Hilda would say, "Why are you behaving like that?" When I showed attachment to other relatives, I felt Hilda's disapproval and jealousy with her comments and tone of voice. I believed that if I had a mother she would be sweet, kind and loving, not harsh like Hilda. I attached myself briefly to other women also. I spent time with Aunt Blanche, my mother's sister, and her children during the summers on the beach in Rockaway. She had a kind, pretty face, and gentle manner. As I got older, the need to find a mother substitute did not abate. It tapered off, but never disappeared.

I had never seen my mother's body in a bathing suit until Aunt Blanche gave me a photo one day over lunch fifteen years ago. Until then I had only seen a headshot of her or fully clothed as a young girl in a gymnasium photo won a beauty contest.

When I had my own children, my mother was not there. Even Aunt Hilda had died when my first of three sons was born. I had no role model, no blueprint for parenting, not even an adopted mother to bond with and share a loving relationship. Having a baby, so beautiful and pure, gave me no hint of how unprepared I was to bring up children. With the demands on my time, energy, and emotions, stress and depression built up and rose to the surface. I was like a ship on the vast unchartered ocean without a compass. I navigated as best I could, not knowing what I lacked.

It has taken time, with the help of my psychoanalysis and antidepressants, to come to terms with feelings of dissatisfaction with myself.

The passage of time has also eased the issues and grievances with Bernard, which loomed so large in youth. As grandparents now we are on very good terms.

As children, my sons did not understand that I could not give what I had not received, nor should they be expected to. Now they are adults and parents themselves. It is my fervent wish they have not only love, but also compassion and forgiveness for me.

On our trip to Poland together, we dredged up horrific memories, events, and family history, but we also made extraordinary discoveries together about my past and their heritage. In a mysterious way, our trip to Poland proved to be a healing and unifying experience for us all.

POSTSCRIPT

JAMES NAMED his eldest son Asher after my father and his middle son Mordechi David after my two uncles. A few months before our trip James and Kricken named their third son Yeruham after my father's younger brother. A few months after our return from Poland, Judson and Sia named their daughter Haya after my father's sister.

To memorialize our travel experiences together, James assumed the task of coordinating all our photographs and videos to make them accessible for viewing and reflection. They will also remain an archive for the family.

In 2010 Jonathan began getting tattoos of significant events in his life. When he returned from our trip, he had a photo of his grandfather Uszer, and his grandfather's signature—copied from my birth certificate—tattooed on his arm. Each of my sons has chosen in a unique way to honor his family history and lost relatives so that they will never be forgotten. Their generation and their children will carry our family into the future.

Left to right: Judson, Gitta, Tomasz, James, Jonathan, Poland, 2010

Jonathan's tattoo of his grandfather

Micah Haya

Micah Haya and Dean Baruh

Gitta and grandchildren Beckett Yeruham and Micah Haya

*"In the end, Hitler did not succeed
in eliminating all European Jewish children
and we and our children and grandchildren
are living proof of that."*

— ROSE GELBART (Child Survivor of the Holocaust)

From left: Liam Asher, Riley Mordecai David, and Beckett Yeruham
(bottom center)

ROSENZWEIG *ROZENCWAJG*
FAMILY GENEALOGY

ROZENCWAJG FAMILY RESIDENCE
Grabanowska Street #8, Biala Podlaska, Poland

GITTA ROSENZWEIG: (born Gita Rozencwajg)
September 15, 1938, Biala Podlaska, Poland

FATHER: Uszer Rozencwajg, June 14, 1906 – 1942
MOTHER: Hudesa Zajgman, September 11, 1904 – 1942
BROTHER: Izrael Itzchak, June 29, 1933 – 1941

UNCLE DAVID (Mother's Brother): David Zajgman, 1907 –
1984
AUNT JENNA: Friedman Zajgman, April 2, 1906 –
January 1, 1948
MOTHER OF JENNA: Miriam Friedman, 1874 – 1957
DAUGHTER OF DAVID AND JENNA: Regine Zajgman
Silbermann, January 13, 1937, Married Marc Silbermann

UNCLE MARTIN (Father's Brother): Motel Wolf Rozencwajg
(changed spelling to Rosenzweig in the U.S.) July 12, 1907
– November 1987
AUNT HILDA: Hilda Gilksberg Rosenzweig March 10, 1908
– September 30, 1969

DAUGHTER OF MARTIN AND HILDA: Marcia Rosenzweig
Goldberg, May 23, 1951
FATHER'S YOUNGER BROTHER: Yeruham Rozencwajg, 1919
– 1942
FATHER'S SISTER: Haya Rivka Rozencwejg Lebenberg,
November 2,1910 – 1942, Married Fiszel Lebenberg
SON OF HAYA: Izrael Lebenberg, September 26, 1936 –1942

GITTA'S GRANDPARENTS AND GREAT GRAND PARENTS

FATHER OF USZER: Abram Jakow Rozencwajg, September
14, 1882 – February 27, 1939 Sokolow, Podlaski
MOTHER OF USZER: Cyrla Rozenbaum
PARENTS OF CYRLA: Srul and Leja
GRANDMOTHER OF USZER: maiden name Josperzon
GRANDFATHER OF USZER: Zurych Nusyn Rozencwajg
GREAT GRANDMOTHER of USZER: Szejna Hofer

FATHER OF HUDESA: Icek Noech Zajgman
MOTHER OF HUDESA: Gitla Rojza Englander, 1869, Janow,
Podlaski. Married 1890
GRANDFATHER OF HUDESA: Jankiel Englander, 1836
GRANDMOTHER OF HUDESA: Jenta/Ita Epelbaum, 1848,
Janow, Podlaski. Married 1865

GITTA'S SONS: *(see Hebrew names)*

JONATHAN ASHER YAKER *(Yonatan Asher Boaz)* July 30,
  1970. Married Magdalena Kasprzyk, September 8, 2011
JAMES ISAAK YAKER *(Jacob Izhak)* January 29, 1972.
  Married Kricken Hering *(Ariel Lior)* July 24, 1999
JUDSON ARI YAKER *(Ari Yehuda)* April 10, 1975. Married
  Sia Kugias December 23, 2010

GITTA'S GRANDCHILDREN

LIAM ARMSTRONG YAKER *(Asher Shalom)* April 14, 2003
RILEY JORDAN YAKER **(***Mordechi David)* March16, 2005
BECKETT EZRA YAKER *(Yeruham Israel)* APRIL14, 2010
MICAH HAYA YAKER, January 22, 2011
DEAN BARUH YAKER, October 12, 2013

NOTE: Many of the names I discovered in various documents
have multiple spellings.

Front row / left to right: Aunt Blanche, Aunt Haya
Back row / left to right: Mother, Yeruham and Father,
Letnisko Domaczewo, Poland

Second from right: Aunt Blanche
Fourth from right, Aunt Haya
Letnisko Domaczewo, Poland

Mother's Mother, Gitla Rojza Englander   Mother's Father, Icek Noech Zajgman

Father's parents and younger brother
Left to right: Cyrla Rozenbaum, Yeruham Rozencwajg, and Abram Jakow
Rozencwajg

Mother's sister, Aunt Blanche, April 18, 1930
Blanche Zajgman Singer (1909-1999)

Mother, Fourth from right: Mother's School Ceremony

Front row center, Father holding sign: Remember the Sick in the Hospital, April 13, 1925 fundraiser

Far left, Father: Father with group in Biala Podlaska

Back row center Father: Flower Day to *Benefit Tarbut Library, Biala Podlaska, November 21, 1926*

BIALA PODLASKA PRIOR TO THE WAR

"AT THE BEGINNING of the 20th century, the Jewish population of Biala constituted about 65% of the total. The Jewish community managed five synagogues, six prayer houses, a Jewish hospital, three tenant houses, a Talmud-Torah, seven shops and a few squares and gardens. In the 1923 regional council elections, Jewish parties managed to secure eleven seats in the Biala City Counsel. In the period 1918 and 1939, between wars, there were four Jewish newspapers published in Yiddish: Zionist *Bialer Wochenblat* and *Poldasier Lebn* as well as *Naj Podlasjer Lebn* and *Podlasjer Sztyme*. Biala, at that time located in central Poland, was a small city, looking proudly into the future as the modern aviation and timber industry developed. The Rozencwajgs were one of the Jewish families in town, long rooted in this Podlaskie soil by the 19th century that had already begun showing the first traces of modernity."

—TOMASZ CEBULSKI AND YAD VASHEM[4]

Political Map of Poland

HISTORY OF BIALA PODLASKA

"BIALA PODLASKA is a town situated 162 km east of Warsaw, 120 km north of Lublin, and 61 km east of Siedlce. In 1931, of the population of 10,697, 6,923 (64.7%) were Jewish. The Jewish community in the town had grown rapidly in the second half of the 19th Century, members owning a nail factory, a tannery, a shoe factory, saw-mills, brick-making furnaces, flour mills, a soap factory, a brewery and various other small factories. However, in common with other towns and shtetls in Poland, there were also many who lived in poverty.

The Jews of Biala Podlaska were typical of the small communities of that time; all were religious to a greater or lesser degree, although some were influenced by the Haskalah (Enlightenment), and Zionist movements.

The Germans captured Biala Podlaska on 13 September 1939, but withdrew on 26 September to allow the Soviets to occupy the town. On 10 October 1939, in accordance with the terms of the Molotov—Ribbentrop pact, the Soviets departed and the town was reoccupied by the Germans.

Six hundred Jews left the town at the time of the Soviet departure to reside in that part of eastern Poland then under Soviet control. A Judenrat was formed in November 1939, with Icchak Pirzyc as its head. Insofar as it was possible, the Judenrat attempted to act as the successor to the Kehillah, the pre-war Jewish Community Council, providing a public kitchen for the poor, supervising the Jewish hospital and providing for other communal needs.

On 1 December 1939, the Germans published a decree requiring all Jews aged 6 and older to wear an armband on their right arm bearing a yellow Star of David. Jews were ordered to move to a separate zone on Grabanow, Janowa, Prosta and Przechodnia Streets. At the same time, a Jewish Police (Ordnungsdienst) was established.

At the end of 1939, 2,000-3,000 Jews, deported from Suwalki and Serock, arrived in the town, increasing the misery in the already overcrowded Jewish quarter. Although there was not a closed ghetto in Biala Podlaska, because of the numbers crammed into the residential area and the appalling sanitary conditions, there was a typhus epidemic in early 1940, causing many deaths.

At about this time, less than 200 survivors of a death march of Jewish POWs, initially numbering some 880 men, arrived in Biala Podlaska, to be interned in a prisoner-of-war camp there.

In July 1940, a number of Jewish men were sent from Biala Podlaska to the forced labour camps at Belzec. In the autumn of 1940, the Judenrat's employment office began to conscript workers for the factories built by the Germans in Biala Podlaska and its environs.

Work camps were built by the Germans nearby the factories. Hundreds of Jewish tradesmen were incarcerated in seven of the Judenrat's labour camps situated at the airfield, the train station, the Wineta camp in the Wola district, and elsewhere.

Hundreds of other Jews worked in heavy manual labour paving roads, draining ditches, and constructing sewage facilities, saw mills, and barracks. Many women worked at Duke Potocki's farm "Halas". On 15 May 1941, the Jewish POW camp was closed down, and the surviving prisoners were transported by sealed train to Konskowola, further west.

During 1940 and 1941, several hundred Jews from Krakow and Mlawa were deported to Biala Podlaska. As a result of the many "resettlements" to the town, the Jewish population had grown to approximately 8,400 in March 1942. On 6 June 1941 an announcement forbade "Aryans" to do business with Jews.

At the end of June 1941 a number of Jews were sent to the concentration camp at Auschwitz as punishment for giving bread to Soviet prisoners of war marching through the town. They were among the first Jewish victims to perish in Auschwitz.

On 6 June 1942, a rumour spread throughout the ghetto that the Jews were to be forced to leave Biala Podlaska and evacuated to the west. Only workers at the forced labour camps or those employed at German factories as well as those possessing a labour permit would be exempt from the deportation.

On 10 June at 5 a.m. 3,000 Jews, among them the elderly, women, and children were assembled in the synagogue courtyard. Many of the Jews did not report as ordered and fled to the forests. German police led the assembled Jews to the railroad station.

The next day, 11 June 1942, the deportees were herded into freight cars and were deported to the death camp at Sobibor. When the deportees disembarked from the train, believing they had been sent to a labour camp, a letter was handed to the SS from the municipality of Biala Podlaska requesting decent treatment for the arriving Jews. For this act of "insolence" and "impudence", 200 of the Jews were selected for "special treatment"; all others were immediately gassed.

The "special treatment" consisted of removing luggage from Camp II and loading it onto a train, whilst running a gauntlet of guards who whipped and clubbed the prisoners as they ran. The Jews who had been the subject of this "special treatment" were then also gassed.

Following the first deportation, the Germans reduced the area of the ghetto. On the night of 4 August 1942, gendarmes, German police and Polish police cordoned off the ghetto area, took men out of their homes and gathered them in the market square, where the men's labour permits were examined. Afterwards the men were freed, but on that same night 19 Jews were executed.

On 12 August, German gendarmes and Ukrainian aux-
iliaries began arresting Jewish men and collected them in a
square in the Wola neighbourhood. The Judenrat complained
to the German authorities and the workers were released.
However after a few days the arrests were renewed. About 400
Jews, including members of the Judenrat were deported to
KL Majdanek. Fifty Jews remained there. The other 350 men
were transferred to work on the railroad at Golab, between
Lublin and Pulawy.

In September 1942, 3,000 deportees from the towns of
Janow and Konstantynow were transported to Biala Podlaska.
The overcrowding in the ghetto became desperate. Glätt, an
SD man, took any valuables the Jews still retained and imposed
a "fine" of 45,000 zlotys. The Jews sensed that the Germans
intended to soon liquidate them. Many attempted to escape
to the forests, to dig bunkers, and prepared hiding places for
themselves or hid themselves in basements.

The second deportation of the Jews of Biala Podlaska
began on 26 September 1942 and ended on 1 October 1942.
Gestapo men, the Gendarmerie, the German and Polish
police and soldiers from the nearby airport all participated
in this Aktion. The night before the Aktion the Germans
encircled the ghetto.

The following morning the Jews were driven from their
homes, and concentrated in the New Market Square (Rynek).

Jews who resisted deportation were shot on the spot.
On the same day, 15 patients and two nurses at the Jewish

Hospital were shot by the Gestapo. A number of Jews were removed from the assembly and were sent as slave labourers to the airport at Malaszewicze, near Terespol.

Most of the people who were left in the market square were driven to Miedzyrzec Podlaski in the wagons of peasants from the surrounding area. On the way many were murdered in the Woronica Forest.

On 6 October 1942, the Germans deported about 1,200 workers from the labour camps in the vicinity of Biala Podlaska to Miedzyrzec Podlaski. Only a few managed to escape to the forests. Upon their arrival at the Miedzyrzec train station, the Germans joined most of those who had been deported a few days earlier to the group of workers and brought all of them to the local ghetto, from where they were subsequently deported to the Treblinka death camp.

The fate of the remaining deportees from Biala Podlaska was shared with the rest of the Jews of Miedzyrzec. In July 1943, after several further Aktionen at the end of 1942 and in May 1943, the Miedzyrzec Podlaski Ghetto was liquidated and its inhabitants were deported to Treblinka, where they were murdered.

The Germans left a group of 300 Jewish workers in Biala Podlaska to clear the ghetto and to destroy the synagogue and the small prayer houses. In May 1944, the surviving workers were transferred to KL Majdanek.

Biala Podlaska was liberated by the Red Army on 26 July 1944. Of the more than 6,000 Jewish residents of the town in 1939, only 300 remained alive at the war's end."

—YAD VASHEM ARCHIVES[4]

Memorial plaque, Miedzyrzes, Podlaski

END NOTES

1 Acknowledgments, http://www.yadvashem.org/yv/en/holocaust/about/index.asp

2 Author's Note, Murder of the Jews in Poland, http://www.yadvashem.org/yv/en/holocaust/about/09/poland.asp

3 Part III, http://www.goisrael.com/Tourism_Eng/WhatToDo/Culture/Pages/Yad-Vashem-Holocaust-Memorial-Museum.aspx

4 Part III – Yad Vashem Archives. http://www.holocaustresearchproject.org/ghettos/bialapodlaska.html

BIBLIOGRAPHY

BOOKS

Arad, Yitzah. *Belzec, Sobibor, Treblinka: The Operation Reinhard Death Camps.* Bloomington, Indiana: Indiana University Press, 1987.

Browning, Christopher R. *Ordinary Men: Reserve Police Battalion 101 and The Final Solution in Poland.* New York: Harper Perennial, 1998.

Feigenbaum. M.J. ed. *Book of Biala Podlaska.* Tel Aviv, 1961

Feigenbaum. M.J. *Podlaska in Extermination: Notes from Destruction.* Munich: Central Historical Committee of Liberated Jews on the American Zone of Germany, Munich: 1948

Feigenbaum. M.J. Podlyashe in the Nazi-Camp: Reports from Destruction. Buenos Aires: Committee of Commrads, 1953

Sanders, Ronald. *Shores of Refuge: A Hundred Years of Jewish Emigration.* New York: Henry Holt and Company, Inc., 1988

Sereny, Gitta. *Into That Darkness.* New York: First Vintage Books Edition, 1983.

Vaynberg, Nakhman. Yizkor Book. 1961

Wiesel, Elie. *Night.* New York: Hill and Wang, 2006.

ARTICLES

Cebulski, Tomasz, Ph.D. *The Double Life of Gitta*. Poland, 2010
http://www.jewish-guide.pl/genealogy/genealogy-research-stories

SPEECHES

Abraham Foxman (Excerpt of Speech – The Hidden Child
Conference, New York 1991)

Robert Krell (Excerpt of Speech – The Hidden Child Conference,
New York 1991)

Elie Wiesel (Excerpt of Speech – The Hidden Child Conference,
New York 1991)

WEBSITES

The Holocaust

http://www.yadvashem.org/yv/en/holocaust/about/index.asp

Murder of the Jews in Poland

http://www.yadvashem.org/yv/en/holocaust/about/09/poland.asp

Biala Podlaska

http://www.holocaustresearchproject.org/ghettos/bialapodlaska.
 html

Yizkor Books

http://library.pdx.edu

http://www.goisrael.com/Tourism_Eng/WhatToDo/Culture/
Pages/Yad-Vashem-Holocaust-Memorial-Museum.aspx

http://www.jewishvirtuallibrary.org/jsource/judaica/
ejud_0002_0003_0_02917.htm

http://www.clevelandjewishnews.com/features/community/article_
bb666828-76c5-11e2-bf88-001a4bcf887a.html

http://kavod.claimscon.org/2013/02/conference-presentation-
survivor-resilience/

http://www.ushmm.org/outreach/en/article.
php?ModuleId=10007706

CPSIA information can be obtained at www.ICGtesting.com
Printed in the USA
LVOW05s1006211015

459131LV00018BB/160/P